THE ROOSEVELT COURT

THE ROOSEVELT COURT

A Study in Judicial Politics and Values
1937–1947

C. HERMAN PRITCHETT

Classics of Law & Society

qp

QUID PRO BOOKS
New Orleans, Louisiana

THE ROOSEVELT COURT

Previously published in 1948 by The Macmillan Company, New York, and in 1969 by Quadrangle Books, Inc., Chicago.

Published in the 2014 edition by Quid Pro Books.

ISBN 978-1-61027-238-4 (pbk)
ISBN 978-1-61027-237-7 (ebk)

QUID PRO BOOKS
5860 Citrus Blvd., Suite D-101
New Orleans, Louisiana 70123
www.quidprobooks.com

qp

This is an unabridged and authorized republication of the original 1948 work, as reprinted in the 1969 Quadrangle Paperbacks edition and subsequent reprints by the successor publisher, Simon & Schuster. It is presented in the new Quid Pro Books edition as part of the *Classics of Law & Society* Series. Page number inserts in brackets have been added to maintain continuity of page references with previous printings. Part of the front cover design of this edition is adapted from one by Raymond Welch appearing in the Quadrangle printing.

FOR MARGUERITE

CONTENTS

[Page numbers in brackets below reference the original pagination of the previous printed editions, retained in this republication for continuity in citation and syllabus, consistency with the new ebook edition, and the convenience of the reader. The original pagination is found embedded into the text by the use of brackets. Numbers to the right below refer to pagination found at the bottom of pages in this new edition.]

I.	AT THE CENTER OF THE TORNADO [1]	1
	The Nine Old Men [2]	2
	The Eight Middle-Aged Men [9]	7
	Justices Without Halos [14]	10
II.	DIVIDED IT STANDS [23]	17
	The Multiplication of Division [24]	17
	The Pattern of Division [32]	23
III.	THE QUEST FOR UNCERTAINTY [46]	37
	Dissents and Concurrences [48]	38
	Stare Decisis [53]	42
	Back to Holmes and Brandeis [58]	46
IV.	ECONOMIC REGULATION AND LEGISLATIVE SUPREMACY [71]	57
	The Constitution Among Friends [72]	58
	A Ceiling for Due Process [77]	61
	Due Process and State Regulation [79]	63
	Local Policies and National Commerce [81]	64
	State Taxation and Commerce [84]	66
V.	CIVIL LIBERTIES AND JUDICIAL SUPREMACY [91]	73
	Jehovah's Witnesses et al. [93]	75
	Freedom of the Press [107]	85
	The Right to Go Left [112]	89
	Freedom in Wartime [117]	92
	Civil Liberties and Political Rights [122]	96
	Anti-Okie and Jim Crow [128]	100
	The Court as Super-Legislature [129]	101

VI.   CRIME AND PUNISHMENT [137]   107
       The Right to Counsel [138]   108
       The Representative Character of Juries [141]   110
       The Third Degree [146]   114
       Federal Protection of Civil Rights [148]   115
       The Search and Seizure Mystery [153]   118
       Military Tribunals and Martial Law [155]   120
       Law in the Making [158]   122

VII. BUREAUCRACY: NO ALIEN INTRUDER [167]   131
       The King Is Dead [168]   132
       Long Live the King! [177]   139
       Rudder and Bowsprit [189]   148

VIII. LABOR'S DAY [198]   155
       The Wagner and Fair Labor Standards Acts [199]   155
       Labor and the Sherman Act [208]   163
       Picketing as Free Speech [218]   170
       The States and Labor Regulation [224]   174
       Labor versus Civil Liberties [229]   178
       John L. Lewis and the Law of the Pendulum [232]   180

IX.   ALIGNMENTS AND ISSUES [239]   187
       The Alignments [240]   188
       The Issues [253]   196

X.   THE PLIGHT OF A LIBERAL COURT [264]   205
       Liberalism and Judicial Pragmatism [267]   207
       Economic Liberalism [270]   209
       Liberalism and Individual Rights [273]   212
       Activism versus Self-Restraint [277]   215

       NOTES [288]   223
       DECISIONS OVERRULED BY THE SUPREME COURT [300]   237
       TABLE OF CASES [302]   239
       INDEX [311]   249

ABOUT THE AUTHOR

C. Herman Pritchett (1907-1995) was born in Latham, Illinois, and studied at Millikin University and the University of Chicago. His books include *Congress versus the Supreme Court*; *Courts, Judges and Politics* (with Walter Murphy); *The American Constitution*; and *The American Constitutional System*. Dr. Pritchett was for generations a Professor of Political Science at the University of Chicago and, for thirteen years, the chair of its renowned department of political science. He was former president of the American Political Science Association as well as a fellow of the American Academy of Arts and Sciences.

Pritchett worked for the Tennessee Valley Authority and the U.S. Department of Labor before joining the University of Chicago faculty. In addition to his long-time appointment at Chicago, he was a visiting professor at Makerere University, Uganda, in 1963 and at Stanford in 1966. He also taught at the University of California, Santa Barbara, from 1966 to 1974. With this book and other often-cited research, he became universally recognized as one of modern political science's founding figures: the originator of the modern study of judicial behavior.

The life of the law has not been logic: it has been experience. The felt necessities of the time, the prevalent moral and political theories, intuitions of public policy, avowed or unconscious, even the prejudices which judges share with their fellow-men, have had a good deal more to do than the syllogism in determining the rules by which men should be governed.

—OLIVER WENDELL HOLMES, JR.,
The Common Law

At present we know little more of the craft of judgment than can be gleaned from the words and between the lines of the reports. An increase in understanding must await materials concerned with and a psychology relevant to deliberation in process. But at this point the quest of the "how and why judges decide cases" runs into the larger search for the ways of the mind.

—WALTON HAMILTON, "Judicial Process,"
Encyclopaedia of the Social Sciences

PREFACE

I AM not sure now what case it was, but sometime in the fall of 1940 I was reading the current issue of the *Supreme Court Reporter* in my office at the University of Chicago, one floor above and some thirty feet west of the inscription on the Social Science Research Building which quotes Lord Kelvin's statement that "When you cannot measure, your knowledge is meager and unsatisfactory," when I was struck by what seemed a peculiar combination of justices who had joined in a dissent to one of the Supreme Court's opinions. I began to wonder what it was in that case and in the autobiographies of those justices that led them to disagree with the majority of the Court on the issue there raised. I decided that it might be profitable to examine into the actual patterns of disagreement among the justices, and so went back to preceding terms of the Court for additional data. What I found seemed very revealing, and supplied a challenge to discover explanations for the voting behavior of the justices and methods of presenting the record on judicial divisions, which ultimately resulted in this book.

Clemenceau once said that war was too important a matter to be left to the generals. By the same token I regard law as too important a matter to be left to the lawyers. Though I have spent a good share of my life in the study and teaching of constitutional and administrative law, I am not a lawyer. My approach to this particular subject is that of a political scientist interested in the social and psychological origins of judicial attitudes and the influence of individual predilections on the development of law. For an interest of this sort the Supreme Court of the United States is the obvious focus. For it is a court predominantly engaged in hearing public law controversies, and its judges have an opportunity to influence public policy which seems shocking to those familiar with the more limited scope for judicial discretion found in the legal systems of most other countries.

This book, then, undertakes to study the politics and the values of the Roosevelt Court through the nonunanimous opinions handed down by its justices. A unanimous judicial decision throws little light upon what Walton Hamilton calls "deliberation in process." It tells nothing of the conflicts around the judicial conference table, the alternative lines of argument developed, the accommodations and the compromises which went into the final result. A unanimous opinion is a composite and quasi-anonymous product, largely valueless for purposes of understanding the values and motivation of individual justices.

A nonunanimous opinion admits the public to the Supreme Court's inner sanctum. In such a case the process of deliberation has failed to produce a conclusion satisfactory to all participants. Having carried the argument as far as they usefully can, the justices find it necessary finally to take a vote, state and support the winning and losing positions, and place the arguments before the world for judgment. In informing the public of their divisions and their reasons, the justices also supply information about their attitudes and their values which is available in no other way. For the fact of disagreement demonstrates that the members of the Court are operating on different assumptions, that their inarticulate major premises are dissimilar, that their value systems are differently constructed and weighted, that their political, economic, and social views contrast in important respects. These differences and contrasts are not always evident on the surface of the conflicting opinions. It may be necessary to search out the true causes of dispute, and not all the searchers will come back with the same findings. But that the search is appropriate and essential to a fuller understanding of the judicial process, few will doubt.

Accommodatingly enough for one interested in tracing judicial attitudes as revealed in divided opinions, the Court began about 1941 to step up its production rate of dissents until previously unheard of levels of disagreement were attained. These divisions did not help the reputation of the Court, but they were grist to my mill, and made it possible to develop a full-scale inductive and statistical inquiry into the nature and operation of the process of judicial decision making.

I have been sorry to learn that my pursuit of this interest has not been a cause of unalloyed satisfaction to all members of the present Court. For the last couple of years Charles E. Merriam has been predicting gleefully that I would wind up before the bar of the Supreme Court on a contempt charge. I hope it will be obvious to anyone who reads this book that I am *amicus curiae,* with a deep respect for the judicial process and a great sympathy for the present Court. The attempts made here to examine into the personal foundations of judicial decisions may be wide of the mark, but in any event they are honest attempts and not intended to suggest that the present justices are motivated by their own preferences to any greater extent or are more politically minded than their predecessors. It is my view that the Supreme Court inevitably acts in a political context, and that the greatest danger to the Court and from the Court comes when that fact is inadequately realized. Felix Frankfurter wrote in 1938 that we need a "more continuous awareness of the role of the Court in the dynamic process of American society." I agree with that, and with Konefsky's conclusion that "only by acknowledging that the Supreme Court is a political institution performing a political function can we hope to escape from naive notions as to the nature of our Constitution and to foster a more informed public understanding of the Court's place in the American system of government."

Anyone who undertakes to appraise critically the product of the Supreme Court should have the graciousness to admit the difficult character of its responsibilities. Every sentence that the justices write, every argument that they offer, moves into as searching a spotlight as falls upon perhaps any printed word except the Bible or Shakespeare in the present day. Thousands of judges, attorneys, scholars, law students examine every decision. The opinions are torn apart and built into briefs, they are fought over in court, their main points are condensed in headnotes, they are expatiated upon in the law reviews, they are reprinted in casebooks. In few other fields are men who work with such imprecise verbal symbols held to such strict account. As Walton Hamilton so well says, the decision of a court "represents in a highly artificial form the act of personal judgment; it differs from the ordinary decision of everyman about an everyday matter as a critical intellectual process differs from a half intuitive experience. If the ways of jurists seem unusually prone to inconsistency and error, it is because the way of abstraction is made hard by unanticipated causes. If the categories of statistics or the methods of philosophy or the principles of economics were continually tested by cases fresh from life, the outward integrity of these disciplines would be seriously disturbed."

The use of the phrase "Roosevelt Court" perhaps needs some defense, or at least explanation. Possibly supporters of the late President may object to the term as impliedly alleging improper executive control over the judiciary, while his enemies may lick their chops in anticipation of the same possibility. I hope that both sides will discover they are wrong. The phrase is used purely for descriptive purposes; it is shorthand for "the Supreme Court as reconstituted and redirected by President Roosevelt's appointees."

A question may well be raised as to whether it is proper to call the Court of the last two terms the "Roosevelt Court." His appointees, of course, still dominate that body, and presumably will continue to do so for some time. But already the temper of the Court is changing, and a swing to the right is apparent in several fields. The perspective of a few years will aid greatly in fixing the metes and bounds of the Roosevelt era, but until we have that perspective it seems not unreasonable to consider the decade from 1937 to 1947 as being that of "the Roosevelt Court." At the moment my own guess is that the Roosevelt Court came to an end on that Thursday in March, 1947, when the John L. Lewis decision was handed down.

I want to say a word about Lord Kelvin's influence on this book. In the first place, the statistics employed are of a relatively simple order. For the most part they involve nothing more than counting, and as William Anderson once observed in undue deprecation of his very useful study of the units of government in the United States, counting is perhaps the lowest form of scholarly activity. I am not a statistician and I have certainly not exhausted the possibilities of applying statistical methods to judicial data. My colleague Louis L. Thurstone has some ambitions to use factor analysis on the Supreme Court, and I wish him luck.

In the second place, I am fully aware of the limitations of statistical methods in dealing with materials of the kind involved here. The greater precision and certainty which such methods appear to yield may, under the circumstances, be in part illusory. Nevertheless, I am convinced that the counting and the charting have a positive contribution to make to an understanding of the motivations of the present Court. I have been influenced by what Max Lerner said when he reviewed Ewing's book on the Supreme Court which used statistical methods, but which Lerner considered "truncated" by too much reliance on the "statistical technique by itself." He said: "What is obviously needed is a method in which the analysis is kept from shooting off into the void by being moored to a statistical and factual base, and in which fact-gathering is kept from becoming meaningless by being related to significant analysis." I have no illusions about having achieved this goal, but at least that is what I have been trying to do.

I have a good many obligations to record in connection with this book, and first of all to Leonard D. White and my other colleagues in the Department of Political Science at the University of Chicago, whose goodwill and sympathetic interest provide a continuously helpful setting for productive research. I have been much encouraged by the favorable comments upon my annual Court articles made by a number of my colleagues, and particularly by Carl B. Swisher of Johns Hopkins University. The audience which turned out to hear the substance of this book in a series of lectures at the University of Chicago during the autumn quarter, 1946, supplied a considerable stimulus to the completion of this work. I am of course greatly indebted to the standard works on the Supreme Court, and more particularly to the writers who have discussed its recent experience, such as Carl B. Swisher, Robert K. Carr, Edward S. Corwin, Max Lerner, Arthur M. Schlesinger, Jr., and Charles P. Curtis, Jr., to the latter of whom I owe the quotation with which the book ends. I have made considerable use of the annual analyses of Supreme Court opinions prepared by Robert E. Cushman for the *American Political Science Review*, and I do not guarantee that I have not sometimes used his language in summarizing a decision.

This business of admitting one's intellectual obligations to others always reminds me of some verses written by my favorite poet when he was considerably younger. The poem was called "Sad Plight of an Open Mind," and it was stimulated by the query of a character in Aldous Huxley's *Crome Yellow:* "Would, he ever be able to call his brain his own . . . or was it simply an education." The poem went, as I recall it:

> My whole life long I have heard praise
>   For the receptive spirit.
> The man who never read, who closed
>   His mind, was one to jeer at.
>
> So I have up and crammed my skull
>   With gems from books and teachers;
> Till now I find that my own thoughts
>   Are non-existent features.
>
> My discourse often seems to ev-
>   Idence deep lucubration.
> Be not deceived. The chances are
>   I read it in *The Nation.*

The profit motive—is it sound,
    Or will it send us flooey?
I couldn't say, but I can quote
    From Veblen, Chase, or Dewey.

My pessimism's not inborn.
    Ah no, my sirs and madams!
I picked it up from chaps such as
    O. Spengler and H. Adams.

So you can see to what extreme
    This business has been carried.
Why, I can't call my mind my own—
    And I'm not even married.

None the less, for what follows there is really no one to blame but myself.

C. HERMAN PRITCHETT

THE ROOSEVELT COURT

CHAPTER ONE

At the Center of the Tornado

B ROOKS ADAMS, like his brother Henry, tended to interpret social data in terms of mechanical concepts and the laws of the natural sciences. On one page of his book, *The Theory of Social Revolutions*, which deals primarily with the relationship of American courts to American capitalism, this habit leads him to talk of "the social centre of gravity," "the mass and momentum of modern society," and the social transition "from an unstable to a stable equilibrium."[1] Whether this transplanting of mechanical notions to describe social phenomena is a useful or reliable device may be subject to question, but when Adams speaks of the American bench as having, contrary to the teachings of experience that courts must be withdrawn from politics, been set "at the focus of conflicting forces," the words admittedly have a physical impact which promotes understanding.

Brooks Adams' view of "American courts as legislative chambers" (the title of one of his chapters) is of course almost as old as American national politics, but few others had, by the time his book was published in 1913, thought as seriously as he about the interrelationships of a society and a judicial system in which the lines of force inevitably "converge upon the Supreme Court." His conclusion was that "capitalistic government" was on its way to collapse because of the inability of the "privileged classes" and the "semi-political" courts they controlled to "protect themselves by adaptation when nature turns against {2} them." American experience, he contended, demonstrated that the courts stood as the last line of defense against social change. Consequently, "so long as our courts retain their present functions no comprehensive administrative reform is possible."[2]

Here, of course, Adams was in error. The sweeping movement of administrative reform known as the New Deal was after 1937 given the blessing of a Supreme Court unchanged in its functions, changed only in its composition. It may seem strange that Adams should have foreclosed the possibility of such an overturn, for according to his thesis the Supreme Court was a semi-political body upon which the forces of American life converged. Consequently, how could it in the long run fail to take its direction from the prevailing winds of political, economic, and social doctrine?

The difficulty in the operation of this process was that the long run invariably took too long to run. As Robert H. Jackson wrote before his own elevation to the Supreme Court:

> Life tenure was a device by which the conservatives could thwart a liberal administration if they could outlive it. The alternations of our national moods are such that a cycle of liberal government seldom exceeds eight years, and by living through them the Court could go on without decisive liberal infusions. So well has this strategy worked that never in its entire history can the Supreme Court be said to have for a single hour been representative of anything except the relatively conservative forces of its day.[3]

On March 4, 1933, the stage was set for a repetition of this strategy.

The Nine Old Men

When Chief Justice Charles Evans Hughes administered the oath of office to Franklin D. Roosevelt, the Court over which he presided was composed of nine justices whose average age was nearly 68 years. One justice, Willis VanDevanter, aged 73, dated back to the Taft administration, and the Chief Justice himself had had an earlier term on the Court under appointment from Taft. President Wilson had a woefully mismated pair of representatives on the 1933 Court, James C. McReynolds (aged 71) and Louis D. Brandeis (76). President {3} Harding's short and disastrous term bequeathed to the Roosevelt administration George Sutherland (70), a former conservative Republican Senator, and Pierce Butler (66), Minnesota Democrat and reactionary railroad lawyer. President Coolidge gave the Court one of its most distinguished justices, Harlan F. Stone (60). President Hoover had appointed the remaining members of the Court, Chief Justice Hughes (70) and two associate justices, Benjamin N. Cardozo (62) and Owen J. Roberts (57).

These were the "nine old men" who were to pass judgment on the constitutionality of the New Deal's experimental but far-reaching program of governmental intervention in the economic life of the country. At least four of the nine justices had revealed in their previous decisions a profound disbelief and distrust in considerably milder essays into governmental control. In 1918 VanDevanter and McReynolds had helped to declare the first federal child labor act unconstitutional.[4] In 1923 these two had been joined by Sutherland and Butler, and they constituted four-fifths of the majority which struck down the District of Columbia minimum wage law for women as an unconstitutional invasion of the freedom of contract.[5] In 1928 the same four horsemen rode over a New Jersey statute fixing the fees of private employment agencies, holding that these exchanges were not "affected with a public interest."[6]

Three other members of the Court—Justices Brandeis, Stone, and Cardozo—were on the other hand commonly rated as liberals and had rather consistently approved state and federal efforts at economic regulation. The remaining two members of the Court, Chief Justice Hughes and Justice Roberts, fell somewhere between these two groups in their thinking, and no one could predict just how they would line up on particular legislative issues.

The contrasting complexes of attitudes and values which go by the confusing tags of liberalism and conservatism are not to be accounted for, of course, by so simple an explanation as chronological age. "The devil himself knoweth not the mind of man," said an early English judge.[7] The oldest member of the Court was the liberal Brandeis, while the youngest was Roberts, soon to establish himself as the Court's middleman. Nor was it nominal party allegiance which divided {4} the justices. The hard-shelled McReynolds was a Democrat, Stone a Republican.

If any of the more obvious autobiographical characteristics accounted for the divisions among the justices, it was, as Charles P. Curtis, Jr., suggests, their geographical origins. VanDevanter from Wyoming, McReynolds from Tennessee, Sutherland from Utah, Butler from Minnesota—all had "grown up and made great careers for themselves out of the pioneer life of Turner's frontier." Curtis continues:

> That was their America and they loved it. When a man starts from nothing in a pioneer community and emerges with a great career or a fortune or both, it is impossible for him to believe there is anything really wrong with the society in which he did it. In the best and soundest sense he is conservative.[8]

In contrast, the other five justices had built their careers in Boston, Philadelphia, New York—far from the frontier, where men were more accustomed to the limitations imposed by a settled community and to the use of public instrumentalities for community purposes. It is an interesting speculation, and as good an explanation as any.

Jackson reports that President Roosevelt's advisers were well aware of the "brooding omnipresence" of the Court as they worked out the initial legislative measures of the New Deal. While the brain trusters made "a conscious and conscientious effort to keep within the Constitution," they none the less "knew that the constitutional doctrine on which they were relying had theretofore won adherence from only a minority of the Court. But they acted on it from conviction as well as necessity."[9] The result was that the legislative output of that celebrated and hectic first "one hundred days" of the Roosevelt administration was headed for an inevitable rendezvous with the Court.

It required about two years for this emergency legislation to work itself onto the Supreme Court calendar. In the meantime the Court's decisions were carefully watched for signs as to the direction of judicial thinking. The first significant indication of the Court's position on depression legislation came in January, 1934, when the Minnesota mortgage moratorium law was declared valid.[10] Chief Justice {5} Hughes' recognition of the fact that while an emergency does not create power, it may furnish the occasion for the exercise of power, seemed a favorable omen, but his language expressed the views of only five of the nine justices. Two months later the Court upheld a New York state milk price control law in an opinion by Justice Roberts, but again there was an ominous dissent from Sutherland, VanDevanter, Butler, and McReynolds holding that the Court should consider the "wisdom" of such enactments, and expressing their own belief that the price control law was a "fanciful scheme" and clearly unconstitutional.[11]

In the following term the New Deal cases began to appear on the docket for the long awaited test. On January 7, 1935, the Court, with only Justice Cardozo dissenting, held unconstitutional the section of the National Industrial Recovery Act authorizing a code to govern the petroleum industry, on the ground that it involved an undue delegation of legislative power to the President.[12] On February 18 the congressional resolution voiding gold payment requirements in private contracts squeaked past the Court by a 5 to 4 vote, McReynolds concluding an indignant dissent for the four conservative brethren by blurting out to the packed court room: "As for the Constitution, it does not seem too much to say that it is gone."[13] On May 6, however, the McReynolds version of the Constitution was revived as Justice Roberts swung back to the conservative side of the Court to cause the invalidation of the Railroad Retirement Act by a 5 to 4 vote.[14]

But it was on May 27 that the deluge struck. A unanimous opinion held the Frazier-Lemke Act for the relief of farm mortgagors unconstitutional.[15] Another unanimous opinion reversed the doctrine of one of the Court's earlier decisions to hold the President without inherent power to remove a member of the Federal Trade Commission.[16] By far the most important, however, was a third unanimous opinion in *Schechter Corp.* v. *U. S.*, declaring the National Industrial Recovery Act invalid on the double ground of unconstitutional delegation of legislative powers and over-expansion of the federal commerce power. These leads from the Supreme Court were promptly followed by the lower federal courts, which proceeded to grant during 1935 and 1936 {6} some 1600 injunctions restraining officers of the federal government from carrying out acts of Congress.

The worst was yet to come. Early in the Court's next term, on January 6, 1936, the Court ruled the Agricultural Adjustment Act of 1933 unconstitutional by a 6 to 3 vote in the case of *U. S.* v. *Butler.* Justice Roberts wrote the perplexing majority opinion, which Stone charged in one of his greatest dissents with being based on a "tortured construction of the Constitution." There was wide speculation that Chief Justice Hughes would have preferred to vote with Stone, Brandeis, and Cardozo in dissent, but joined the majority to prevent the spectacle of another 5 to 4 division. Then there was an interlude as the TVA won a limited victory, only Justice McReynolds dissenting, covering its right to sell power generated at Wilson Dam.[17] But in a return to normalcy on May 18, 1936, the Court invalidated the Bituminous Coal Conservation Act of 1935 in the *Carter* v. *Carter Coal Co.* decision. While the Court split 6 to 3 in ruling the labor provisions of the act unconstitutional, Chief Justice Hughes joined the three-judge minority in holding that the price-fixing provisions of the statute were valid and should be allowed to stand, so that another 5 to 4 vote was recorded. On May 26 the same lineup was in effect as the Municipal Bankruptcy Act was declared wholly unconstitutional, the five-judge majority reasoning that the statute invaded the rights of the states to deal with their municipalities, even though it was purely permissive legislation and could not be invoked by a city unless state law authorized it.[18]

The Court then climaxed its work for the term with still another 5 to 4 vote ruling unconstitutional the New York state minimum wage law for women in an opinion by Justice Butler completely denying state power to pass legislation of this kind in any form.[19] Chief Justice Taft had protested when the Court first took its position against a minimum wage law for women in 1923,[20] and now Chief Justice Hughes added the weight of his authority against such a perversion of the due process clause. Probably more than any other action this New York minimum wage decision revealed the grim and fantastic determination of the narrow Court majority to preclude legislative intervention in economic and social affairs. {7}

The resulting constitutional crisis was by no means the first executive-judicial clash in American history, although it was easily the most important, since it was the first time that the Supreme Court had imposed such a blanket veto on executive and legislative powers. Jefferson, Jackson, Lincoln, Theodore Roosevelt—all the strong Presidents had had their difficulties with the Court. Jefferson's feud with Marshall and the Federalist-dominated Court culminated in the attempted impeachment of Justice Chase. Jackson refused to support the Court's decision in the Cherokee Indian case. Lincoln disobeyed a writ issued by Chief Justice Taney. All three of these Presidents denied the Court's status as a final constitutional authority. Theodore Roosevelt, during his Progressive Party period, suggested the recall of judicial decisions.

It was apparently the Agricultural Adjustment Act decision in January, 1936, which first "turned the thoughts of men in the Administration toward the impending necessity of a challenge to the Court" as a way out of the New Deal's constitutional stalemate.[21] The overwhelming victory for President Roosevelt in November, 1936, gave the encouragement and support required for such an assault. The choice of the form which the challenge should take was not an easy one, however. The fact that much of the damage had been done by 5 to 4 decisions tended to revive proposals, made many times previously in American constitutional history, that a two-thirds vote of the Court, or even 7 votes out of 9, be required to declare an act of Congress unconstitutional. Another method previously discussed whenever judicial review had been under fire was the granting to Congress of power to re-enact a statute which had been declared unconstitutional. Senator LaFollette had supported this reform during his 1924 campaign for the Presidency. Senator Burton K. Wheeler, his running mate in that campaign, brought the proposal forward again in 1937 as a way out of the New Deal constitutional crisis.[22]

The device President Roosevelt finally determined upon, an increase in the size of the Court, did not bring into question the fundamental premise of judicial supremacy. He did not propose any limitation on the power of the

Court to review legislation. His theory was that it was a personal, not an institutional, failure that had resulted {8} in this constitutional impasse. In other words, there was nothing wrong with the Supreme Court that a few new justices would not cure. In the normal course of events, President Roosevelt would have had at least one or two vacancies to fill during his first term. Harding had named four justices in three years. Taft in his one term as President had the opportunity to make no less than six appointments to the Court, including that of the Chief Justice. But Roosevelt still had Hoover's Supreme Court.

The Court reorganization message which President Roosevelt sent to Congress on February 5, 1937, chose to state this problem of personal failure on the Court in an indirect and maladroit fashion. There was no reference to the course of recent Supreme Court decisions, nor to the constitutional crisis resulting from them. There was instead a general discussion of the problems of delay in federal court litigation, of the heavy burden on the Supreme Court and the many petitions for review which it was forced to deny for want of time to hear them, and of the need for a "constant infusion of new blood" into the courts. The one positive proposal made to achieve this goal was a request that the President be given authority to appoint a new justice in any federal court where an incumbent reached the retirement age of seventy but failed to retire. There was a proviso that the Supreme Court should not be increased beyond the size of 15 by this method.

The President's unwonted lack of skill in presenting the issue no doubt had much to do with the eventual defeat of his "court-packing" proposal. By appearing to charge the entire Court with inefficiency and inadequacy in the performance of its functions, he alienated even the liberals on the Court. Brandeis, himself eighty years old at the time, joined with the Chief Justice in vigorously and correctly denying that the Supreme Court was in arrears with its work or that its older justices needed younger "assistant judges" to help them with their duties. On March 9 the President made a radio speech in which he put the real issue directly, but by that time his cause had been irreparably damaged.

While one of the bitterest debates in American political history raged on, the Court itself began to prove the truth of Mr. Dooley's {9} conclusion that that estimable body generally, if belatedly, "follows th' illiction returns." On March 29, the Court amazingly held constitutional a minimum wage act of the state of Washington closely similar to the New York law which had been so ruthlessly invalidated only ten months earlier.[23] The reversal in position resulted from Roberts' changing of sides. On April 12 the "switch in time that saved nine" took on the proportions of a revolution as the controversial National Labor Relations Act was declared constitutional by the same 5 to 4 lineup in *N.L.R.B.* v. *Jones and Laughlin Corp.* Six weeks later the Social Security Act was upheld in two decisions.[24] And about the same time Justice VanDevanter announced that he would retire from the Court at the end of the term. For the President it looked like a battle lost and a war won.

The Eight Middle-aged Men

Once the charm which protected the Court had been broken by VanDe-vanter's retirement, vacancies on the Court came thick and fast. In the six years between 1937 and 1943 President Roosevelt named the Chief Justice and eight associate justices. When the process of re-making the Court was completed, only one member, Owen J. Roberts, did not owe his commission to President Roosevelt. Harlan F. Stone, who had been elevated to the chief justiceship by Roosevelt, had of course received his original appointment from President Coolidge.

The first of the eight Roosevelt-appointed associate justices was Hugo L. Black, appointed in 1937 to fill the VanDevanter vacancy. Justice Black, U.S. Senator from Alabama since 1926, took his seat on the Court under extremely unfavorable circumstances. He was charged with having been a member of the Ku Klux Klan, and a lawsuit was brought to bar him from the Court on technical constitutional and statutory grounds.[25] The furor gradually subsided as his fellows on the Court ruled that the legal questions had not been properly brought before the Court, and Black himself made a radio address admitting his one-time membership in the Klan, but giving {10} assurance that it had long been terminated and repudiating the prejudices for which that organization stands.

Justice Sutherland retired in January, 1938, and Stanley Reed of Kentucky was appointed as his successor. Reed had come to Washington on appoint-ment from President Hoover as general counsel of the Federal Farm Board. Under the New Deal he had been first general counsel for the Reconstruction Finance Corporation, and then Solictor General of the United States. He had defended the principal New Deal measures before the Supreme Court, but had succeeded in keeping pretty well out of the Court reorganization fight, and his nomination had no important opposition.

Justice Cardozo died in July, 1938, and in January, 1939, Felix Frankfurter, from the Harvard Law School was appointed to his seat. Frankfurter had long been famous for the power he was reputed to wield behind the scenes of the Roosevelt administration and for his influence in the making of important federal appointments. His activities in defense of labor and civil liberties, particularly in the Sacco-Vanzetti and Tom Mooney cases, had given him a wholly unjustified reputation for radicalism, and he felt it necessary to declare at the Senate hearings on his nomination that he was not a communist.

The venerable Justice Brandeis resigned in February, 1939, and the follow-ing month forty-year old William O. Douglas, then chairman of the Securites and Exchange Commission, and a former professor at Yale Law School, was nominated for his place. Justice Butler died in November, 1939, thus giving President Roosevelt the opportunity to name his fifth justice and secure a clear majority on the Court. His selection was Frank Murphy, Attorney General, appointed in January, 1940. Murphy had had previous service as high commis-sioner to the Philippines and as governor of Michigan during the sit-down strikes which had been successfully terminated without the drastic action urged upon him from many quarters.

The last of the Court's Old Guard, Justice McReynolds, retired in January, 1941, and his vacancy was filled the following summer by the appointment of James F. Byrnes, U.S. Senator from South Carolina since 1931, and a man who had been a tower of strength for the Roosevelt administration in the Senate. Then Chief Justice Hughes {11} tendered his resignation effective at the end of the term in June, 1941. In a move which was widely applauded President Roosevelt elevated Associate Justice Harlan F. Stone to the chief justiceship. To fill the Hughes vacancy Robert H. Jackson, Attorney General, was appointed in July, 1941. Jackson was known as an ardent New Dealer and apparently had been considered by President Roosevelt as a likely Democratic nominee for the Presidency in 1940 before Mr. Roosevelt decided on a third-term candidacy for himself. Jackson had joined the administration in 1934 as general counsel for the Bureau of Internal Revenue, and had served thereafter as assistant attorney general and Solicitor General before becoming Attorney General in 1940.

Justice Byrnes, after one term on the Court, resigned in October, 1942, when the President requested him to take the important wartime post of director of economic stabilization. Early in 1943 this vacancy was filled by the appointment of Wiley B. Rutledge. Formerly dean of the University of Iowa Law School, Rutledge had served two years as a member of the circuit court of appeals for the District of Columbia at the time of his elevation to the Supreme Court.

The Rutledge appointment was the last which President Roosevelt had occasion to make to the Court, but barring some holocaust of deaths or resignations the Roosevelt members may be expected to dominate the Court for some time to come. Two changes have occurred in the Court's composition since President Roosevelt's death. Republican Senator Harold Burton of Ohio began his service on the Court in the fall of 1945 as President Truman's first appointee, replacing Justice Roberts who had resigned. Chief Justice Stone's great services to the Court were terminated by his death on April 22, 1946, his post going to Secretary of the Treasury Fred M. Vinson of Kentucky.[26]

How do Roosevelt's eight appointees (excluding Chief Justice Stone) compare in character, ability, and mental caliber with past members of the Court? Of the eight nominations made, serious question was raised about only two at the time of appointment, the selection of Justices Black and Frankfurter. However, the charges made by Justice Jackson against his colleague Justice Black in the Nuremberg {12} statement of June 10, 1946, were the occasion for considerable moralizing in the anti-administration press about the general unfitness of the Roosevelt appointees for judicial posts. It was variously alleged that the Court had been packed "with men temperamentally and judicially unfitted for the duties to which they were assigned"; that the appointees were "political lawyers and small-town judges of limited experience" elevated to the highest court in the land; that they "were not selected because of their judicial experience—for they had virtually none—but because they were partisans of a particular economic and political philosophy held by the man who appointed them"; that the nominees received their appointments "for their ability to deliver votes—or as reward for having done the same." These are random selections from the editorial page of a single, rather moderate Republican newspaper. Much juicier examples could have been culled from the more rabid press.

Any judgments as to general character or judicial temperament of the Roosevelt appointees, which are difficult matters to assess, must await the examination of the record of the Roosevelt Court which this book proposes to give. But there are other respects as to which the appointments can be assayed more readily. It is true that the justices are small town men, at least by birth. Justice Frankfurter was born in Vienna, but all the others came from small American towns or farms, which is generally regarded as an asset in a country where the log cabin tradition is nostalgically honored.

It is true that the group contains several "political lawyers." Reed was Solicitor General, and Murphy and Jackson were Attorneys General at the time of their appointments. The promotion of men from these posts to the Supreme Court is quite in line with previous practice. Stone and McReynolds, to name only two of the more recent pre-Roosevelt examples, were both appointed from the Attorney General's post. In fact, 9 of the 20 appointees to the Court between 1897 and 1937 had been "political lawyers" previously connected in some way with the Department of Justice.[27]

It is true that there were some "vote-getters" among the Roosevelt choices. Three of the justices had held elective office—Byrnes and Black in the Senate, Murphy as governor of Michigan. It is sufficient {13} comment to note that six of the Court's justices prior to 1937 had also been governors of their states, this number including Charles Evans Hughes; and that ten ex-senators had been appointed to the bench prior to 1937.

It is true that the Roosevelt appointees had relatively little judicial experience. Justice Rutledge had spent two years on the important bench of the Court of Appeals for the District of Columbia, while Justice Black, as his detractors were fond of pointing out, also had prior judicial experience—18 months as a police judge in Birmingham. There were no other former judges among the eight Roosevelt choices. In comparison with this record, 12 of the 20 justices appointed between 1897 and 1937 had prior judicial experience. However, of the 8 men on the Court when Roosevelt made his first appointment, only one, Justice Cardozo, had ever sat on an inferior court, although Chief Justice Hughes had had an earlier term on the Supreme Court itself. Thus the Roosevelt practice of largely avoiding judges as appointees had also been employed by his immediate predecessors.

The derogatory remarks quoted above did not attack the Roosevelt Court on a score where it might be considered vulnerable, namely, over-representation of academic lawyers. Three of the eight appointees—Douglas, Frankfurter, and Rutledge—had been law school professors or deans, although the academic curse had been partly removed from Douglas by his work on the SEC, while Rutledge had moved on from Iowa Law School to the federal bench. The law school professoriat has not of course been without previous representation on the Court, Stone and Holmes being the two most illustrious examples in this century.

Another factor worth mentioning in appraising the Roosevelt appointees is their relative youthfulness. The previous Court with its nine old men had reached the average age of 72 by 1937. In 1943, when Roosevelt's last appointment had been made, the average age of the Court was 56 years. The average age of the Roosevelt appointees when the appointments were made, including the age of Stone when he was promoted to the chief justiceship, was less than 48 years. In contrast, President Taft's six appointees averaged slightly over 56 years of age.[28] So far as these more obvious criteria go, then, the Roosevelt {14} appointees were exceptional, if at all, only in their comparative lack of judicial experience and in their relative youth.

Justices Without Halos

The Court as thus re-made by President Roosevelt has turned out to be perhaps the most controversial in American history. In part this controversy has been of its own making, and is on its own head. But for a balanced view it is necessary to recognize that to a considerable extent the problems and troubles of the Roosevelt Court have been the problems and troubles of the times, an inheritance which could scarcely have been avoided. The Court has presided over the destinies of the American constitutional system under conditions of unparalleled perplexity. The period has been almost entirely of war or preparation for war, and in such times the voice of the law has difficulty in making itself heard above the din of arbitrament by force. The Court, moreover, inherited a structure of American constitutionalism sadly in need of repair and remodeling. Its predecessors had failed to carry out the program of continuous adaptation required to fit an eighteenth century document to the facts of twentieth century industrialism and politics. This meant that the adjustments, which should have taken place by a gradual and almost imperceptible process of growth, had to be effected without proper ideological preparation and so on occasions seemed shockingly abrupt.

By the time this process had been fairly well completed, the Court was in new difficulties. As the fervor of the original New Deal waned, and as energies were consumed in the tasks of war, and as war's illusions and unities were dissolved by contact with the bitter realities of a so-called peace, the Court found itself in the unprecedented situation of being the most liberal branch of the government, and thus in an exposed position subject to attack from the forces which in former times had been most active in promoting veneration for the Court. Every Court prior to the Roosevelt Court had enjoyed the protection of perhaps the most potent myth in American political life—the myth that the Court is a non-political body, a sacred institution on which politics must not lay its profane hands. "For the last three-quarters of {15} a century," Ewing noted in 1937, "the public has, in increased degree, sacerdotalized the court."[29] When justices went onto the Court they somehow became depersonalized and disembodied of all ordinary prejudices and passions. In the rarefied atmosphere of their chambers they were presumed to sit divining the law and applying it without regard for the feelings or interests of any person or class. As the official keepers of the Constitution, the justices shared in the reverence and awe with which that document has so generally been regarded. Felix Frankfurter, before his own induction into these mysteries, wrote:

> . . . multitudes of Americans seriously believe that the nine Justices embody pure reason, that they are set apart from the concerns of the community, regardless of time, place, and circumstances, to become the interpreter of sacred words with meaning fixed forever and ascertainable by a process of ineluctable reasoning.[30]

According to the myth, interpretation of the Constitution was not a task allowing of individual interpretation or judicial discretion, and it was precisely because of this assumption that it was believed safe to grant the Court such extraordinary powers. The justices did not make law; they simply discovered the law and applied it in the circumstances of individual cases. No less acute an observer than Lord Bryce accepted the explanation that in passing on the validity of legislation, the Supreme Court was merely "declaring and applying" the law, not passing on the policy or reasonableness of legislation.[31] Indeed, the Supreme Court itself has adopted a similar view, in what may be termed the "yardstick theory" of constitutional interpretation. The most recent occasion on which this theory was propounded with a straight face for a Court majority was by Justice Roberts in his strange 1936 opinion holding the Agricultural Adjustment Act unconstitutional, when he said:

> It is sometimes said that the court assumes a power to overrule or control the action of the people's representatives. This is a misconception. The Constitution is the supreme law of the land ordained and established by the people. All legislation must conform to the principles it lays down. When an act of Congress is appropriately challenged in the courts as not conforming to the constitutional mandate the judicial branch of the Government has only one duty,—to lay the article of the {16} Constitution which is invoked beside the statute which is challenged and to decide whether the latter squares with the former. All the court does, or can do, is to announce its considered judgment upon the question.[32]

Thus the myth has received official judicial confirmation. Yet the plain fact of the matter is that the Supreme Court of the United States always has been and, so long as it retains its present powers, always will be a political institution. The notion that the Court's justices are political eunuchs quietly going about their work of applying permanent canons of interpretation in the settlement of individual disputes, with no relation to the province of government or the formulation of policy, has never corresponded with the facts. If there is quiet in the Supreme Court chamber it is, as Max Lerner says, the quietness which prevails at the center of a tornado.[33]

The Supreme Court has been from the first an active participant in the power struggles of American politics. It could not well be otherwise when the most important political questions must sooner or later be couched in the form of a lawsuit and presented to the Court for adjudication before the legality of governmental action is known. The American constitutional system is one in which, as in the gold clause cases of 1935, the entire economy of the country may be shaken to its foundations by a $16.00 lawsuit.[34] Where the potential consequences of judicial decisions are so great, judges must be politicians in the higher sense of that much abused word. President Roosevelt (Theodore, not Franklin D.) put it very well when, in a letter to Senator Lodge in 1902 concerning the appointment of Judge Oliver Wendell Holmes to the Supreme Court, he wrote:

> In the ordinary and low sense which we attach to the words "partisan" and "politician," a judge of the Supreme Court should be neither. But in the higher sense, in the proper sense, he is not in my judgment fitted for the position unless he is a party man, a constructive statesman, constantly keeping in mind his adherence to the principles and policies under which this nation has been built up and in accordance with which it must go on; and keeping in mind also his relations with his fellow statesmen who in other branches of the government are striving in cooperation with him to advance the ends of government.[35] {17}

That the Court's members have a political role to fulfill has been recognized by the Presidents who appoint them, by the Senators who confirm them, and by the justices themselves. Probably no other figure in American history supplies better documentation for this statement than William Howard Taft, who demonstrated his concern for the politics of the Court in all three situations. The accomplishment of which he was proudest as President, so he confided to the newspaper correspondents at his last press conference before giving way to the dreaded liberalism of Woodrow Wilson, was the fact that six members of the Supreme Court bore his commission. "'And I have said to them,' Taft chuckled, 'Damn you, if any of you die, I'll disown you.'"[36] In fact, only one of his select six did die during the next eight years, but that opening gave Wilson an opportunity to nominate Louis D. Brandeis for the Court. Taft was quick to challenge this threat to the conservative policies which he had done so much to ensure on the Court. With five other past presidents of the American Bar Association, Taft fought to persuade the Senate to refuse confirmation, by issuing a statement to the effect that Brandeis was "not a fit person to be a member of the Supreme Court of the United States."

In the election of 1920, Taft had no hesitancy in using the Supreme Court as a political argument for the election of the Republican ticket:

> Four of the incumbent Justices are beyond the retiring age of seventy, and the next President will probably be called upon to appoint their successors. There is no greater domestic issue in this election than the maintenance of the Supreme Court as the bulwark to enforce the guaranty that no man shall be deprived of his property without due process of law.[37]

Harding's election made Taft himself a candidate for the Supreme Court, or rather for the chief justiceship, for he let it be known that his past attainments would make it impossible for him to accept any lesser post. Taft's expectations had a sound basis, for he had when President appointed the Court's Chief Justice, Edward Douglass White, nominally a Democrat, and White, grateful for the appointment, had told Taft that he was holding the office for him and "would give it back to a Republican administration."[38] Taft called on the aging White after Harding's election, and was disturbed no little to {18} find that White was apparently not contemplating resignation. However, White's death occurred shortly, but even then, in spite of the political pressure Taft brought to bear, Harding kept the candidate on the anxious seat for days before making the appointment.

As Chief Justice, Taft continued to play party politics of a fairly mundane sort. He was Coolidge's emissary to Harry L. Daugherty to persuade him to resign the Attorney Generalship. He sought to sabotage Senator Walsh's investigation of the aluminum trust. He was ringleader of a group which endeavored to persuade Coolidge to run for a third term, and which fought the early Hoover boom. When the great engineer, who was too liberal for Taft's taste, was elected anyway, it became Taft's mission to outlast him. In a personal letter Taft wrote on November 14, 1929:

> I am older and slower and less acute and more confused. However, as long as things continue as they are, and I am able to answer in my place, I must stay on the court in order to prevent the Bolsheviki from getting control . . .[39]

But he finally had to surrender, and permit the Bolshevik Hoover to appoint his successor.

Politics on the Court, it would appear, was unobjectionable so long as it was played by conservatives. Certainly conservatives showed no hesitation in offering the Court political arguments to defeat liberal legislation. There was Joseph H. Choate's famous appeal to the Court in 1895 to invalidate the federal income tax and thus forestall the "communist march" that was threatening private property. In the same case former U.S. Senator George F. Edmunds asked the Court: "What will become of a country, and how long will it last, where taxation and all its burdens and expenses are imposed, by those who pay nothing, upon a small minority of their fellow citizens?"[40] In our own day George Wharton Pepper's peroration when arguing against the Agricultural Adjustment Act stands as a classic political argument:

> But I do not want your Honors to think that my feelings are not involved, and that my emotions are not deeply stirred. Indeed, may it please your Honors, I believe I am standing here today to plead the cause of the America I have loved; and I pray Almighty God that not {19} in my time may "the land of the regimented" be accepted as a worthy substitute tor "the land of the free."[41]

The political history of the United States Supreme Court has thus been written so that all who run might read. But apparently the writing was not plain enough, or else we ran too fast. With respect to the operation of the judicial power most Americans remained politically untaught. The Supreme Court itself had to teach them—by its 5 to 4 decisions in 1935 and 1936, by McReynolds' melodramatic wail that the Constitution was gone, by Stone's ringing rebuke that "courts are not the only agency of government that must be assumed to have capacity to govern," and most of all by Roberts' strange waverings and wanderings as the odd man on the Court. A public which sat through this performance could be, as Max Lerner says,

> no longer in complete innocence about the functioning of the judicial process. They began to see that judicial decisions are not babies brought by constitutional storks, but are born out of the travail of economic circumstance. They learned that judges are human, and that the judicial power need be no more sacred in our scheme than any other power. . . . If only for a moment, they peered beyond the symbol of the divine right of judges to the realities of the judicial power. They dared look upon the judicial Medusa-head, and lo! they were not turned to stone.[42]

Such an experience is likely to yield the cynicism which so often follows the smashing of a cherished illusion. All those who believe in justice as a value of civilized society must regret an improper devaluation of the judicial symbol. One runs a considerable risk of overpersuading when speaking of justices as politicians and of the Supreme Court as a "legislative chamber." There is, true enough, a considerable similarity between the task of a Supreme Court justice and that of a congressman. Each is confronted periodically with important issues of public policy, upon which he must formulate a conclusion and register a vote. In form, the justice is adjudicating a current dispute between named parties, whereas the legislator is adopting future rules for unnamed millions, but in each instance the product is law, whether case or statute. Theoretically, the congressman speaks as a representative of his particular constituency, whereas the responsibility of the judge {20} is to the universal constituency of reason and justice. Theoretically, the legislator's discretion is

14

much wider than that of the judge, who is obligated to achieve a pattern of consistency in his votes. However, from the accumulation of one hundred and fifty years, precedents can be found to support almost any judicial decision.

None the less, in spite of these similarities, not even on the Supreme Court is the judicial function to be equated with that of the legislator. Judges operate under severer, if not different, requirements as to methods, as to ethics, and above all as to responsibility for basing their decisions on the fundamental principles by which their society has agreed to be bound or upon rules rationally developed from those basic principles to meet new situations. The concept of the "rule of law" has been much obfuscated by untenable contrast with the "rule of men," but it remains the core of a system of democratic constitutionalism, and the responsibility for its achievement rests especially on the courts.

The Supreme Court thus faces the dilemma that, to perform its duties properly, it must be of politics without being in politics. It must hang its clothes on the hickory limb of political principle, but it must resist the lure of a dive into the pond of practical politics. This necessity of distinguishing between the higher and lower levels of politics is a strain upon judges. Brooks Adams felt that the strain was, indeed, humanly impossible to support, and he regarded it as self-evident "that a bench purposely constructed to pass upon political questions must be politically partisan." To his way of thinking the founders of the American constitutional system had been blind to the age-old teaching of experience that the judiciary must be "studiously withdrawn . . . from politics."[43] But tears on that issue are water long under the bridge. Any examination of the present-day Court must accept the fact that its decisions inevitably have a political character, and the real question is not whether, but how well, its justices perform political functions.

Two criteria may be suggested for judging the Court's competence in its political role. The first is the representative quality of its decisions. The federal judiciary is alone among the three branches of the government in the absence of any direct responsibility to a constituency, {21} enforceable through periodic elections. Whereas the executive and the legislature have a representative character thrust upon them, the Supreme Court must labor to achieve representativeness. The process is not an easy one, for a change in the temper of the times filters relatively slowly into the ranks of a life-term judiciary. But filter it must, for there are other devices than that of election for enforcing the Court's responsibility. There is a tendency to forget the extent to which the Supreme Court's supremacy is grounded in psychological rather than legal foundations. Its function is extremely limited—to decide "cases" and "controversies"—and even its jurisdiction to do that can be largely taken away by Congress. It lacks power to execute its commands, and must rely on the executive for their enforcement. Its members receive their offices by action of the President and Senate, and hold them "subject to an undefined, unlimited, and unreviewable Congressional power of impeachment."[44] Their salaries are constitutionally irreducible, but payment is contingent upon congressional appropriations. Dependent as it is, the Supreme Court enjoys the privilege of becoming unrepresentative only at its peril, for the methods of retaliation are readily available should the representative branches of the government have cause to resort to them.

Even greater than the Supreme Court's responsibility for being representative, however, is its responsibility for being *right*. It is not the theory of the American Constitution that the ballot box is always right. That document purposely put beyond the reach of what Madison called "the superior force of an interested and overbearing majority"[45] certain protections deemed essential to the maintenance of a free political community, certain safeguards against the discriminatory or abusive use of governmental authority. As McIlwain says, "the most ancient, the most persistent, and the most lasting of the essentials of true constitutionalism still remains what it has been almost from the beginning, the limitation of government by law. 'Constitutional limitations,' if not the most important part of our constitutionalism, are beyond doubt the most ancient."[46]

Rightness for the Supreme Court consists in being able to distinguish those constitutional limitations which are necessary conditions for the healthful operation of a free democratic society, from limitations {22} which have no firmer basis than custom or class advantage or vested interest. A Supreme Court which grounds itself on such fundamental values as tolerance and free discussion and the right of assembly can hope to preserve these principles and to maintain itself against a popular wave of intolerance and frenzy. But a Court whose politics and values lead it to the proposition that an economic depression is constitutional and that efforts to combat it are unconstitutional puts itself in the grave peril of being neither right nor representative.

This book, then, is frankly concerned with the politics and values of the Court which was born out of the New Deal constitutional crisis, the politics and values of the justices who were named to that Court by President Roosevelt. This is an examination of the record of men at work making and applying the law without the benefit of judicial halos, before a public taught at last by the events of 1937 that the meaning of the Constitution is determined by counting noses.

CHAPTER TWO

Divided It Stands

PRESIDENT ROOSEVELT was reputed to have selected as nominees for the Supreme Court men who were partisans of his own social and political philosophy, which they were expected to write into law in their decisions. The new justices were regarded by many as "yes-men" who were to transform the Court into a monolithic instrument for justifying the goals of their leader in true totalitarian fashion. Yet the Court out of which such enthusiastic unanimity was anticipated has become, by statistical tests at least, the most *un*unanimous Court in American history. Dissenting opinions have been turned out on a mass production basis. The Roosevelt justices have freely rebuked one another with such charges as that they were resting "their interpretation of statutes on nothing but their own conceptions of 'morals' and 'ethics,'" that they were making "wholly gratuitous assertions as to constitutional law," or that they were willing to enforce constitutional provisions "only if the outcome pleases." Critics who had prepared themselves to blast away at the Court's unanimity have found its open and sometimes bitter differences an equally attractive target. Jonathan Daniels reports one of the justices as saying, within the seclusion of his office: "Hell, they said the Court lost prestige because we were all Rooseveltian rubber stamps. Now they are giving us the devil because we're divided."[1] {24}

The Multiplication of Division

The only indications of disagreement among the justices normally made public are in dissents registered to the decisions of the Court. Contrary to the more restrictive practices of some other legal systems, the traditions of the American judiciary have never insisted that justices sitting en banc should hide the existence of division among themselves behind a façade of pretended unanimity. Justices who disagree with a decision of their brethren have been permitted to say so, and to give their reasons. This practice has had an immeasurably great effect in facilitating the growth of the law and in promoting a personalization of the responsibility of the judge.

17

There are, it is true, powerful factors normally operating to achieve unanimity in the decisions of the Supreme Court. Leaving aside such all-important matters as the generally settled character of the American legal system, fairly strict adherence to the principle of stare decisis, and the broad similarities in training and background which tend to characterize Supreme Court justices, there are other vital conformist effects in the operating methods of the Court itself. Probably the most important of these is the discussion which goes on around the judicial conference table, out of which consensus can often be achieved. The influence of a strong and skillful Chief Justice is of great importance in leading to the discovery of solutions satisfactory to all members of the Court. The assigning to one judge of responsibility for writing the Court's opinion, rather than following the practice of the early Court where the justices read their individual opinions seriatim, is another influence strengthening the institutional element in the decision-making process. Justices who have only minor reservations as to the language or holding of the Court's opinion customarily maintain silence under these conditions, or merely note that they concur in the result. A more vigorous difference in views will of course normally be expressed by a dissent, but even here justices tend to feel that, having once made public their disagreement with a position supported by a majority of the Court, they should thereafter be ruled by the majority view and refrain from dissenting when succeeding cases involving the same question arise. {25}

During past years the influence of factors such as these has customarily resulted in the Supreme Court achieving unanimity in all except ten to twenty per cent of its full opinions. On the Roosevelt Court, however, the dissenting opinion has multiplied and flourished until it has become more common than the unanimous, or garden variety, opinion. The increase in disagreement on the Court since 1930 is indicated in Table I. During the 1930 term,* 11 per cent of the opinions were not concurred in by the entire Court, and for 1935 the figure was 16 per cent. The early years of the Roosevelt Court saw this record doubled, with nonunanimous opinions 34 per cent of the total during the 1938 term. Then a slight recession in dissents ensued, but the armistice was ended and a new increase got under way in the 1941 term, the rate of dissent reaching 58 per cent in the 1943 and 1944 terms, {26} dropping slightly to 56 per cent for the 1945 term, and then reaching a new peak at 64 per cent in the 1946 term.[2]

---

* Throughout this book, Court terms are identified by the year in which they began. The 1930 term refers to the term beginning in the fall of 1930 and closing in the spring of 1931.

TABLE I

DISAGREEMENT ON THE SUPREME COURT, 1930-1946 TERMS

Term	Total Opinions	Non-Unanimous Opinions		Dissenting Votes		5 to 4 Votes
		Number	Per Cent	Number	Per Opinion	
1930	168	18	11%	46	.27	6
1931	151	26	17	55	.36	2
1932	169	27	16	61	.36	2
1933	166	27	16	66	.40	6
1934	172	22	13	61	.35	8
1935	160	26	16	80	.50	9
1936	162	31	19	82	.51	13
1937	170	46	27	88	.52	3*
1938	149	50	34	116	.78	6*
1939	141	42	30	85	.60	2*
1940	169	47	28	117	.69	3*
1941	162	59	36	160	.99	16
1942	171	75	44	176	1.03	10*
1943	137	80	58	194	1.42	16
1944	163	94	58	245	1.50	30
1945	137	77	56	156	1.14	.. **
1946	144	92	64	246	1.71	26

*Less than a full Court sitting during a considerable portion of the term.
**Only eight justices during the entire term.

Another index of division is the number of dissenting votes cast per opinion, and this measure of dissent tells the same story. As Table I shows, dissenting votes per opinion increased from .27 in the 1930 term to a high of 1.71 for the 1946 term. The number of 5 to 4 decisions, which has often in the past been the basis of criticism of the Court, has also shot up phenomenally on the Roosevelt Court, reaching a peak of 30 such divisions during the 1944 term.

What is the cause, and what is the significance, of this unusual amount of disagreement and division? The easy explanation, since Justice Jackson's embittered blast against his colleague Justice Black delivered from Nuremberg, Germany on June 10, 1946, is that the unprecedented disagreements in decisions are the result of judicial feuds and entangling alliances among the Court members. The Jackson attack apparently confirmed the rumors which had begun to circulate several years earlier about clashing personalities and ambitions on the Court. The facts of the Jackson-Black affair, so far as they have been made public, are as follows.

Chief Justice Stone died on April 22, 1946. Speculation immediately centered upon Justice Jackson, absent from the Court since 1945 to act as chief American prosecutor at the Nuremberg war crimes trial, as his successor. According to some reports, President Roosevelt had led Jackson to believe that he was in line for the post. However, days passed and the appointment was not made. Instead, reports began to circulate that President Truman had been informed that Black (and perhaps Douglas and Murphy as well) would resign if Jackson was appointed Chief Justice. President Truman, as he later told a press conference, did not discuss the appointment with any member of the present Court. He did, however, talk with former Chief Justice Charles Evans Hughes and former Justice Owen Roberts, who were reported in the press to have advised him to go outside the Court to find the new Chief Justice. This the President did, the appointment of Fred M. Vinson being announced on June 7.

On June 10 Justice Jackson's statement, which had been cabled to President Truman in advance and which the President had asked {27} Jackson to withhold until his return to this country, was issued to the press in Nuremberg in disregard of the President's request. The reason given for putting out the statement was a column in the *Washington Star* on May 16, 1946, purporting to give the facts of a Black-Jackson "feud," and tracing it to circumstances growing out of the Court's *Jewell Ridge Coal Co.* decision in 1945.[3] In this case the United Mine Workers' Union, which won the decision by a 5 to 4 vote, had been represented before the Court by Crampton Harris, one-time law partner of Justice Black. The partnership had been dissolved in 1926, when Black was elected to the Senate. Justice Black participated in the *Jewell Ridge* decision and voted with the majority. If he had removed himself from the case, the resulting 4 to 4 vote would have had the effect of affirming the decision of the circuit court of appeals, which was also in favor of the union.

The coal company sought a rehearing, alleging that Black should not have participated in the case because of the presence of his former law partner. According to Jackson, the Chief Justice proposed a two sentence opinion denying rehearing on the ground that "this Court is without the authority and does not undertake to pass upon the propriety of the participation by its members in the decision of cases brought here for review." Jackson reports that he was willing to accept this statement, but that Black declared "any opinion which discussed the subject at all would mean a declaration of war."[4] Jackson, angered at this "bullying," said that he would himself write an opinion "to keep self-respect in the face of his threats." The opinion he prepared, concurred in by Justice Frankfurter, was on its face a temperate, unobjectionable statement, concluding that "there is no authority known to me under which a majority of this Court has power under any circumstances to exclude one of its duly commissioned Justices from sitting or voting in any case."

This was the cause of Black's war on Jackson, according to the latter, a war carried on with the methods of a "stealthy assassin," by "mysteriously and irresponsibly" feeding out "stories of feuds" to the newspapers. Jackson's Nuremberg statement concluded by saying that he was not attacking Black's "honor" but his judgment. He felt that the continued employment of judges' ex-law partners as counsel before {28} the Court[5] would "bring the Court into disrepute," and, he blustered, "if it is ever repeated while I am on the bench I will make my Jewell Ridge opinion look like a letter of recommendation by comparison."

The purpose of his statement, Jackson said, was to answer the attacks made on him in his absence and to give the facts to "the responsible committees of Congress." The responsible committees considered Jackson's facts and concluded that no basis was offered for congressional action. Many suggestions were heard, both in and out of Congress, that both Black and Jackson should resign. A preposterous constitutional amendment was proposed by Senators Eastland and Bridges which would limit any President to three Supreme Court appointments, any remaining vacancies to be filled temporarily by House election from among lower court judges. This plan was to be retroactive, forcing the retirement of the last four Roosevelt appointees from the Court.[6] Its operation, incidentally, would have forced Jackson's retirement but not that of Black, Roosevelt's first appointee.

Throughout the whole affair, Justice Black, acting in accordance with his concept of judicial propriety, refused to comment publicly in any way on the Jackson charges. It is consequently impossible to present his side of the story. It may be noted, however, that the question of appropriateness of participation in decisions has always been considered a matter for the discretion of the individual justice, and that other justices have participated in cases argued by their former law partners or firms.[7] A Supreme Court justice with an active public life behind him is likely to bring many attachments with him to the bench, and it seems doubtful whether a man is fit to be a Supreme Court justice unless he can be trusted to decide for himself whether these previous contacts are likely to prejudice his decision of a case. Justice Jackson admitted that the matter was not one over which the Court had any jurisdiction, but he none the less made it his business, choosing a method of so doing which was bound to harm the Court infinitely more than the practice of which he was complaining. The kindest course is to dismiss the incident, as Arthur M. Schlesinger, Jr., does, as

> the act of a weary and sorely beset man, committed to a harassing {29} task in a remote land, tormented by the certainty that the chief justiceship had now passed forever out of his reach. Only someone who has lived the unreal life of an army of occupation can understand the violence of his response to the fragmentary reports of Washington intrigue; he reacted as a G.I. would to rumors of his wife's infidelity.[8]

There have of course been feuds on the Supreme Court before. The late Justice McReynolds, whom Taft characterized as having "a continual grouch," was one of the best haters the Court has ever had. It is reported that he did not speak to Justice Clarke for many years, and when Justice Brandeis retired from the Court, McReynolds refused to sign the letter which the other seven members of the Court sent to him in appreciation of his services.[9] But such personal vendettas were not brought to public attention, nor did they have ramifications extending throughout the Court. In the Jackson-Black controversy, on the other hand, there appeared to be no doubt that other justices had aligned themselves to some degree around these two focal personalities. With such a state of affairs, the authority and prestige of the Court was bound to suffer.

Other personal factors probably have had their place in the picture of division on the Court. The comparative youth of the Roosevelt appointees has undoubtedly meant that they chafe at the restrictions of their judicial office and give more thought to the possibility of reentering political life than is normally the case on the Court. Jackson has been regarded as politically ambitious, and was willing to accept the controversial war guilt prosecution assignment. Douglas' name apparently would have been offered for the Democratic vice-presidential nomination at Chicago in 1944 if he had permitted it, and he has also been discussed in connection with cabinet posts as well as with the 1948 campaign. Justice Murphy took leave from the Court for a few months of military service in 1942. President Roosevelt drafted Justice Roberts for the Pearl Harbor inquiry, took Byrnes off the Court to serve as wartime "assistant President," and was reportedly restrained from using justices for other war assignments only by the vigorous protest of Chief Justice Stone. Political ambitions are of course tempting apples of discord in a judicial Eden. When lobbies form, uninvited but perhaps not sufficiently discouraged, to promote {30} the fortunes of individual justices, additional strain is put upon judicial otherworldliness.

When all these factors are taken into account, however, it would still be much too simple to conclude that the dissents of the Roosevelt Court have been founded on nothing but feuds, conflicting ambitions, and personal animosities. Take the simple fact that during the 1944 term, which was the last before Jackson's war-guilt assignment, he and Black managed to agree in only half (53 per cent) of the decisions where there was division of opinion on the Court. But during the same term Chief Justice Stone, who presumably did not figure in any feuds, agreed with Black in only 41 per cent of the Court's nonunanimous opinions. And it was certainly no personal feud which caused Justice Roberts to disagree so persistently with the bulk of his colleagues during the last years he spent on the bench. Clearly there are larger and more powerful forces at work on the Supreme Court than injudicial spleen and disgruntlement.

One of the factors usually overlooked, because it is less sensational than talk of quarrels in explaining the disagreements among the justices, is that the Court is getting continually a greater percentage of "hard cases." Hard cases, it has been said, make bad law; certainly they make for divided decisions. With its jurisdiction very largely discretionary, the Supreme Court's grist now comprises, for the most part, cases it chooses to hear precisely because they do present difficult questions. The clear cases in settled fields, where the Court would naturally be unanimous, and which under the system as it existed before 1925 often came up to the Supreme Court as a matter of right, are now increasingly refused Supreme Court consideration when review is sought by writ of certiorari, granting of which is within the Court's discretion. The increase in hard cases is well illustrated by the persistence of the Jehovah's

Witnesses sect in pushing their claims for religious freedom up to, if not well beyond, the extreme allowable limits of heterodoxy in an organized community. The resulting difficulty and soul-searching for a court desperately concerned about civil liberties are symptomatic of the increased present-day complexity of judicial life.

Another factor complicating the process of achieving unanimity is {31} that to an increasing degree the task of the present Court has been interpretation of regulatory statutes novel and complex in character. As the broader constitutional challenges to such legislation have been disposed of, the narrower but more thorny questions as to what Congress meant by a particular word or phrase rise to plague and divide the Court. Judges intent on putting the legislative will into effect must set off on a chase after an elusive and probably non-existent "legislative intent," which is sought in such places as legislative committee reports, remarks on the floor of Congress, earlier drafts of the bill, contemporaneous construction given the statute by the executive arm of the government, and the like. The method is reminiscent of the tactics employed in hunting the Snark, for in that venture, it will be recalled:

> They sought it with thimbles, they sought it with care;
>> They pursued it with forks and hope;
> They threatened its life with a railway-share;
>> They charmed it with smiles and soap.

It is not surprising if the legislative intent discovered by judges employing somewhat similar devices is often the subject of controversy, and usually bears a strong resemblance to what they feel the intent of the legislature should have been.

Finally, it may be argued that the amount of disagreement on the Court is overstressed by the statistics of dissent. Certainly it is true that in many areas where the Court was formerly divided it has now reached almost unprecedented unanimity. For example, the constitutionality of practically all federal legislation can be taken for granted under present interpretations. To a certain extent, also, the statistics of dissent on the Roosevelt Court have been artificially inflated by the fact that one or two justices were so far separated from the body of the Court on many issues. Particularly was this true of Justice Roberts during his last term on the Court, and earlier McReynolds had presented a similar problem. None the less, it is not to be denied that all the justices have participated with a will in the big push which has carried dissent to new highs in the past few years. {32}

The Pattern of Division

Dissent is usually not a game played in solitaire; the great majority of all Supreme Court dissents are concurred in by two, three, or four justices. The agreements and disagreements thus recorded can be examined to determine whether any regular pattern of alignments is evident in these votes. The existence of such a pattern would be evidence that disagreement in decisions is not a random process but is, as Thomas Reed Powell put it, indicative of "some underlying differences of gospel."[10] One useful method of presenting data on judicial alignments is in the form of a table showing the relationship between the dissenting votes of every pair of justices. Such an analysis is set forth in Table II, covering the five terms from 1931 through 1935.[11] It indicates the number of dissents cast by each justice during that period and the number of times that the other justices on the Court were also in dissent in the same cases. Dissents in which only a single justice participated are given in parentheses. The justices are arranged in the table in such a manner that, so far as interrelationships permit, each justice is placed closest to those with whom he dissented most often, and farthest from those with whom he dissented least often. {33}

TABLE II

1931-1935 TERMS	Stone	Cardozo	Brandeis	Hughes	Roberts	VanDe- vanter	Suther- land	Butler	McReyn- olds
No. Dissents	67	55	57	15	15	17	23	36	33
Stone	(4)	51	53	12	6			1	
Cardozo	51	(3)	40	12	2	1		1	
Brandeis	53	40	(1)	10	8		1	3	
Hughes	12	12	10	(2)	1	1			
Roberts	6	2	8	1	(1)		5	7	3
VanDevanter		1		1		(1)	13	13	11
Sutherland			1		5	13	(1)	19	13
Butler	1	1	3		7	13	19	(5)	17
McReynolds					3	11	13	17	(13)

In part this table merely confirms what was already clear concerning the nature of the divisions on the Court between 1931 and 1936. The affinity among Stone, Cardozo, and Brandeis is emphasized by the table, which shows that these three justices were normally in dissent together. On the other side of the Court another coherent bloc was operating, composed of VanDevanter, Sutherland, Butler, and McReynolds. In the center of the Court were Chief Justice Hughes and Justice Roberts. It is significant, however, that when the Chief Justice was driven to dissent, he did so in company with the Stone-Cardozo-Brandeis wing, whereas Roberts' dissents were distributed between both groups, thus confirming his position as the middle man on the Court as it then stood. The result was that "as goes Roberts, so goes the Court."

The table shows not only direction but also intensity of dissent. The location of control on the Court during the period is amply indicated by the fact that Stone, Cardozo, and Brandeis were forced into dissent about twice as often as the justices on the other side of the Court. The relative positions of the justices in the conservative group are rather accurately revealed by the number of their dissents, with VanDevanter showing the least amount of deviation from the center, and McReynolds taking such an extreme position that in 13 cases none of his colleagues would join him.

A point which this table does make crystal clear, and which might not have been anticipated, is the coherence of the judicial blocs. The groups on each side of the Court were almost watertight. In only a very few instances did a justice in one wing find himself dissenting in company with a justice from the other wing. This fact would seem to indicate that there were indeed "underlying differences of gospel" in terms of which decisions in practically all of these controversial matters were given. During the five-year period the justices were unanimous in 85 per cent of their decisions, but where differences did exist they conformed to a regular pattern. Locating the justices along a single attitude scale in terms of relative liberalism or conservatism would adequately account for the judicial disagreements manifested during that period.

The terms "liberal" and "conservative," though they remain the {34} labels most generally used to distinguish between opposed complexes of preferences in matters of public policy, have largely lost any precision they may once have had in describing the substance of political attitudes. Consequently, their use will be avoided so far as possible in connection with these tables, and the locations of the justices will be described simply in terms of positions to the left, center, and right of the Court. In accordance with normal usage, "left" will designate the more liberal side of the Court and "right" the conservative, but the terms are to be construed in a strictly relative sense indicating direction of deviation away from the majority view of the Court at any given time, and are not intended to convey any fixed connotation or impute the possession of any definite set of political principles.

When the interrelationships between judicial dissents during the 1936 term are reduced to tabular form, the change which occurred in the balance of power on the Court during that eventful period is clearly visible. The votes of Hughes and Roberts gave the left side of the Court control of the situation, and the four right-wing justices were now the ones pushed into dissent. The division between the two sides was absolutely clear-cut, no dissents being filed in which members of both wings were involved. McReynolds continued to hold {35} down the extreme right, with 6 solo dissents. The number of nonunanimous opinions did not increase markedly, however, 81 per cent of all decisions being concurred in by the entire Court.

TABLE III

1936 TERM	Stone	Cardozo	Brandeis	Hughes	Roberts	VanDe-vanter	Suther-land	Butler	McReyn-olds
No. Dissents	3	7	5	2	4	11	14	16	20
Stone	..	3	2	1	1				
Cardozo	3	(1)	4	2	1				
Brandeis	2	4	..	1	2				
Hughes	1	2	1	..					
Roberts	1	1	2		(2)				
VanDevanter						..	11	10	9
Sutherland						11	(1)	12	11
Butler						10	12	(1)	14
McReynolds						9	11	14	(6)

When the Supreme Court opened its 1937 term, there was only one change in personnel from the preceding year, Black having replaced VanDevanter. The eight hold-over justices generally maintained their previously established positions during the term. Black naturally fitted into the existing left-wing group, though his location was quickly revealed as substantially farther to the left than the older justices by the fact that on 11 occasions he dissented by himself. Chief Justice Hughes was so perfectly balanced in the center of the Court during this term that he was in agreement with every one of the 170 opinions it rendered. Justice Roberts, however, began to edge over to the right of the Court.

The 1937-38 Court was definitely under the control of its center and moderate left-wing members (Hughes, Roberts, Brandeis, Cardozo, and Stone) who cast a total of only 12 dissenting votes during the entire term. Justices Butler and McReynolds on the right were pushed into dissent 22 and 28 times respectively, while Black dissented from the far left on 15 occasions. Nonunanimous opinions {36} during the term amounted to 27 per cent of the total, an increase of 8 per cent over the preceding year. Replacing Justice Sutherland, Justice Reed joined the Court somewhat too late in the term to figure in many dissents, and he is not included in the table, but he did give indication of a position slightly to the left of center.

TABLE IV

1937 TERM	Black	Stone	Cardozo	Brandeis	Hughes	Roberts	Suther-land	Butler	McReyn-olds
No. Dissents	15	5	4	1	0	2	9	22	28
Black	(11)	3	2	1					
Stone	3	..	4	1					
Cardozo	2	4	..	1					
Brandeis	1	1	1	..					
Hughes					..				
Roberts						..	2	2	2
Sutherland						2	..	7	9
Butler						2	7	(1)	21
McReynolds						2	9	21	(5)

TABLE V

1938 TERM	Black	Reed	Frank-furter	Doug-las	Bran-deis	Stone	Hughes	Roberts	Butler	McReyn-olds
No. Dissents	17	6	3	2	0	4	5	13	32	34
Black	(7)	6	3	2		1		2		
Reed	6	..						1		
Frankfurter	3		..	2				1		
Douglas	2		2	..				1		
Brandeis					..					
Stone	1					(1)	2		2	2
Hughes						2	..	3	5	5
Roberts	2	1	1	1			3	..	11	11
Butler						2	5	11	(2)	30
McReynolds						2	5	11	30	(4)

The 1938 term of the Court saw the passing of the two most venerated members of the Court's left-wing group, as Justice Cardozo died before the term opened and Justice Brandeis retired midway in the term. Justices Frankfurter and Douglas were appointed to replace them. With four Roosevelt appointees on the Court, and constituting its entire left wing, the general leftward direction of the Court's movement began to be evident. The famous dissenter, Justice Brandeis, long accustomed to being on the Court's left, found that the new Court had moved so fast that he was left squarely in the center during his last days on the Court, with no occasion for participating in a single dissent during the part of the term which he served. Even more indicative of developments was the topple of the Chief Justice from his delicately balanced position in the center of the Court. But the most striking change of all came as Justice Stone crossed the continental divide to take up a position on the outskirts of the right-wing group. {37} Naturally Butler and McReynolds found the Court's decisions even more unpalatable than in the preceding term. Roberts definitely committed himself to the right wing, while Black continued to play rather deep in left field, dissenting by himself in 7 cases. Disagreement was up 7 per cent for the term, dissents being registered in 34 per cent of all opinions. However, there was a surprising amount of unanimity among the five most centrally located justices, with Reed, Frankfurter, Douglas, Stone, and Hughes casting only 20 dissenting votes among them during the term.

The 1939 term saw the Roosevelt justices achieving a clear majority, as Murphy came on the Court after Butler's death. These five justices operated during the term as a markedly homogeneous group in clear command of the situation, as is evidenced by the fact that they found it necessary to register dissent so seldom. Justice Black was completely at home for the first time on the Court, with no need to voice any solo dissents. The amount of disagreement dropped to 30 per cent, as the six justices from Black to Stone were impelled to dissent only 16 times in all. The three justices to their right, however, registered a total of no less than 69 dissents. Justices Roberts and {38} Hughes were deeper than ever in the right wing, but they hesitated to associate too closely with McReynolds, who dissented by himself on 13 occasions.

TABLE VI

1939 TERM	Black	Douglas	Frank-furter	Murphy	Reed	Stone	Hughes	Roberts	McReyn-olds
No. Dissents	4	4	2	1	1	4	14	23	32
Black	..	4	2	1					
Douglas	4	..	2	1					
Frankfurter	2	2	..						
Murphy	1	1		..					
Reed					(1)				
Stone						(1)	3	3	2
Hughes						3	..	14	12
Roberts						3	14	(2)	19
McReynolds						2	12	19	(13)

The composition of the Court was unchanged for the 1940 term, except that McReynolds gave up the battle in February, 1941, his position remaining vacant for the remainder of the term. His absence was largely responsible for the fact that the rate of dissent showed a slight drop to the figure of 28 per cent. Substantial dissent reappeared on the left of the Court as Black, after one term of comparative quiet, erupted with 15 dissents. Now, however, he had a partner, Justice Douglas, who agreed with Black in every decision during the term. As a matter of fact, the two justices had not been on opposite sides of a decision since Douglas joined the Court during the 1938 term. Murphy was considerably less enthusiastic in his leftward deviation. Frankfurter maintained his position only faintly to the left of center. The temper of the Court had been eminently satisfactory to him ever since he joined it, and he had found it necessary to dissent only 7 times during his first three terms on the Court. Justice Reed who, like Frankfurter, had never been very deep in the left wing, consolidated his central position by dissenting on occasion with each wing. Stone was still located on the outer fringe of the right wing, but Hughes and Roberts had moved more sharply to the right, Roberts {39} taking up McReynolds' torch on the far right and dissenting by himself 8 times.

TABLE VII

1940 TERM	Douglas	Black	Murphy	Frank-furter	Reed	Stone	McReyn-olds	Hughes	Roberts
No. Dissents	15	15	6	2	8	7	9	24	31
Douglas	..	15	6	2	4				2
Black	15	..	6	2	4				2
Murphy	6	6	..	1					
Frankfurter	2	2	1	..					
Reed	4	4			..	1	2	3	3
Stone					1	..	2	7	2
McReynolds					2	2	..	8	7
Hughes					3	7	8	..	19
Roberts	2	2			3	2	7	19	(8)

With the opening of the 1941 term, Justices Byrnes and Jackson brought the number of Roosevelt appointees up to seven, and Stone took over the chief justiceship. Some startling changes in judicial divisions occurred under this reorganized lineup, and the Court began to give the appearance of flying apart in all directions. The rate of disagreement shot up to 36 per cent. Roberts, previously the most active dissenter, was eclipsed by Douglas, Black, and Stone. Frankfurter issued more than twice as many dissents in this one term as he had during his three preceding terms. Even Black and Douglas, the Damon and Pythias of the Court, disagreed with each other for the first time. Douglas,

Reed, Byrnes, and Stone participated in dissents with every other member of the Court, while Frankfurter and Jackson dissented with every other justice except one.

In spite of the general melee, a definite liaison was preserved on the left among Douglas, Black, and Murphy. Reed, Jackson, and Byrnes spread themselves rather evenly over the entire spectrum of judicial opinion. Frankfurter slipped definitely into the right wing, developing a close affiliation with the Chief Justice, who in turn found himself agreeing with Roberts in 12 dissents. {40}

TABLE VIII

1941 TERM	Black	Douglas	Murphy	Reed	Jackson	Byrnes	Frank-furter	Stone	Roberts
No. Dissents	21	28	18	14	10	12	16	22	19
Black	..	21	13	5	2	6		1	
Douglas	21	(2)	15	8	3	6	2	2	1
Murphy	13	15	..	4		3	3	5	
Reed	5	8	4	..	2	1	4	5	4
Jackson	2	3		2	(2)	2	2	2	4
Byrnes	6	6	3	1	2	..	5	6	4
Frankfurter		2	3	4	2	5	(1)	10	4
Stone	1	2	5	5	2	6	10	(1)	12
Roberts		1		4	4	4	4	12	(5)

Looking backward, it is clear that the 1941-42 term was definitely a turning point for the Roosevelt Court. Several hypotheses may be hazarded to explain what occurred during that term. First of all, with seven New Deal appointees this group may have felt a certain sense of relief from the previous constraint of being only a bare majority, or less than a majority, of the Court. The battle being won, they broke ranks. Second, the practical disappearance of the old conservative bloc (now represented only by Roberts, who a few years earlier had been at the Court's center) may have operated to remove the polarizing force which had kept the Court divided into two definite blocs. Third, the term saw the debut of Stone as Chief Justice. Stone was one of the greatest and most respected justices who ever sat on the Supreme Court, but it seems to be agreed that as presiding officer he lacked some of the talents of his very able predecessor. Jonathan Daniels writes:

> The late Chief Justice Stone . . . was affectionately regarded by the court, but liberal and conservative justices alike looked back beyond

him to the skill as presiding officer of Chief Justice Hughes. Hughes stated the case and his opinion and then let the other justices state theirs, but Stone continued argumentatively from justice to justice around the table. The Saturday conferences stretched long into the evening. And in such a process antagonism sharpened in exasperation.[12]

Finally, in view of the later dispute between Jackson and Black, it may be relevant to note that 1941 was the year when Jackson joined the Court. However, he certainly gave no evidence of disruptionist tendencies at the time. In fact, he dissented less often than any other member of the Court that first term. Nor were his later alliances foreshadowed then, for he dissented only twice with Frankfurter, and the same number of times with Black.

The 1942 term saw Byrnes completing his short stay on the Court, with Rutledge replacing him. The rate of disagreement continued its upward climb to 44 per cent. Bloc divisions were a little more definite than those of the preceding term, principally because Jackson and Reed tended toward a closer affiliation with the right-wing group. The extent of Frankfurter's swing to the right is shown by his 14 dissents in company with Roberts, as compared with his mere 7 dissents with the more moderate Stone. Rutledge did not participate in enough {41} dissents to give much hint as to his eventual position. It is noteworthy that the three left-wing justices were more dissatisfied with the Court's decisions than anyone else except Roberts, who dissented 9 times by himself.

TABLE IX

1942 TERM	Black	Douglas	Murphy	Rutledge	Stone	Jackson	Reed	Frankfurter	Roberts
No. Dissents	24	23	26	2	15	17	17	21	31
Black	(3)	20	16	1	1	1	2		1
Douglas	20	..	16	1	1	1	1	2	1
Murphy	16	16	(1)	1	3	3	2	3	3
Rutledge	1	1	1	...				1	1
Stone	1	1	3		(3)	4	4	7	10
Jackson	1	1	3		4	(3)	6	6	8
Reed	2	1	2		4	6	(2)	10	10
Frankfurter		2	3	1	7	6	10	..	14
Roberts	1	1	3	1	10	8	10	14	(9)

On the 1943 Court, unchanged in composition, disagreement {42} reached a peak of 58 per cent. The principal new development was Rutledge's definite alignment with the left wing, bringing its membership up to four. Jackson and Reed continued their predominantly right-wing affiliations. Every justice dissented at least once with every other justice, except for the Frankfurter-Rutledge combination.

TABLE X

1943 TERM	Black	Douglas	Murphy	Rutledge	Jackson	Reed	Stone	Frank-furter	Roberts
No. Dissents	19	22	20	16	22	18	16	22	39
Black	(1)	15	10	7	3	2	1	1	1
Douglas	15	(1)	12	8	5	3	1	1	1
Murphy	10	12	(2)	10	1	1	1	1	3
Rutledge	7	8	10	(1)	2	2	1		3
Jackson	3	5	1	2	(4)	6	1	10	8
Reed	2	3	1	2	6	..	8	9	9
Stone	1	1	1	1	1	8	(1)	7	8
Frankfurter	1	1	1		10	9	7	..	15
Roberts	1	1	3	3	8	9	8	15	(13)

For the 1944 term the figure on disagreements remained at 58 per cent. A considerable part of this record was attributable to Roberts, who celebrated his last term on the Court with the astounding output of 57 dissents (21 of them solos). On the left the general alignment was unchanged, but on the right Frankfurter, Stone, and Roberts coalesced somewhat more tightly, with Jackson and Reed on the fringes of their group, though Reed also maintained substantial contacts with the left as well. Again every justice was found in dissent with every other justice at least once except for the brethren at the two extremes of the Court, Black and Roberts.

TABLE XI

1944 TERM	Black	Douglas	Rutledge	Murphy	Reed	Jackson	Frank-furter	Stone	Roberts
No. Dissents	30	23	23	23	17	17	24	31	57
Black	(4)	16	17	14	6	1	2	2	
Douglas	16	(1)	12	10	6	2	1	4	3
Rutledge	17	12	..	13	3	2	3	2	2
Murphy	14	10	13	(3)	4	1	2	2	4
Reed	6	6	3	4	..	2	5	11	9
Jackson	1	2	2	1	2	(4)	8	9	11
Frankfurter	2	1	3	2	5	8	..	15	22
Stone	2	4	2	2	11	9	15	..	26
Roberts		3	2	4	9	11	22	26	(21)

The 1945-46 Court was composed of only eight justices, due to Jackson's absence in Nuremberg. In spite of this gap and the replacement of Roberts, the Court's most active dissenter, by Burton, the rate of disagreement dropped only slightly to 56 per cent. Maintenance {43} of dissent at this high level is explicable only in terms of a further atomization of opinion on the Court, evidenced by the fact that for the first time every member dissented by himself at least once. Coherent left- and right-wing blocs practically disappeared. Instead there remained only attachments between certain pairs of justices, the principal combinations being Frankfurter-Rutledge, Stone-Burton, Burton-Frankfurter, and Black-Douglas.

The disintegration of the left wing is seen in the fact that only 9 of Douglas' 22 dissents were in company with his one-time inseparable, Justice Black. Murphy dropped away from Black and Douglas, but maintained his ties with Rutledge. Rutledge in turn found his closest relations to be with Frankfurter, erstwhile of the far right. The axiom that things equal to the same thing are equal to each other proved not to apply to the 1945 Court, for Frankfurter was in 11 dissents with Rutledge and 9 with Burton, but Rutledge and Burton did not dissent together once. Chief Justice Stone, who had begun his Supreme Court career on the far left, closed it on the far right.

TABLE XII

1945 TERM	Black	Douglas	Murphy	Rutledge	Frankfurter	Reed	Burton	Stone
No. Dissents	18	22	13	22	30	15	21	15
Black	(4)	9	3	4	2	2	3	
Douglas	9	(7)	3	5	5	1	2	
Murphy	3	3	(3)	7	3			
Rutledge	4	5	7	(4)	11	1		1
Frankfurter	2	5	3	11	(5)	6	9	6
Reed	2	1		1	6	(1)	6	6
Burton	3	2			9	6	(3)	9
Stone				1	6	6	9	(2)

For the 1946 term, the Court celebrated Vinson's appointment to the chief justiceship with a record-breaking 64 per cent rate of dissent. A rightward swing of the Court tended to restore a certain amount of coherence to the left-wing bloc. The affinity between Rutledge and {44} Murphy was further developed, as this pair took positions considerably more extreme than those of Black and Douglas on several occasions. The Court's center was composed of Reed, Burton, and Vinson, with Jackson and Frankfurter pairing off on the right in a substantial number of cases. For the first time in Court history every justice dissented at least once with every other justice.

To supplement this term-by-term account of the divisions on the Court, Table XIV shows the extent of each justice's disagreement with the Court's decisions since the 1940 term.

* * *

This account of the divisions on the Roosevelt Court and how they grew undoubtedly raises more questions than it answers. It does of course make quite obvious the leftward movement of the Court, typified by the progressive-ly rightward position taken by Roberts, Hughes, and Stone as the Court moved away from them. This series of charts presents an accurate picture of judicial behavior, but does little to explain that behavior. The clear-cut nature of the divisions down through the 1940 term was similar to that characterizing the pre-Roosevelt Court, except that the balance of power had shifted {45} from the right wing to the left. Beginning in 1941, however, something happened which had the effect of blurring previous patterns and softening up the blocs.

C. Herman Pritchett

TABLE XIII

1946 TERM	Rutledge	Murphy	Black	Douglas	Reed	Vinson	Burton	Jackson	Frank-furter
No. Dissents	43	34	29	29	17	13	21	27	33
Rutledge	(4)	28	23	15	6	2	7	5	8
Murphy	28	(2)	22	19	2	2	2	4	5
Black	23	22	(1)	14	2	1	3	1	1
Douglas	15	19	14	(3)	3	·2	4	1	4
Reed	6	2	2	3	(1)	1	7	6	6
Vinson	2	2	1	2	1	..	5	5	8
Burton	7	2	3	4	7	5	(3)	6	9
Jackson	5	4	1	1	6	5	6	(4)	16
Frankfurter	8	5	1	4	6	8	9	16	(3)

TABLE XIV

DISSENTS OF SUPREME COURT JUSTICES, 1940-1946 TERMS

	1940	1941	1942	1943	1944	1945	1946
Stone	4%	14%	9%	12%	19%	15%	..
Roberts	19	16	18	30	36	..	..
Black	9	13	13	14	19	13	21
Reed	5	9	10	13	10	11	12
Frankfurter	1	10	12	16	15	22	23
Douglas	9	17	14	16	15	16	21
Murphy	4	11	17	15	15	10	24
Jackson	..	7	11	17	11	..	20
Rutledge	..	..	3	12	14	16	30
Burton	..	..	..	..	..	15	14
Vinson	..	..	..	..	..	..	9

Was this because the Court was being confronted with new kinds of questions? Was it because New Dealism had such a heterogeneous intellectual content? Was it because the oracle of liberalism had grown tired and befuddled and gave incoherent answers when her followers came to the shrine? Was it because the justices had differing views as to the judicial function and the proper role of judges? For an answer to these and similar questions, it is necessary to move on from statistics to semantics, from counting dissents to analyzing the issues causing dissents, from charting judicial alignments to discovering judicial attitudes. The following chapter is devoted to a consideration of the Roosevelt Court's practices in the handling of precedents. Chapters IV through VIII examine the decisions and the divisions of opinion in five general areas—governmental power to regulate economic affairs, civil liberties, procedure in criminal trials, federal regulation, and labor—in which the majority of the nonunanimous opinions handed down by the Roosevelt Court have been registered.

CHAPTER THREE

The Quest for Uncertainty

ON APRIL 3, 1944, eight justices of the Roosevelt Court decided that Lonnie E. Smith, a Negro, had been unconstitutionally denied an opportunity to vote in the 1940 Texas Democratic primary election. This holding overruled the decision in an earlier Texas "white primary" case which Justice Roberts had written less than a decade earlier for a unanimous Court, and Roberts, protesting the liquidation of his brain child, produced what was probably the only successful bon mot of his judicial career. "The reason for my concern," he said in his dissenting opinion, "is that the instant decision, overruling that announced about nine years ago, tends to bring adjudications of this tribunal into the same class as a restricted railroad ticket, good for this day and train only."[1]

Justice Roberts went on to charge that it is "the present policy of the court freely to disregard and to overrule considered decisions and the rules of law announced in them." Such an indictment, coming from a member of the Court itself, is more alarming, though somewhat less insulting, than the comment of one pundit to the effect that:

> What the members of the Supreme Court will do with matters that are laid before them is as predictable, these days, as what a cage of chimps would do with a bunch of bananas. Inasmuch as the principal function of courts is to enunciate principles so that all men may be {47} treated alike, today and tomorrow, and be able to conduct their affairs accordingly, the simian gymnastics of the judges are not so terribly amusing.[2]

Certainly, certainty is one of the primary values of a judicial system. But there are competing values which on occasion take precedence over certainty. A legal system cannot be static in a dynamic world. The late Chief Justice Stone once said that the major problem of modern jurisprudence was the "reconciliation of the demands that law shall at once have continuity with the past and adaptability to the present and the future."[3] This task of reconciliation is primarily one for legislatures, but the courts must also participate,

37

particularly in a system such as ours where judicial rulings on matters of constitutional interpretation can be overridden only with the greatest difficulty.

An interesting example of how certainty may come out second best, which is no longer controversial because it occurred one hundred years ago, concerns the constitutional grant of admiralty jurisdiction to the federal courts. In England, admiralty jurisdiction had extended only to cases arising on the high seas or on rivers as far as the ebb and flow of the tide extended. The principle of certainty and continuity in the law called for the adoption of this rule in American law. But it soon became evident that a rule valid on a small island where tide water and navigable water are practically identical, was hardly appropriate for a continent with tremendous navigable rivers and lakes which never feel the ebb and flow of the tide. Under these circumstances the Supreme Court concluded that the claims of certainty were outweighed by the necessity of adopting a realistic rule for federal admiralty jurisdiction, and so in the famous case of *The Genessee Chief,* decided in 1851, it overruled the earlier cases and adopted actual navigability as the test of admiralty jurisdiction.

This example is scarcely needed to prove that there must always be in the law some uncertainty, some room for play, some provision for growth.[4] The objections that have been heard against the Roosevelt Court on this score are that it has been responsible for an unreasonable amount of uncertainty, and the case that can be made on this point deserves examination. {48}

Dissents and Concurrences

The contention that the Court's recent interpretations have provoked uncertainty in the law is based, first, on the unusual proliferation of dissenting and concurring opinions. "Today," says Arthur Ballantine, "the practicing lawyer finds himself dizzy with dissents and confused with concurrences."[5] The phenomenal increase in dissents on the Roosevelt Court has already been pointed out, but the rise in the number of concurring opinions has not been remarked upon. Concurring opinions are usually written by justices who agree with the Court's disposition of a case, but who have different reasons or wish to stress different points than those stated by the justice designated to write the Court's decision. The practice of filing concurring opinions has, it is true, sharply increased on the Roosevelt Court. During the 1945-46 term, 37 of the 137 decisions handed down by the Court saw the majority viewpoint represented by more than one opinion. Robert E. Cushman concludes that "the Court seems to be moving toward the old practice of the pre-Marshall period by which the justices wrote *seriatim* opinions," and he feels this to be a depressing trend.[6]

What with divisions and concurrences in Supreme Court decisions, then, the lawyer and the interested layman find themselves confronted with more to read, and because of this fragmentation of opinion are left in greater doubt as to the rule of law which the Court is likely to enforce in the future. One may sympathize with the plight of the practicing lawyer who, facing the necessity of giving advice to his clients, is uncertain how much reliance to place on a 5 to 4 decision where even the majority justices may not have been in full agreement with each other.

In passing, a demonstration of how complicated judicial divisions may become is found in two recent cases where the Court was split three ways, with the result that two justices were prevented from voting their own convictions by the necessity of achieving a majority disposition of the case. The first of the decisions was *Screws* v. *United States*, which will be the subject of later and more extended comment. It concerned the federal criminal prosecution of a Georgia sheriff who {49} had beaten to death a Negro he had taken into custody. One group of four justices, led by Douglas, held that the sheriff was entitled to a new trial. Three justices—Roberts, Frankfurter, and Jackson—concluded that the conviction should be set aside. Two justices, Murphy and Rutledge, wanted to uphold the conviction, but in order to permit the formation of a five-judge majority Rutledge voted with the Douglas group. An earlier instance where Roberts was the victim of a Hobson's choice came in *Addison* v. *Holly Hill Fruit Products*, a 1944 decision involving application of the Fair Labor Standards Act. Roberts did not agree with either of the two four-judge groups of his colleagues on this issue, but he had to concur with the bloc whose view he disliked least.

There is little doubt that the Roosevelt Court has developed a different attitude toward dissent than formerly prevailed. In the past the tendency has been to regard the dissent as a rather formidable weapon to be reserved only for situations of deep disagreement, while minor differences were passed over in silence. Undoubtedly one of the reasons for the effectiveness of the great dissents by Holmes and Brandeis was their relative infrequency. In part this was a result of the way the Court operated. As Schlesinger points out:

> In the time of Chief Justice Taft, even Holmes and Brandeis might vote against a decision in conference without writing a dissent, and sometimes without even formally registering their disagreement. Similarly, an opinion of the Court, instead of expressing the clear-cut views of two or three Justices, would be diluted until it was palatable for all the Justices who concurred in the result. Holmes, gazing mournfully upon the wreck of one of his own original drafts, described this process as pulling out all the plums and leaving the dough; but the system did produce a greater impression of unity, even if it sacrificed individualities of style and doctrine.[7]

On the other hand, Chief Justice Stone's "respect for the other person's view made him tolerant on the question of multiple concurrences and dissents," and often he "would not let cases hang over long enough to allow emotions to subside and compromises to emerge." This is scarcely the whole story, but in any case it is true {50} that on the present Court dissents appear to be registered with complete lack of restraint over differences that are not always vital ones. John Chamberlain comments that "many practicing members of the bar think the dissents are too frivolously undertaken, with the kazoo or piccolo note often substituted for the old organ tones of Holmes, Brandeis and Cardozo."[8]

Criticism of this sort, however, must take into account the fact that one of the great principles of the Anglo-Saxon judiciary is at stake. Arthur Krock suggested a few years ago that "in the interests of democracy at war, dissenting brethren should disagree in silence, or at least eschew personalities."[9] With the latter part of this advice few would disagree, but the right to express dissent is an invaluable feature of the American heritage, for Supreme Court justices as for other men. As Alexander Pekelis has pointed out:

> It must be kept in mind that the very existence of separate opinions is a characteristic common-law feature. A French judge who would dare to add the single word "dissenting" to his signature would be deemed guilty of a grave disciplinary infraction and subject to removal from office. The only country on the European continent where the individual opinions of the judges composing a court are known, is Switzerland, which is an island of devotion to the principles of democratic federalism and to the law-making function of the judiciary.

Considering these facts, Pekelis is inclined to think that

> irritation against the Justices' frequent and vocal disagreements among themselves is rooted in a conception profoundly alien to the contrapuntal common-law approach to law, society and government. . . . Quite possibly the dislike of seeing our Justices manifest their disagreement on vital issues is rooted in the failure to grasp the deeper and essential philosophy of which the First Amendment is only one manifestation.[10]

Right though Pekelis undoubtedly is, the dissenting opinion is easily over-romanticized. As Justice Jackson has said:

> Dissenting opinions . . . have a way of better pleasing those who read as well as those who write them. They are apt to be more individual {51} and colorful. Opinions which must meet the ideas of many minds may in comparison seem dull and undistinguished.[11]

As for the notion that dissenting opinions are always ahead of their time and point the way for the development of the law, Jackson is skeptical. "In judicial thinking as elsewhere two good heads will average better results than one, and time more often vindicates majority opinions than minority ones."

None the less, the dissenting opinion has important uses. Far from confusing, it often clarifies the issues in a case and aids the lawyer or student by giving additional indication of the range over which judicial discussion traveled. One may sometimes feel that the dissents reveal differences which further conferences might have composed. It may seem strange that Justice Rutledge should have to say of an opinion written by the late Chief Justice Stone, who produced some of the Court's best-reasoned arguments in his day, that "I am unable to comprehend the Court's decision."[12] But the process of conference table discussion can as a practical matter proceed for only a limited period, and then respective views must be stated, majority and minority opinions written, and the argument turned over to the interested public for further consideration. Thomas Reed Powell has stated excellently the important role which dissents play in the development of legal logic:

> Dissenting opinions have their uses, and not only as food for com-
> mentators. They may put in sharper focus the issues raised by a case
> though not solved by it. It might be assumed that majority authors
> have an opportunity to revise their script if they insist on doing so in
> order to correct misapprehensions of the minority, and it might
> therefore be supposed that egregious misrepresentations would not
> go uncorrected. Yet it would be difficult to run the business of the
> Supreme Court if there were to be in every hotly contested case a
> verbal interchange of battledore and shuttlecock. So it may be that
> in fact the majority in many instances refrain from alterations or
> additions or subtractions to defend the target from the shafts of the
> minority, and that it must be left to outsiders to spot the shots.[13]

In a larger sense, the possibility of dissent encourages and protects the independence of the judiciary, and permits the development and {52} maturing of alternative constitutional and legal theories which, though held by a minority today, may in time prove their greater vitality and become the majority view. Former Chief Justice Hughes well stated this great function of the dissent when he said:

> A dissent in a court of last resort is an appeal to the brooding spirit
> of the law, to the intelligence of a future day, when a later decision
> may possibly correct the error into which the dissenting judge be-
> lieves the court to have been betrayed.[14]

The operation of this process has been demonstrated in its most perfect form as the classic dissents of Justice Holmes have one by one been adopted as the controlling view of the present Court, a process which will be examined in more detail presently. The two high points in the career of the late Chief Justice Stone were undoubtedly his dissents in the *Butler* case and in the first flag salute decision.[15] Although Stone stood alone in his flag salute dissent, a majority of the Court had come round to his way of thinking within three years, and the philosophy of the *Butler* decision did not long survive his eloquent protest.

Something of the same case can be made for the concurring opinion. Justice Frankfurter said, in introducing his concurring opinion in *Graves* v. *O'Keefe,* where in the Court was announcing the overthrow of a long-established rule on intergovernmental tax immunity:

> The volume of the Court's business has long since made impossible the early healthy practice whereby the Justices gave expression to individual opinions. But the old tradition still has relevance when an important shift in constitutional doctrine is announced after a reconstruction in the membership of the Court.

There are other circumstances which justify concurring opinions. A justice may agree with the disposition of a case but disagree vigorously as to the reasons for reaching that conclusion. Concurring opinions are the mark of judges who believe in the influence and importance of reason and who have a serious concern for their personal responsibility in the development of the law. Basically the dissents and the concurrences which characterize the Roosevelt Court reflect the conflicts {53} of a society faced with unprecedented new problems of public policy and the deadly earnest in which the Court is considering proposed solutions.

Stare Decisis

In the second place, the Roosevelt Court is charged with promoting uncertainty and unpredictability in the law by abandoning the rule of *stare decisis* and ignoring the responsibility for a judicial system to honor its precedents. *Stare decisis,* it has been said, is

> the doctrine that a court will give a word or phrase in a contract or statute the same meaning tomorrow that it did yesterday, that it will resort to the same principles to fashion future judgments that it employed in past ones. Of course, even at its best the endless variation in the facts of cases makes any prediction from precedent an imperfect one. But in its absence, or before judges with no regard for the true function of the precedent, there is no law but that day's opinion of the judge who perhaps accidentally gets the case.[16]

Observance of precedents is the means whereby certain traditional restraints are imposed on the personal preferences of justices, the instrument for making law into a rule by which men may live. But a strict interpretation of the requirements of *stare decisis* would stifle growth and development in the law. The decision in *The Genessee Chief,* to use our earlier example, adjusting the rule of admiralty jurisdiction to the facts of American geography, could not have been arrived at without violating precedents. No rule can be honored which condemns the law to sterility, and *stare decisis* is not to be interpreted to require that result. It is not, as Justice Brandeis once pointed out, "a universal, inexorable command," but simply a rule of policy, and usually, he added, "the wise policy, because in most matters it is more important that the applicable rule of law be settled than that it be settled right."[17]

In the field of constitutional interpretation, however, a policy of *stare decisis* has especially significant limitations. It is now almost a century since Chief Justice Taney announced in the *Passenger Cases:*

> I . . . am quite willing that it be regarded as the law of this court, {54} that its opinion upon the construction of the Constitution is always open to discussion when it is supposed to have been founded in error, and that its judicial authority should hereafter depend altogether on the force of the reasoning by which it is supported.

The practice of the intervening years was summed up by Justice Brandeis in 1932 when he said:

> . . . in cases involving the Federal Constitution, where correction through legislative action is practically impossible, this Court has often overruled its earlier decisions. The Court bows to the lessons of experience and the force of better reasoning, recognizing that the process of trial and error, so fruitful in the physical sciences, is appropriate also in the judicial function.

Not only, he added, may the decision of the previous case

> have been rendered upon an inadequate presentation of then existing conditions, but the conditions may have changed meanwhile. . . . Moreover, the judgment of the Court in the earlier decision may have been influenced by prevailing views as to economic or social policy which have since been abandoned. In cases involving constitutional issues of the character discussed, this Court must, in order to reach sound conclusions, feel free to bring its opinions into agreement with experience and with facts newly ascertained.[18]

When, in accordance with these principles, the Supreme Court determines that it must refuse to give effect to a particular precedent, there are three broad possibilities open to it. First, it may simply ignore the conflicting precedent in writing the decision in the current case. This course of action has the merit of letting sleeping dogs lie, but it hardly promotes certainty or predictability, since the dogs may be awakened for purposes of any succeeding decision. An excellent example of this practice is furnished by the now-you-see-it-and-now-you-don't history of *Lochner* v. *New York.* In this famous 1905 decision the Court held unconstitutional a New York ten-hour law for bakers. Then in 1917 a somewhat differently constituted Court upheld an Oregon ten-hour law for factory workers in a decision which avoided any mention of the

Lochner case, although it seemed squarely {55} incompatible with that ruling.[19] The result of this silence was that when a Court majority of five justices decided to invalidate a District of Columbia minimum wage law for women in 1923, it was able to dig up the *Lochner* case as a precedent, contending that "the principles therein stated have never been disapproved." Chief Justice Taft, dissenting, found this all very confusing, for he had always supposed that the *Lochner* decision had been "overruled *sub silentio.*"[20]

A second course open to the Court when it wishes to avoid the effect of an earlier ruling is to distinguish the precedent from the case at hand, or to qualify its doctrine. This process is usually not too great a strain on the capacities of a clever justice, for the facts of two cases are never identical. For example, in upholding the constitutionality of the Wagner Act under the commerce clause in 1937, the Court had the embarrassing problem of deciding what to do about its 1935 and 1936 decisions holding the National Industrial Recovery Act and the Bituminous Coal Act not justified under the commerce clause. Chief Justice Hughes apparently decided that these two decisions were too young to die, like the princes in the Tower, and that it would be preferable to distinguish rather than extinguish them.[21] And so in four sentences he was able to put aside as not controlling the two rulings which six lower courts and fifty-seven Liberty League lawyers had relied on in declaring the National Labor Relations Act unconstitutional. Incompatible as they are with present interpretations of the commerce clause, the *Schechter* and *Carter* decisions remain unreversed to this day, though the Court did find it necessary in 1941, when upholding the Fair Labor Standards Act, to note that the *Carter* case was somewhat inconsistent with other decisions of the Court and that its doctrine was correspondingly "limited in principle."[22]

A precedent distinguished, like a precedent ignored, may live to fight another day. *Munn* v. *Illinois*, decided in 1877, found the Supreme Court deciding, just before big business won control of the Court in the eighties, that under its police power the state of Illinois could regulate rates charged for storing grain in elevators, because this was a type of business historically considered to be "affected with a public interest." Subsequently the more conservative Court repented of this hands-off policy toward state price-fixing and regulation, but {56} *Munn* v. *Illinois* was still honored, though in the breach rather than in the observance. There was no denying that legislatures could regulate businesses affected with a public interest. What the Court did was simply to find that theater ticket brokers and private employment exchanges and gasoline dealers and ice manufacturers were not "affected with a public interest."[23] But throughout this period *Munn* v. *Illinois* remained a candle in the window which finally lighted the wandering Court home in 1934 when it upheld the New York milk price-fixing statute.

Finally, of course, a precedent which the Court finds it necessary to depart from may meet the fate of a short sharp shock on a big black block by being specifically overruled by name. This treatment definitely liquidates a decision. Like old Marley, the decision is dead, and there is no doubt about it. The corpus delicti is exhibited to public view. Certainty on the point is as great as anything can be in as inexact a science as the law. To be sure, the ghost may walk, as Marley's did. There may even be a flesh-and-blood resurrection, but that approaches the miraculous, and miracles do not happen often.

The Roosevelt Court has done its share of ignoring, distinguishing, and qualifying. Some of its most significant changes in direction have been effected without any direct challenge to precedents which seemed to stand in the way. But it has generally not hesitated at outright reversals, which have been more numerous and enthusiastic than in any other period of Court history. To some the Roosevelt Court has seemed to assume the power of the Roman praetor who by his edicts suppressed inconvenient precedents and thus maintained flexibility in the law. The sterner standards of Anglo-Saxon justice have frowned upon this practice, and the high death rate among the precedents entrusted to the care of the Roosevelt Court has convinced many that it is not a safe guardian for the law. Thomas Reed Powell, no worshipper of sacred cows, feels that the Court has been somewhat immoderate in its zeal, and warns:

> The fact that judges exhibit readiness to undo the work of their pre-decessors in this field, whenever they would not have made the initial determination, has wide repercussions. Who can tell what other landmarks {57} will be similarly obliterated? Where shall confidence be placed? How far will transactions become a mere gamble as to their legal results?[24]

The *American Bar Association Journal,* considerably more outraged than the professor, produces an outrageous pun, the "new guesspotism," to convey its view of the present regime.[25]

A closer look at the record on reversals is called for, however, before the Court is condemned as a menace to the law. According to the author's count, some 32 previous decisions of the Supreme Court were overruled during the ten terms from 1937 through 1946.[26] This reckoning includes only decisions which the Court flatly stated that it was overruling, plus a few where the intimation was so clear that it could not be misunderstood, even though the word "overruled" was not used. In *Phelps-Dodge Corp.* v. *N.L.R.B.,* for example, the Court said of two earlier decisions that they had been "completely sapped . . . of their authority." Of these 32 precedents dumped overboard, 8 had been unanimously adopted, 4 had been originally objected to by one judge, 5 by two judges, 7 had found three justices in opposition, and 8 had been 5 to 4 decisions. They date back as far as 1842, but over half were sired by the conservative Court of the twenties and early thirties. The actual temporal distribution is as follows:

Terms	Number
1842–1900	4
1901–1910	3
1911–1920	6
1921–1930	8
1931–1936	9
1937–1946	2
	32

But the fact that the Roosevelt Court has abandoned 32 precedents in ten terms, some of them going back one hundred years, must be supported by further evidence before it stands as a serious indictment. There is general agreement that the law must grow, and an omelet cannot be made without breaking eggs. Justice Field, scarcely one of the Court's radical thinkers, said in 1894: {58}

> It is more important that the court should be right upon later and more elaborate consideration of the cases than consistent with previous declarations. Those doctrines only will eventually stand which bear the strictest examination and the test of experience.[27]

Perhaps during recent years examination and experience have disclosed an unusual number of errors in the doctrines espoused by earlier courts, particularly the Court of the 1920s and the early 1930s. If the Court has succeeded in getting itself "right" on these issues, then the overruling of certain contrary decisions is not only understandable but is to be welcomed. If, on the other hand, the overrulings have been the work of a bare majority of the Court taking advantage of its perhaps temporary authority to break down established doctrines of American constitutionalism and to set up new standards for which previous thinking on the Court has furnished no ideological preparation or doctrinal support, then the Roosevelt Court has indeed rendered a disservice to the rule of law and the claims of certainty.

Back to Holmes and Brandeis

An examination of the record on this score may well begin in a field where the precedents overturned have been most ancient and most numerous—intergovernmental tax immunity. The theory that American federal and state governments and their instrumentalities should enjoy reciprocal immunity from taxation dates back to Marshall's famous dictum in *McCulloch* v. *Maryland* that "the power to tax is the power to destroy." While that case concerned state taxation of a federal instrumentality, state immunity from federal taxation speedily developed as a corollary of the McCulloch doctrine. Once established, this principle was applied by the Supreme Court to one field of governmental concern after another. In 1842 *Dobbins* v. *Erie County* held that a state had no power to tax the office, or the emoluments of the office, of a federal officer. In 1871 *Collector* v. *Day* ruled that the salary of a Massachusetts judge was not subject to the federal Civil War income tax. In 1895 *Pollock* v. *Farmers Loan & Trust Co.* exempted from federal taxation state and local government bonds, and the interest therefrom. {59}

It was not until the 1920s, however, that the Court began to expand intergovernmental immunity to preposterous extremes. In the 1922 case of *Gillespie* v. *Oklahoma,* a state tax applied to income accruing to the lessee of some Indian oil lands was held invalid by a 5 to 4 vote, the majority reasoning that the lessee was an instrumentality of the United States used by the government "in carrying out duties to the Indians." In 1928 another 5 to 4 decision in *Panhandle Oil Co.* v. *Mississippi* invalidated a state gasoline tax collected on gasoline sold to the federal government. Another 5 to 4 decision, *Long* v. *Rockwood,* in the same year held it unconstitutional for a state to tax royalties received from a patent granted by the United States. Justice McReynolds sought to support this amazing decision by arguing that taxing the royalties from federal patents would interfere with the federal efforts to promote science and invention by issuing patents and copyrights. In 1929 *Macallen Co.* v. *Massachusetts* held a corporate franchise tax invalid because interest from national and state bonds was included in measuring the tax. The 1931 decision of *Indian Motorcycle Co.* v. *U. S.* ruled invalid a federal sales tax as applied to the sale of a motorcycle to a municipal police department. And in 1932 the Court ruled—again by a 5 to 4 vote—in *Burnet* v. *Coronado Oil & Gas Co.* that a federal tax imposed on the income which private persons derived from leasing state-owned oil lands was invalid.

This unprecedented extension of the immunity principle rested on the thinnest kind of a Court majority, and represented an extreme view as to what constituted a "burden" on governmental operations. A return to saner judgments was clearly called for, and in fact the reaction set in as early as 1931. In that year *Educational Films Corp.* v. *Ward* impliedly overruled the *Macallen* decision. The next year *Fox Film Corp.* v. *Doyal* specifically disposed of *Long* v. *Rockwood,* decided only four years earlier. But the other immunity cases remained in effect, and the *Panhandle* decision was even reaffirmed by a 1936 case, *Graves* v. *Texas Co.* The Roosevelt Court thus inherited the problem of an intergovernmental immunity doctrine only slightly reduced from its 1930 inflation.

The basis for reversing these views had been laid by the dissenting {60} opinions which Justices Holmes and Brandeis, later joined by Stone, had written. It was Holmes who effectively disposed of Marshall's dictum when he rejoined in his *Panhandle* dissent: "The power to tax is not the power to destroy while this Court sits." Holmes left the Court in 1932, and Brandeis early in 1939, so that the major task of translating the minority view of the preceding decade into the majority position of the Roosevelt Court fell to Stone.[28] He had consistently argued that immunity from intergovernmental taxation was not to be supported by merely theoretical conceptions of interference with the functions of government. He demanded that any "burdens" alleged to result be proved by economic data. This view had already won victories in the *Educational Films* decision, which Stone wrote, and in the *Fox Film* case, both of which involved private corporations seeking tax exemption for income derived from business relations with a governmental agency or enterprise.

The Roosevelt Court resumed operations along this same line, and in March, 1938, *Helvering v. Mountain Producers Corp.,* decided by a 5 to 2 vote with Chief Justice Hughes writing the opinion, overruled the *Gillespie* and *Burnet* cases. Here Wyoming had leased certain school lands to an oil corporation on terms which gave the state a substantial share of the royalties. Reversing its earlier view, the Court held that where one operating under a government contract is merely being taxed on his profits in the same way that others engaged in the same business are taxed, he cannot show that the effect of the tax on the state "is other than indirect and remote."

Two months later the Court moved in closer to the heart of the immunity doctrine to reconsider the long-standing reciprocal exemption of state and federal employees from taxation on their income. The rule in this field went all the way back to the *Dobbins* case in 1842 and *Collector v. Day* in 1871, and had been reaffirmed as late as 1937 in two decisions, *New York el rel. Rogers v. Graves* and *Brush v. Commissioner.* When the Court was asked in 1938, however, in the case of *Helvering v. Gerhardt,* to rule on the liability of certain employees of the Port of New York Authority to federal income taxation, it was prepared to reverse the time-honored rule on the ground that immunity from federal taxation should not be allowed beyond what {61} was vitally necessary for the continued existence of the states. A non-discriminatory tax on the net income of state employees, concluded Justice Stone for the Court, could not possibly obstruct the performance of state functions.

The opinion in this case carefully avoided direct challenge of any of the precedents in this field, though Justice Black in a concurring opinion urged their complete re-examination. The process he suggested was not long deferred. The following year New York's effort to tax the salary of an attorney for the Home Owners Loan Corporation was upheld by a 7 to 2 vote in the case of *Graves v. O'Keefe.* Following the logic of the *Gerhardt* decision, the Court, again through Justice Stone, held that the old theory "that a tax on income is legally and economically a tax on its source is no longer tenable." This time, however, the argument went on to make a clean sweep of the past opinions which had ruled to the contrary. Stone's decision specifically overruled *Collector v. Day* and *Rogers v. Graves,* but Frankfurter added in his concurring opinion that he assumed the *Dobbins* case had also been liquidated, while Butler's dissent lamented that in addition to these three the Brush decision had also gone down. It appears that Butler for once was correct, and that Stone was entitled to cut four notches in his gun after the *O'Keefe* case.

Finally, in 1941 the Court got around to eliminating one of the few remaining relics of the immunity boom. The case was *Panhandle Oil Co. v. Mississippi,* and its continued existence was challenged by *Alabama v. King & Boozer,* which raised the question whether a state might validly levy a sales tax on the purchase of materials by a contractor for use in building an army camp for the United States under a cost-plus contract. The Court held that Congress had granted no immunity covering such a situation, and that the Constitution did not extend it.

All in all, the Roosevelt Court directly overruled no less than eight precedents, and left several others with doubtful authority, in establishing its new rule on intergovernmental tax immunity. The justification for its action is overwhelming. That the immunity doctrine had been over-expanded was clear even to the pre-Roosevelt Court, which overruled two of its own precedents in this field. The Roosevelt Court {62} was scarcely invading the legislative sphere in engineering these reversals, for the immunity barrier was a judge-made one, and if it was unwise, it was up to the Court to remove it. The dissenting opinions of Holmes, Brandeis, and Stone had served as clear warning of the excesses being committed in the name of this principle. No personal inequities resulted from the abandonment of the old rules, though the cooperation of Congress was required to adopt legislation precluding the states from seeking to collect back taxes from federal employees. Finally, the Court kept the new principle within definite bounds, as was demonstrated when it refused to accede to the Treasury's claim that the income from "tax-exempt" municipal bonds should be held subject to federal taxation.[29]

A second field in which the Roosevelt Court was responsible for a major overturn in the law by overruling a long-established precedent attracted little public attention at the time, though it was of considerable moment to lawyers. In April, 1938, when there were only two Roosevelt appointees on the Court, it discarded a rule first announced by Justice Story for a unanimous Court in the 1842 case of *Swift* v. *Tyson*. The holding there was that in cases which arise under state laws but which are tried in the federal courts because of the diverse citizenship of the parties, the federal courts are not bound by the unwritten or common law of the states, but are free to base the decision on their own independent judgment as to matters of "general law." Under this ruling there was built up what became virtually a body of federal common law, causing considerable confusion because it produced varying rules of common law administered in a given state by state and federal courts. Justice Holmes attacked the doctrine of *Swift* v. *Tyson* in a 1910 decision, declaring it to be "an unconstitutional assumption of powers by the courts of the United States," based on the unsound theory that there is "a transcendental body of law outside of any particular state but obligatory within it unless and until changed by statute."[30]

Justice Brandeis wrote the 1938 decision in *Erie Railroad Co.* v. *Tompkins* which made Holmes' dissent the law of the land. *Swift* v. *Tyson* was attacked on the ground that Story's interpretation of the Judiciary Act of 1789 was inaccurate in the light of more recent researches. {63} More important, it had prevented uniformity and produced uncertainty in the law, had resulted in denial of equal protection of the laws, and had supported the position that there can be a body of law established without any definite authority behind it. The legal profession is still divided as to whether the reversal of this century-old precedent was a wise move, but it can be said in its favor that it was based on a proposition stated years earlier by Holmes, it had a sounder theoretical foundation than the opposing principle, and it was opposed only by two of the Court's least impressive intellects, Butler and McReynolds.

The last of the nineteenth century precedents to be abandoned was the famous 1869 insurance case of *Paul* v. *Virginia*. Its reversal in 1944 was one of the most controversial of the Roosevelt Court's decisions, and may appear to render the Court subject to criticism on the basis of the standards stated previously. Not only was the reversal felt to undermine the entire structure of state regulation and taxation of the insurance business, but there was the additional fact that this major overturn was accomplished by less than a majority of the Court, the vote being 4 to 3.

Paul v. *Virginia* had concerned the validity of a Virginia statute regulating insurance companies doing business in that state, which was resisted by out-of-state companies on the ground that their business in Virginia was interstate commerce. The Court concluded, however, that insurance contracts are local transactions, even though the parties are domiciled in different states, and consequently are subject to local regulation. On this decision the American system of state insurance regulation was built, and a business with assets exceeding 37 billions, annual premium receipts of 6 billions, touching vitally the interests of practically every person in the country, and carried on through interstate operations on a gigantic scale, continued in legal theory to be a merely "local" business.

The theory was challenged when the Department of Justice in 1942 secured indictments against the South-Eastern Underwriters Association (representing a membership of nearly 200 private stock fire insurance companies) alleging conspiracies to fix prices and monopolize trade and commerce in violation of the Sherman Anti-Trust Act. The {64} federal district court, bound by three-quarters of a century of precedents, held the statute inapplicable.

The Supreme Court, however, was free to re-examine the precedents. What Justice Black, speaking for the Court in *United States* v. *South-Eastern Underwriters Association*, found as a result of this reexamination was that all the precedents holding the insurance business not to be commerce were cases where the validity of *state* statutes had been at issue, and the question had been the extent to which the commerce clause automatically deprived states of the power to regulate insurance. It was in these circumstances that the Court had consistently upheld state regulatory authority. The *South-Eastern* case was the first in which the Court had been asked to pass on the applicability of a *federal* statute to companies doing an interstate insurance business. "Past decisions of this Court," Black noted, "emphasize that legal formulae devised to uphold state power cannot uncritically be accepted as trustworthy guides to determine Congressional power under the Commerce Clause."

Coming at the problem from this angle, an entirely different line of precedents became applicable. All the cases in which the transportation or movement across state lines of lottery tickets, stolen automobiles, kidnapped persons, women for immoral purposes, diseased cattle, and radio waves had been held to be interstate commerce and subject to federal regulation were the controlling authorities. If activities of these variegated sorts were interstate commerce, then Black felt that "it would indeed be difficult now to hold that no activities of any insurance company can ever constitute interstate commerce." While a contract of insurance might not in itself be interstate commerce, the entire transaction of which it is a part is a chain of events crossing state boundaries. "No commercial enterprise of any kind which conducts its activities across state lines has been held to be wholly beyond the regulatory power of Congress under the Commerce Clause. We cannot make an exception of the business of insurance."

This was the conclusion of four members of the Court—Justices Black, Douglas, Murphy, and Rutledge—one less than a clear majority. But the three other justices who participated in the decision, and who wrote dissenting opinions (Stone, Frankfurter, and Jackson), were in {65} agreement with the majority that the insurance business constituted interstate commerce or affected it so vitally as to justify congressional regulation under the commerce clause. It is true that Chief Justice Stone wavered somewhat on this point. While he agreed to this proposition at the beginning of his dissent, he still clung to the view that insurance contracts could be considered as separate local incidents, and consequently that rate-fixing or other restraints on competition in entering into such contracts were not subject to federal control. But at least six members of the Court were in agreement that *Paul* v. *Virginia* misstated the present constitutional situation of the insurance business.[31]

The real disagreement between the majority and two of the dissenters, Stone and Frankfurter, was as to whether Congress had *intended* the Sherman Act to apply to insurance. *Paul* v. *Virginia* was decided in 1869. The Sherman Act was passed in 1890. Did Congress, which was well aware of the existence of the decision and the constitutional exemption it gave insurance, intend to adopt the status quo as a permanent limitation on the Sherman Act, or did it mean to use its constitutional power to any extent that judicial decision might subsequently expand it to cover?[32] An answer to this question was sought by examination of the congressional reports and debates on the Sherman Act at the time of its adoption. Justice Black's conclusion for the majority from this study was: "We have been shown not one piece of reliable evidence that the Congress of 1890 intended to freeze the proscription of the Sherman Act within the mold of then current judicial decisions defining the commerce power." Chief Justice Stone, confronted with the same absence of satisfactory indication of congressional intent, appeared to assume that the burden of proof should fall on those who sought to hold the act applicable to insurance, and the absence of such proof was taken as evidence that Congress had not "intended the Act to apply to matters in which under prevailing decisions of this Court, commerce was not involved.

Justice Jackson, the third dissenter, was little concerned with what Congress had or had not intended in 1890. His opinion was frankly devoted to a discussion of the public policy most appropriate for the Court to adopt in this confused situation. Agreeing that as a matter of fact {66} insurance was interstate commerce, he felt that as a matter of law a "constitutional fiction" had been developed holding insurance not to be commerce. Until Congress itself destroyed that fiction by new legislation specifically applicable to insurance, he believed that the Court should continue to observe it. For the Court to validate federal control when there was no federal legislation covering the insurance business on the statute books would force Congress to act immediately to provide such legislation, and he felt that "a poorer time to thrust upon Congress the necessity for framing a plan for nationalization of insurance control would be hard to find." He concluded his admittedly "political" argument with these words:

> To use my office, at a time like this, and with so little justification in necessity, to dislocate the functions and revenues of the states and to catapult Congress into immediate and undivided responsibility for supervision of the nation's insurance business is more than I can reconcile with my view of the function of this Court in our society.

The chaos which Justice Jackson foresaw happily did not eventuate. Even in the midst of war Congress proved resourceful enough to deal with the situation, quickly passing the McCarran Act confirming state regulation and taxation of the insurance business and its exemption from any federal statutes not specifically covering the business of insurance, with the exception of the Sherman Act and three other federal statutes specifically named. In 1946 the effectiveness of the new statute was tested both by a state taxation case and by a state regulation case,[33] and the Court unanimously upheld state powers on both counts.

Examination of other decisions overruled by the Roosevelt Court reveals that in several instances the cases it abandoned as precedents had themselves been established in disregard of still earlier precedents. For example, in the 1935 case of *Colgate* v. *Harvey*, the pre-Roosevelt Court had invalidated a Vermont income tax act which exempted from taxation income from money loaned inside the state while taxing income from loans outside the state. One of the grounds for the Count's conclusion, stated by Justice Sutherland, was that this provision {67} abridged the privileges and immunities of citizens of the United States, contrary to the Fourteenth Amendment.

This interpretation did violence to the long-established rule, laid down when this part of the Fourteenth Amendment was first discussed in the famous *Slaughter House Cases* of 1873, that the clause protects only those privileges and immunities peculiarly attaching to national citizenship as distinguished from state citizenship. The great mass of ordinary and fundamental rights of citizens which they enjoy by virtue of the common law or of state statutory or constitutional provisions remained, according to this view, within the protection of the states. Justice Sutherland made scarcely any pretense of citing any authority or justification for his surprising reversal of this doctrine, and Justice Stone, with Brandeis and Cardozo concurring, riddled the decision as "feeble indeed" in relying upon "the almost forgotten privileges and immunities clause" which on 44 previous occasions the Court had refused to utilize for invalidating state legislation.

It is consequently not surprising that when the first opportunity offered, the Roosevelt Court disposed of Sutherland's pipe dream. *Madden* v. *Kentucky,* decided in 1940, involved a Kentucky statute taxing citizens of that state at a higher rate on bank deposits kept outside the state than on deposits within the state. The Court by a 6 to 2 vote held the tax valid, saying: "We think it quite clear that the right to carry out an incident to a trade, business or calling such as the deposit of money in banks is not a privilege of national citizenship." *Colgate* v. *Harvey* was specifically overruled, the Roosevelt Court thus honoring a 67-year-old, and reversing a 5-year-old, precedent.[34]

A second instance of this sort involves the famous, or infamous, case of *Hammer* v. *Dagenhart,* decided by a 5 to 4 vote in 1918. The Court majority there declared unconstitutional the federal Child Labor Act of 1916, which sought to close the channels of interstate commerce to goods produced by child labor, on the ground that regulation of production was a local affair reserved to the states by the Tenth Amendment. Probably no federal statute has ever been invalidated on weaker grounds. The Court had earlier approved other statutes excluding lottery tickets and impure foods from interstate commerce, but those precedents were not relevant, the majority opinion by Justice {68} Day urged, because in those cases the articles shipped were intrinsically harmful, while goods produced by child labor "are of themselves harmless."

The dissent from this view, written by Justice Holmes and concurred in by McKenna, Brandeis, and Clarke, was generally regarded as a complete refutation of the Court's reasoning, and subsequent decisions deprived the *Hammer* case of much of its authority. Congress deliberately challenged its validity by passing the Fair Labor Standards Act of 1938, a statute which, with its regulation of wages and hours of persons engaged in commerce and in the production of goods for commerce, could not be upheld if *Hammer* v. *Dagenhart* was still controlling. The test came in 1941, and the statute won. Justice Stone, speaking for a unanimous Court in *United States* v. *Darby Lumber Co.,* obviously regarded the 1918 decision as so contemptible as scarcely to merit a decent burial.

> The distinction on which the decision was rested that Congressional power to prohibit interstate commerce is limited to articles which in themselves have some harmful or deleterious property—a distinction which was novel when made and unsupported by any provision of the Constitution—has long since been abandoned. . . . The conclusion is inescapable that *Hammer* v. *Dagenhart* was a departure from the principles which have prevailed in the interpretation of the commerce clause both before and since the decision and that such

vitality, as a precedent, as it then had has long since been exhausted. It should be and now is overruled.

In situations of this sort the Roosevelt Court has been the conservator of constitutional traditions and the upholder of precedents against the conservative Court of the two preceding decades which in its zeal to protect property and limit government activity did not hesitate to override doctrines set up by *its* predecessors.

It is not feasible to continue the roll call of overruled decisions farther at this point. Most of the cases not yet mentioned will be dealt with at the appropriate place in succeeding chapters. But careful examination of all 32 of the overruled decisions scarcely seems to support Justice Roberts' jibe that the Roosevelt Court has been characterized by "an intolerance for what those who have composed this court in {69} the past have conscientiously and deliberately concluded," or that it is proceeding on "an assumption that knowledge and wisdom reside in us which was denied to our predecessors."[35] It would seem more accurate to say that the Roosevelt Court has simply been picking different predecessors by which to be guided. For it is a striking fact that 22 of the 32 decisions which the Roosevelt Court has reversed had been originally announced over the objection of Holmes, Brandeis, or Stone, singly or in combination. Specifically, 19 of the 32 decisions had been handed down while Justice Holmes was a member of the Court, and he had registered dissents against 14 of them. As for Justice Brandeis, he was on the Court when 20 of the subsequently discarded decisions were made, and he had objected to 17 of them. Justice Stone was a participant in 13 of the 32 decisions, and in 10 of them he had dissented.

Thus during the 1920s and early 1930s Holmes, Brandeis, and Stone were in their dissents pointing the way on a significant number of issues to a different course of constitutional development than that espoused by the Court majority of that time. The road of that majority led straight to the constitutional impasse of 1935 and 1936. The Roosevelt Court has since 1937 been registering its conviction that this road was not a wise or necessary one. But it has not had to do much trail-breaking of its own, for an alternative road had already been mapped out by "Holmes, Brandeis, and Stone, dissenting."

* * *

The compulsion exercised by the principle of *stare decisis is* the compulsion of the beaten track. The beaten track is normally the safest and most satisfactory road. The pressures that keep a Court close to it are very great. Fortunately, the track beaten by one hundred and fifty years of constitutional interpretation is a broad one. All things considered, the Roosevelt Court has strayed very little from it, nor has it denied the value of precedents or ignored society's psychological need for security and the practical need for continuity in the development of rules of law. Justice Frankfurter has recently said: "We recognize that *stare decisis* embodies an important social {70} policy. It represents an element of continuity in law and is rooted in the psychologic need to satisfy reasonable expectations."[36]

And already the Roosevelt Court has begun to stress the necessity of honoring its own precedents. When an interpretation laid down in the 1941 case of *United States* v. *Classic* came up for reconsideration in 1945, Justice Douglas, speaking for the Court, reminded the minority: "The rule adopted in the *Classic* case was formulated after mature consideration. It should be good for more than one day only."[37] Thus precisely the same argument which Justice Roberts employed against the Roosevelt Court in an attempt to restrain it from an alleged disregard of the rules of its predecessors is appropriated by the Court for the defense of its own new line of decisions, and the deviation of one term becomes the rule for the next. So quickly does the living stuff of the law harden into the crust of precedent.

CHAPTER FOUR

Economic Regulation and Legislative Supremacy

THE HISTORIC POSITION of liberalism on judicial review has been that the judicial function is a limited one and that, as Justice Stone said in his memorable *Butler* dissent, "courts are not the only agency of government that must be assumed to have capacity to govern." Liberals have long criticized the Supreme Court for its chronic inability to remember that it is not the policy-forming organ of the government and that it must refrain from substituting its judgment for that of Congress or the state legislatures. It was on this point that Justice Holmes insisted particularly in his series of great dissenting opinions charging his colleagues with invalidating legislation because they did not agree with its philosophy, and it was on this ground that Holmes' reputation for liberalism was largely based. Whether he himself approved of many of the legislative policies for which his dissenting opinions spoke may well be doubted, but he was firmly convinced that it was not the province of a judge to veto legislative judgments merely because they did not conform with his own social and economic views.

Most of Holmes' classic pronouncements on the necessity for judicial self-limitation came in cases where business regulation, taxation, or experimental economic legislation was at issue. It is in this area that the Roosevelt Court has adopted the Holmes philosophy of legislative supremacy most wholeheartedly. His doctrines have been {72} re-stated, and in some respects applied in new ways. There has been a new emphasis on the restricted competence of the judge, who is accepted as an expert only in matters of law, able to claim little authority when other than legal issues are involved. There has been a new stress on the inherent limitations of a lawsuit as a vehicle for the formulation of broad public policies. A legal controversy, it has been pointed out, allows the presentation only of those facts that are judicially cognizable about a particular situation, and they may be far from representative. If the Court uses this individual instance for formulation of a sweeping general rule, as it does when it enunciates a principle of constitutionality, there may be consequences totally unpredictable from the limited information the Court had at its disposal. This acceptance by the Court of its limitations as a policy-forming agency, fortified by the fact that the members of the Roosevelt Court were favorably inclined toward the general economic and social goals of the New Deal, has combined to produce a marked judicial deference toward Congress and an almost unbroken record of upholding congressional interpretations of federal regulatory powers.

The Constitution Among Friends

The unique position of the Supreme Court is built in no small measure upon its power to declare acts of Congress unconstitutional. Recognition of the existence of this power tends to dominate all discussions of the Court, like the death's-head at a feast. In fact, American thought on constitutional problems has tended to be preoccupied, as Carl Swisher has recently pointed out, with the negative problem of unconstitutionality, with what cannot be done, rather than with the positive problems of developing and adjusting our constitutional system. It has practically been assumed that unless the Supreme Court declares a law unconstitutional every now and then, it is failing to perform its duty. There has been a tendency to regard the fact that the Roosevelt Court has made almost no use of this power as a kind of reflection upon its competence or as a sign of lack of independence.

Many learned volumes have been written about the Supreme Court's power to declare acts of Congress unconstitutional, but the {73} lessons learned in a century and a half of experience were pretty well foreshadowed in the first two uses which the Court made of its weapon. In *Marbury* v. *Madison*, decided in 1803, John Marshall showed how a declaration of unconstitutionality could be used against the other branches of the government as a political attack which, in *the short run,* they could not counter. Thomas Jefferson fumed about judicial usurpation, and Congress threatened impeachment, but the victory remained with Marshall. Once its existence had been established, the genie was not called on again until the *Dred Scott* decision of 1857, when a Court representing the slavocracy conjured it out of the bottle to strike down the Missouri Compromise and thus helped to insure the Civil War. Here the moral is that, in spite of its power, when the Court attempts to thwart the political decisions of American democracy, it will be overridden—sooner or later, peacefully or with violence. The pre-Roosevelt Court, faced with the challenge of the Roosevelt New Deal, showed that it had learned the lesson of *Marbury* v. *Madison,* but had failed to grasp the meaning of *Dred Scott* v. *Sandford.*

Through the years Supreme Court justices, like the atomic scientists, have developed certain precautions to be observed in handling their explosive power. A violation of the Constitution must be "plain and clear" before the Court so declares it. As Marshall said in *Fletcher* v. *Peck*:

It is not to be on slight implication and vague conjecture that the legislature is to be pronounced to have transcended its powers, and its acts to be considered as void. The opposition between the constitution and the law should be such that the judge feels a clear and strong conviction of their incompatibility with each other.

Likewise the Court has ruled that it must avoid passing on constitutional questions unless such a ruling is absolutely necessary for the disposition of the case. If there is any construction of a questioned statute which will render it constitutional, that interpretation is to be adopted, for every presumption is in favor of the validity of the act. Another restriction stated by Marshall was that the Court would not, except in a matter of absolute necessity, deliver any judgment in cases {74} where constitutional questions were involved in which a majority of the entire Court did not concur, although ordinary questions may be settled by the majority of a quorum. Then there is the doctrine of "political questions," which affords the Court an opportunity to escape embarrassingly difficult problems by holding certain acts of the executive and the legislature to be "political" in character and so beyond judicial control.

Such rules and doctrines, however, are of much less consequence for an understanding of the processes of judicial review than an insight into what Holmes called the "inarticulate major premises" of the judges called on to exercise these powers. The major premise of the Roosevelt Court in this respect has been a disposition to construe the American Constitution broadly, giving the legislature and the executive wide scope of authority in meeting problems unforeseen by the founding fathers in 1787. This premise is not, of course, peculiar to the Roosevelt Court. It has motivated all the great interpreters of the document. John Marshall was the first to warn that the Constitution was not to be entrusted to pettifoggers who would appraise it as though it were a will or an agency agreement. "We must never forget," he said in *McCulloch* v. *Maryland*, "that it is a constitution we are expounding"—and a constitution, moreover, "intended to endure for ages to come, and consequently, to be adapted to the various crises of human affairs."

At times this spirit has been lost. The Court was not acting in the Marshall tradition when, between January 7, 1935, and May 25, 1936, it struck down eleven major pieces of legislation adopted by Congress for dealing with the problems of the depression. In this holocaust the federal government's power over interstate commerce was seriously restricted, its taxing power was challenged, undue delegation of legislative powers to the President was discovered for the first time in American constitutional interpretation, the limitations of due process were extended, and in the name of the doctrine of "dual federalism" the Tenth Amendment with its reservation of powers to the states was used to block action by the federal government in fields where the Constitution expressly grants power to act.

The liquidation of these doctrines, most of them announced {75} in decisions where the vote was 5 to 4 or 6 to 3, got under way even before the first Roosevelt appointee appeared on the bench. The commerce clause, on which nearly all the important federal regulatory statutes are based, was released from the confines of the Schechter and the Carter cases by the *Jones & Laughlin* decision in April, 1937. Other liberal interpretations of the scope of the commerce power followed this lead. The Fair Labor Standards Act of 1938 was approved by a unanimous Court in 1941, a step requiring, as already noted, the overruling of *Hammer* v. *Dagenhart* in the process. The registration provisions of the Public Utility Act of 1935 were upheld with but a single dissenting vote in 1938,[1] and other provisions of the same act, including the "death sentence," were unanimously accepted as constitutional in two 1946 decisions.[2] In contrast with the sad fate of the first Agricultural Adjustment Act of 1933, which was done to death by the *Butler* decision, the A.A.A. of 1938 and other agricultural legislative programs were held clearly valid as regulations of interstate commerce.[3] Where the Coal Act of 1935 had been liquidated, the Bituminous Coal Act of 1937, omitting the earlier statute's labor provisions, was approved in 1940 with but one dissent.[4] The Municipal Bankruptcy Act, little changed from the version declared unconstitutional in 1936, was upheld in 1938.[5] The first Railroad Retirement Act had its head chopped off in 1935, but the second, and quite similar, act was not even carried to the Supreme Court for a constitutional test. In the *Appalachian Electric Power Co.* decision of 1940 the Court pushed to its widest possible extent the plenary control of the federal government over navigable waters and the hydroelectric power derived from them. How the insurance business was brought under the wing of the federal commerce clause has already been described.

Under the interpretations of the Roosevelt Court, it is not easy to say what the limits are on federal regulatory control under the commerce clause. When a farmer raising 23 acres of wheat, none of it intended for interstate commerce but all to be consumed on the farm or fed to stock, is held to have such an effect on interstate commerce as to be liable to marketing penalties imposed under the Agricultural Adjustment Act of 1938,[6] then it is pretty clear that agricultural production, {76} which as recently as 1936 had been held by the Court to be a local matter, has been completely federalized.

Almost the only recent occasions where the Court has discovered business activities free from federal regulation under the commerce clause have been in situations where Congress had deliberately chosen not to use its full range of regulatory authority. Thus in *Federal Trade Commission* v. *Bunte Brothers,* decided in 1941, the Court refused to allow the Commission to forbid the use of unfair methods in local sales on the ground that they handicapped interstate competitors. The Interstate Commerce Commission has long had power in comparable situations under the doctrine of the *Shreveport* case, but the Court concluded that Congress had not intended the F.T.C. to have similar authority. A more recent instance where the Court failed to push the commerce clause as far as it was urged to do came in a 1947 ruling to the effect that taxicab service available at Chicago railroad stations was not part of interstate commerce.[7]

In fields other than commerce the Roosevelt justices have shown the same tendency to reverse the doctrines which their predecessors sought to establish in 1935 and 1936, and have confirmed the constitutional basis of broad congressional and executive action programs. The taxing power, challenged by the *Butler* decision in 1936, was firmly re-established when the Social Security

Act tax provisions were upheld in 1937.[8] The notion that the reserved powers of the states can have the effect of limiting the federal government in the exercise of its specifically granted powers gave up the ghost when *Hammer* v. *Dagenhart* was liquidated in 1941.[9] The authority of Congress to aid municipalities in establishing publicly owned power systems was upheld in *Alabama Power Co.* v. *Ickes.* Charges that federal regulatory statutes unconstitutionally delegated legislative powers to administrative agencies were for the most part taken seriously on the Roosevelt Court only by Justice Roberts.[10] The constitutionality of wartime price and rent controls was practically assumed by the Court without discussion.[11] What might have been the most important decision with respect to presidential power in wartime, arising from Army seizure of the Montgomery Ward properties, failed to materialize when the issues became moot before the case reached the Supreme Court.[12] {77}

So far as congressional exercise of authority in the economic field is concerned, then, the policy has been strictly hands off. Like Marshall, the Roosevelt Court has interpreted the Constitution as a document intended to be "adapted to the various crises of human affairs."

A Ceiling for Due Process

While the Court has been conforming the Constitution to a greatly expanded federal power, it has been seeking to give the same kind of leeway to the states by adopting a lenient attitude in applying the standards of the federal Constitution to state economic legislation. The pre-Roosevelt Court made a show of protecting states' rights by using the Tenth Amendment to strike down federal legislation "invading" local concerns, but it was at the same time taking away from the states their taxing and regulatory powers by exaggerated interpretations of the limitations imposed by the Fourteenth Amendment, the commerce clause, and other provisions of the Constitution. It was particularly the due process clause which the Court relied upon in its crusade against state legislation, a practice against which Holmes had protested in his classic *Baldwin* v. *Missouri* dissent:

> I have not yet adequately expressed the more than anxiety that I feel at the ever increasing scope given to the Fourteenth Amendment in cutting down what I believe to be the constitutional rights of the States. As the decisions now stand, I see hardly any limit but the sky to the invalidating of those rights if they happen to strike a majority of this Court as for any reason undesirable. I cannot believe that the Amendment was intended to give us *carte blanche* to embody our economic or moral beliefs in its prohibitions.

The Roosevelt Court has followed Holmes completely in eliminating the due process clause as a barrier to state taxing or business regulatory legislation. Since the 1938 term not a single state law in these categories has been invalidated on due process grounds. If the sky was the limit before, now there is a ceiling.

The most important due process controversy over state taxing powers settled by the Roosevelt Court concerns the constitutionality {78} of double taxation by state inheritance levies. Competition among states in taxing intangible property has long posed problems for the courts. A state must, of course, have jurisdiction of such property in order to tax it, and the general rule has been that the situs of intangible property for taxing purposes is in the state where the owner or creditor has his domicile. But there are at least three other competing theories concerning situs which have been followed to some extent, yielding the possibility that the same property in intangibles may be taxed by more than one state. In 1903 the Supreme Court, speaking through Justice Holmes in the case of *Blackstone* v. *Miller,* specifically admitted this possibility in ruling that debts are taxable both at the domicile of the debtor and at that of the creditor.

To the property-minded Court of the late twenties, double taxation of intangibles looked exceedingly dangerous, and they set about to declare it unconstitutional, at least in the field of inheritance taxation. Inheritance taxes are levied not upon the property inherited but upon the privilege of succession to the property. The state of the deceased person's domicile may consequently levy inheritance taxes in an amount determined by the value of the property transmitted. Other states may, however, have control of some of the property involved, and may also seek to levy taxes measured by the value of such portion of the estate.

A case of this sort arose in 1930, involving a resident of New York who died leaving a large amount of bonds issued by the state of Minnesota. New York of course taxed the transfer of the bonds, but Minnesota sought to levy an inheritance tax on the same transfer. The latter tax was held void by the Court in *Farmers' Loan & Trust Co.* v. *Minnesota,* on the ground that Minnesota had no jurisdiction over the bonds and so was seeking to take property without due process of law. The Court, which divided 7 to 2, specifically overruled *Blackstone* v. *Miller* in establishing its new view that double taxation of intangibles was unconstitutional.

The same position was taken a little later in *Baldwin* v. *Missouri,* a decision made noteworthy by the famous Holmes dissent previously referred to. And the prohibition on double taxation was given a definitive statement in the 1932 decision of *First National Bank of Boston* v. *Maine,* {79} where the Court held that Maine had no power to tax the transfer of shares of stock in a Maine corporation owned by a citizen of Massachusetts and located in Massachusetts. A three-judge minority of Holmes, Brandeis, and Stone contended that Maine should be permitted to tax the transfer since the nature and extent of the decedent's interest in the shares were "defined by the laws of Maine, and his power to secure the complete transfer" was dependent upon them.

This dissenting view soon became the law on the Roosevelt Court. In 1939 the Court, by a 5 to 4 decision in the case of *Curry* v. *McCanless,* drastically limited the recently evolved no double taxation rule, Justice Stone's opinion noting that "there are many circumstances in which more than one state may have jurisdiction to impose a tax and measure it by some or all of the taxpayer's intangibles." The facts of the Curry case were such as not to require a direct overruling of the earlier decisions. But in 1942, *State Tax Commission of Utah* v. *Aldrich* presented a factual situation identical with that in the *Maine* case, and by a 7 to 2 vote (Jackson and Roberts dissenting) the 1932 decision was overruled, presumably taking down with it others in that same line.

Further developments on taxation of intangibles came in 1947, when the Court in *Greenough* v. *Tax Assessors of Newport* held that a state may tax intangibles in the hands of a trustee of an out-of-state trust who resides in the state. This decision split the Court wide open, and along unfamiliar lines, Jackson and Vinson from the right joining with Murphy and Rutledge from the left in contending that the tax was really upon the trust corpus, which was outside the state, not on the trustee, and so unconstitutional because measured by the value of property wholly beyond the reach of the state's power, to which the state gave no protection or benefit. The close margin by which this case was decided indicates that the limits of the Court's tolerance on double taxation or intangibles have about been reached.

Due Process and State Regulation

As for application of the due process clause to state business regulation, perhaps the principal accomplishment of the Roosevelt Court {80} has been to terminate one of the most notorious and disreputable lines of cases ever developed by the Supreme Court. In 1898 the Court opened a Pandora's box when in the famous decision of *Smyth* v. *Ames* it laid down the rule that rate-making calculations for public utilities must be based on the "fair value" of the utility property, but gave only the vaguest sort of notion as to how fair value was to be determined. Through the years the Court came to espouse the "reproduction cost" theory, which was one of the several standards mentioned in *Smyth* v. *Ames,* and the basis most favorable for utilities during a period of rising prices, as over against the "prudent investment" theory promoted by Justice Brandeis.[13]

In one of the first important state rate cases which the Roosevelt Court received, *Driscoll* v. *Edison Light & Power Co.,* decided in 1939, rates established by the Pennsylvania commission were upheld against a charge that the statute did not require use of the reproduction cost method. The decision was not a clear-cut reversal of *Smyth* v. *Ames,* and in fact Justice Frankfurter objected that the Court had in a left-handed fashion given renewed vitality to the "mischievous formula" stated in 1898. None the less, the *Driscoll* decision seems to have achieved its purpose, for not a single important state rate-making case has come to the Court since that time, although there have been some important federal rate cases arising under the Natural Gas Act.

The only outright reversal of a previous due process decision in the state regulatory field which the Roosevelt Court has had occasion to make came in

1941. It involved the 1928 case of *Ribnik* v. *McBride* where the Court, over the protest of Holmes, Brandeis, and Stone, had ruled unconstitutional a New Jersey statute regulating the fees charged by employment agencies. This was one of several decisions during that period invalidating price-fixing or other types of regulation of businesses not in the traditional public utility field, on the ground that these businesses were not "affected with a public interest." By 1934, however, the pre-Roosevelt Court had repented of these decisions, and in upholding the New York milk price control law had indicated its return to the notion of public interest first stated in the 1877 decision of *Munn* v. *Illinois*. *Ribnik* v. *McBride* and the other decisions related to it still remained theoretically on the books, {81} however, and a literal-minded Nebraska court adopted the *Ribnik* rule in striking down a Nebraska statute fixing maximum charges of employment agencies. The Supreme Court was thus given an opportunity specifically to overrule the *Ribnik* case, which it did in a unanimous holding to the effect that "the drift away from *Ribnik* v. *McBride* has been so great that it can no longer be deemed a controlling authority."[14]

The practical unanimity which the Roosevelt justices had achieved in their support of state legislation against due process claims was finally shattered in 1947 by an interesting equal protection case, *Kotch* v. *Board of River Port Pilot Commissioners*. Louisiana had a scheme of licensing pilots through a state board of river pilot commissioners. These commissioners were themselves pilots, and they operated the certification process in such a way that only selected relatives and friends of present pilots could secure licenses. In the conflict between respect for state powers and distaste for discriminatory state action which was thus posed for the Court, state power won out, but by the narrow margin of a 5 to 4 vote.

This case was a particularly difficult test for the left-wing justices, with their somewhat greater crusading spirit and less inhibited approach to the redress of injustices, and three of them—Douglas, Rutledge, and Murphy— voted along with Reed to hold the state action unconstitutional. They relied on the principle of the *Yick Wo* case, decided sixty years earlier, where an attempt to prevent Chinese from operating laundries had been thwarted on equal protection grounds. Justice Black, however, voted with the right wing to give a majority for upholding, as he put it, "the right and power of a state to select its own agents and officers." The case constituted the most serious challenge for a decade to an exercise of state regulatory powers on Fourteenth Amendment grounds.

Local Policies and National Commerce

State legislation affecting interstate commerce presents a somewhat more difficult problem for a liberal court than was found in the due process cases. The presumption favoring the validity of {82} legislative action is still operative, but there are competing values at work also, particularly the need to prevent state action from interfering with federal regulatory programs or burdening national commerce. There is a well-known passage in which Justice Holmes gave vigorous expression to his concern for the maintenance of judicial control over state legislation affecting commerce. He said:

> I do not think the United States would come to an end if we lost our power to declare an act of Congress void. I do think the Union would be imperiled if we could not make that declaration as to the laws of the several states. For one in my place sees how often a local policy prevails with those who are not trained to national views and how often action is taken that embodies what the Commerce Clause was meant to end.[15]

Because both liberals and conservatives are sensitive to the need of preserving national commerce from crippling state interference, judicial divisions on state legislation raising a commerce clause issue have tended to be less wide and clear than on due process claims. Nevertheless, there was a distinct tendency during the 1920s for the conservative Court to go far beyond what the liberal minority thought justified in striking down state regulation on the ground that it impinged on interstate commerce. To give only one example, there was the 1927 case of *DiSanto* v. *Pennsylvania* in which the Court, over the protest of Holmes, Brandeis, and Stone, held that a state could not require the licensing of persons selling steamship tickets to or from foreign countries.

The Roosevelt Court quickly reversed such extreme conceptions and returned to earlier views which allow state regulation affecting interstate commerce to stand if the matter dealt with is essentially local, if Congress has not undertaken to regulate it, and if no burden on interstate commerce results. By applying these tests the Roosevelt Court has been able to uphold the great majority of the state regulations questioned on commerce grounds. The *DiSanto* case was unanimously reversed in 1941.[16] A state statute rather stringently limiting the width and weight of motor trucks was upheld in *South Carolina Highway Department* v. *Barnwell Brothers*, as was another state law {83} prohibiting the operation on state highways of "car-over-cab" automobile truck carriers.[17] A California program for controlling the marketing of raisins was held not to conflict with the federal Agricultural Marketing Act nor to obstruct interstate commerce.[18]

In fact, in only four nonunanimous decisions since 1940 has the Roosevelt Court undertaken to invalidate state business regulation on commerce grounds.[19] By far the most interesting of these decisions, *Southern Pacific Railroad* v. *Arizona,* concerned an Arizona train limit law which prohibited operation within the state of trains more than 14 passenger cars or 70 freight cars in length. There is some suspicion that the railroad brotherhoods in sponsoring this legislation were not unmindful of the fact that it would create more railroad jobs. Its official justification, however, was as a safety measure, the hazards to trainmen from "slack action" being allegedly greater on longer trains. The Court majority concluded that the claims for increased safety were slight and dubious, and were outweighed by the "national interest in keeping interstate commerce free from interferences which seriously impede it and subject it to local regulation which does not have a uniform effect on the interstate train journey which it interrupts." If there was to be regulation of train lengths, the Court indicated that it would have to come from Congress, since national uniformity was "practically indispensable to the operation of an efficient and economical national railway system." The *Barnwell* decision was distinguished on the ground that the states were proprietors of the highways and have special rights to regulate their use.

Justice Black, speaking for Douglas as well, dissented from the majority view. He was bitter in his condemnation of this attempt by the Court to weigh for itself the probable dangers to railroad employees on long as compared with short trains, concluding:

> The balancing of these probabilities . . . is not in my judgment a matter for judicial determination, but one which calls for legislative consideration. Representatives elected by the people to make their laws, rather than judges appointed to interpret those laws, can best determine the policies which govern the people. That at least is the basic principle on which our democratic society rests. {84}

State Taxation and Commerce

The doctrine of legislative supremacy has seldom received a more startling statement than in the dissent which Justices Black, Douglas, and Frankfurter appended to a 1940 decision, *McCarroll* v. *Dixie Greyhound Lines*. At issue was the validity of an Arkansas statute which required buses and trucks entering the state to pay the state gasoline tax on all gasoline over twenty gallons which they had in their tanks at the time. The majority of the Court regarded this tax as an unconstitutional burden on interstate commerce, but the dissenting minority frankly doubted the ability of the Court to formulate wise policies as to interstate trade barriers in single cases of this sort, and demanded that the whole problem be left to Congress.

> Judicial control of national commerce—unlike legislative regula-tions—must from inherent limitations of the judicial process treat the subject by the hit-and-miss method of deciding single local con-troversies upon evidence and information limited by the narrow rules of litigation. Spasmodic and unrelated instances of litigation cannot afford an adequate basis for the creation of integrated na-tional rules which alone can afford that full protection for interstate commerce intended by the Constitution. We would, therefore, leave the questions raised by the Arkansas tax for consideration of Con-gress in a nation-wide survey of the constantly increasing barriers to trade among the States. Unconfined by "the narrow scope of judicial proceedings" Congress alone can, in the exercise of its plenary con-

stitutional control over interstate commerce, not only consider whether such a tax as now under scrutiny is consistent with the best interests of our national economy, but can also on the basis of full exploration of the many aspects of a complicated problem devise a national policy fair alike to the States and our Union. Diverse and interacting state laws may well have created avoidable hardships. . . . But the remedy, if any is called for, we think is within the ample reach of Congress.

Although this dissent did not expressly so state, its clear implication was that the commerce clause did not by its own force protect interstate commerce from burdensome taxation, but was merely an authorization to Congress to adopt protective legislation. Only on this theory could a refusal by the Court to apply the commerce clause as {85} a limitation on the power of the states be supported. Perhaps the minority was thinking of using this doctrine only in dealing with the hard cases, but such a limitation was not stated, and considerable alarm was expressed at the time over this proposal for the Court to "abdicate" its functions as umpire of the federal system.

Although the logic of the *McCarroll* dissent was never officially adopted as the majority view of the Roosevelt Court, its early policy certainly allowed a considerably expanded scope for the exercise of state taxing powers without running afoul of the commerce clause. Illustrative of this attitude were two 1941 decisions in which the state of Iowa was upheld in requiring Sears, Roebuck and Montgomery Ward to collect the Iowa "use tax" on mail-order shipments from Chicago to Iowa customers.[20] The tax was held not to be an unconstitutional burden on interstate commerce, since it was levied on use within Iowa, local sales within Iowa were subjected to the same tax, and the state was requiring the companies to collect the tax for it as the price of being permitted to operate retail stores in Iowa. Justices Roberts and Hughes dissented, charging that the task of collecting the tax on over a million mail-order transactions a year with Iowa customers was a direct and serious burden on interstate commerce.

Another instance where the early Roosevelt Court permitted the levying of a local tax which would previously almost certainly have been condemned as a burden on commerce was supplied by the 1940 case of *McGoldrick* v. *Berwind-White Coal Co.* Here the Court upheld a New York City sales tax applied to coal brought from Pennsylvania and sold in New York to public utility and steamship companies, its view being that the tax was not aimed at interstate commerce and did not discriminate against it. "It was not the purpose of the commerce clause," wrote Justice Stone, "to relieve those engaged in interstate commerce of their just share of state tax burdens." Hughes, McReynolds, and Roberts argued on the contrary that, even though non-discriminatory, the tax was a direct burden on commerce since it was laid on the delivery of the coal, an essential part of the interstate transaction, and had the same effect as a tariff on the entrance of coal into New York.

As recently as 1944, in *Northwest Airlines* v. *Minnesota,* the Court {86} showed that it was still willing to go rather far in upholding state taxing power against commerce claims. In this decision, written by Justice Frankfurter, the Court by a 5 to 4 vote upheld the state in assessing taxes on a Minnesota airlines corporation on the basis of its entire fleet of planes coming into the state, although only 16 per cent of the daily plane mileage of the company's interstate planes was within the state. Stone, Roberts, Reed, and Rutledge contended that this was an unconstitutional tax on vehicles of interstate commerce.

With the Northwest Airlines decision the Court's first flush of enthusiasm for abdicating judicial controls over state taxation was waning. In the 1944 case of *McLeod* v. *Dilworth* the Court majority ruled against the application of an Arkansas sales tax under circumstances which Black, Douglas, Murphy and Rutledge said constituted "a retreat from the philosophy of the *Berwind-White* case." In 1945 the same four justices protested as the Court in *Hooven & Allison Co.* v. *Evatt* set down an entirely new limitation on state taxing powers which had not even occurred to the pre-Roosevelt Court. The holding in this case was that bales of hemp imported from abroad and held in a manufacturer's warehouse in the original packages pending their use in the manufacture of rope were not subject to state property taxation. The "original package" doctrine had been first laid down as a test of state taxing power in an 1827 decision involving articles held by an importer for sale.[21] It had not proved too satisfactory a test in all respects, and there was considerable surprise when the Court extended it to cover manufacturers' stocks.

Then in 1946 the Court in *Nippert* v. *City of Richmond* invalidated a local tax affecting salesmen who solicit orders to be filled by subsequent interstate shipment. This decision was more or less in line with a long series of cases protecting drummers against discriminatory local taxation, but Justices Black, Douglas, and Murphy objected to the decision, charging that the majority's reasoning was based on purely speculative or theoretical concepts of interference with commerce. As they saw it,

> one who complains that a state tax, though not discriminatory on its face, discriminates against interstate commerce in its actual operation {87} should be required to come forward with proof to sustain the charge. . . . Cases of this type should not be decided on the basis of speculation; the special facts and circumstances will often be decisive.

The 1946-47 term saw the pendulum picking up even greater speed on its swing back, as the application of state tax laws was invalidated on commerce grounds in three consecutive cases, in each instance over protests from the left of the Court.[22] Justice Frankfurter's majority opinion in the second of these cases, *Freeman* v. *Hewit,* made clear the extent of his retreat from the philosophy of congressional supremacy which he, along with Black and Douglas, had announced in the *McCarroll* case in 1940. His withdrawal from the rather extreme position he had taken then had been accomplished gradually, but it had become clearly evident by the time of the *Northwest Airlines* decision in 1944. While he wrote the majority opinion upholding the state tax in that case, his argument was largely based on a Holmes precedent of many years earlier, and there was no suggestion in his decision that the Court should leave it to Congress to work out the rules in this perplexing field. Frankfurter's apostasy in the *Northwest Airlines* case was so obvious that Black felt obliged to write a concurring opinion there re-stating his *McCarroll* attitude:

> The differing views of members of the Court in this and related cases illustrate the difficulties inherent in the judicial formulation of general rules to meet the national problems arising from state taxation which bears in incidence upon interstate commerce. These problems, it seems to me, call for Congressional investigation, consideration, and action. The Constitution gives that branch of government the power to regulate commerce among the states, and until it acts I think we should enter the field with extreme caution.

But Frankfurter was not re-converted. His 1946 *Freeman* v. *Hewit* decision completely disclaimed any necessity for the Court to wait on congressional action, applying rather

> the principle that the Commerce Clause was not merely an authorization to Congress to enact laws for the protection and encouragement of commerce among the States, but by its own force created an area of trade free from interference by the States. In short, the Commerce Clause {88} even without implementing legislation by Congress is a limitation upon the power of the States.

Frankfurter suggested also that it was not as serious for the Court to invalidate the application of a state tax as for it to strike down a police power measure.

> A police regulation of local aspects of interstate commerce is a power often essential to a State in safeguarding vital local interests. . . . State taxation falling on interstate commerce, on the other hand, can only be justified as designed to make such commerce bear a fair share of the cost of the local government whose protection it enjoys. But revenue serves as well no matter what its source. To deny to a State a particular source of income because it taxes the very process of interstate commerce does not impose a crippling limitation on a State's ability to carry on its local function. Moreover, the burden on interstate commerce involved in a direct tax upon it is inherently greater, certainly less uncertain in its consequences, than results from the usual police regulations. The power to tax is a dominant power over commerce. Because the greater or more threatening

burden of a direct tax on commerce is coupled with the lesser need to a State of a particular source of revenue, attempts at such taxation have always been more carefully scrutinized and more consistently resisted than police regulations of aspects of such commerce.

Three months after *Freeman v. Hewit* came Justice Reed's decision in *Joseph v. Carter & Weekes Stevedoring Co.,* arguing that since Congress had left "intact" the Court's decisions on state taxing powers in relation to interstate commerce, this "acquiescence in our former rulings on state taxation indicates its agreement with the adjustments of the competing interests of commerce and necessary state revenues" which the Court had made. To Justice Douglas it appeared that the Court had come to "the end of one cycle under the Commerce Clause and the beginning of another." Having started out by considering seriously whether the Court should not yield its protective authority over interstate commerce to Congress, the Court soon decided that the constitutional provisions automatically required judicial intervention and needed no congressional mandate to bring them into effect, and finally convinced itself that the failure of Congress to express disapproval of {89} Court decisions in this field was tantamount to positive congressional adoption of the judicial policies.[23]

* * *

The recapitulation of judicial votes in nonunanimous state regulation and taxation cases decided from the 1938 through the 1946 terms, given in Table XV, tells an interesting story. Black, Douglas, and Murphy stand together as strong supporters of the constitutionality of state economic action. Frankfurter, in spite of his recent tendencies toward a stricter rule on state powers in commerce cases, was closest to their position for the entire period. This is one field in which the principal professed disciples of Holmes' liberalism on the present Court have managed to stick fairly close together in putting his principle of respect for state legislative action into effect.

Justices Stone and Reed were emphatic enough in rejecting due process claims, but considerably more receptive to contentions that the federal commerce power was being invaded by state action. Rutledge's {90} record of support for state legislation is probably unrepresentatively low, since he missed out on the early years of the Roosevelt Court when many of these cases were decided. Jackson's position is completely atypical of the Roosevelt justices in both areas, and is comparable with that of Hughes and Roberts. McReynolds supplies a useful reminder of the intransigence that once passed for sound judicial thinking.

TABLE XV

ALIGNMENTS OF JUSTICES IN CASES OF STATE TAXATION AND REGULATION,
1938-1946 TERMS

| | No. Cases | Decisions for State | | Total |
		Due Process	Commerce	
No. Cases		12	25	37
Majority	37	100%	52%	68%
Black	37	100	88	92
Murphy	27	80	88	85
Douglas	32	91	81	84
Frankfurter	33	100	68	79
Stone	27	100	59	74
Reed	37	83	48	59
Rutledge	19	60	57	58
Burton	9	100	14	33
Hughes	16	17	40	31
Jackson	20	50	7	20
Vinson	8	50	0	13
Roberts	24	0	20	13
McReynolds	14	0	0	0

Obviously these decisions on state regulatory policy have brought a welter of conflicting judicial values into play. A justice whose inarticulate major premises dispose him to favor state regulation may yet vote against it because it is administered arbitrarily or appears to limit the effectiveness of federal regulation in the same field. A justice with a fundamental bias against state interference in the economic area may still hesitate to act on this bias if he has a stronger attachment to the conflicting notion that judges should not interfere with legislative decisions.

The record shows that Black has been the most consistent member of the Court in supporting state adoption and administration of regulatory legislation, even in the *Kotch* case where the discriminatory use of state authority must have been extremely distasteful to him. He has reacted sharply against some of the decisions where the Court deserted the policy of legislative supremacy, as in the Arizona train-limit case and in *Nippert* v. *Richmond*, where he warned that the Court was "assuming the role of a 'super-legislature' in determining matters of governmental policy."

These charges have a familiar ring. All this has been said before and, with all due respect to the very great abilities of Justice Black, said better in Justice Holmes' dissents of twenty years earlier. It must be admitted, however, that Holmes had better material to work on, for the super-legislating on economic issues which the Court of his day indulged in was crass and flagrant. Even though the enthusiasm of the Roosevelt Court for legislative supremacy has abated somewhat from that of its early period, there can be no doubt that federal and state economic legislation has less to fear from constitutional tests today than from any previous Court since the Civil War.

CHAPTER FIVE

Civil Liberties and Judicial Supremacy

L ILLIAN AND WILLIAM GOBITIS, aged 12 and 10 respectively, were ex-
pelled from the public schools of Minersville, Pennsylvania, in 1935,
because they refused to salute the American flag as part of a daily school
exercise required by regulation of the Minersville school board. Their reason
was that they had been taught by their parents, members of the sect known as
Jehovah's Witnesses, to regard this observance as the worship of a "graven
image," a practice forbidden by the Bible. Their father, required by the state
compulsory education law to enter them in private schools, but financially
unable to do so, sought an injunction in the federal courts to restrain the
school authorities from making the flag salute compulsory, alleging that it
constituted an infringement of religious freedom guaranteed by the Constitution. Two lower federal courts upheld his contention, but in 1940 the Supreme
Court, with only one justice dissenting, decided that the school board's action
did not deny the constitutional rights of the Gobitis children.[1]

This decision was perfectly consistent with two basic doctrines of the Roosevelt Court discussed in the preceding chapter: first, that governmental
power to act is not to be narrowly limited by constitutional barriers; and
second, that legislative judgments, even at the lowly level of a school board,
are to be respected. One might have been excused for concluding that these
were the only two factors {92} needed in the equation for predicting future
judicial decisions in the civil liberties field—legislative supremacy and judicial
limitation.

As it turned out, of course, the formula was considerably more complex.
By the time the Court had gained a few more Roosevelt appointees and had
wrestled with a few more Jehovah's Witnesses cases, it became apparent that
when civil liberties were up for consideration the Court majority seemed to act
on premises of *legislative* limitation and *judicial* supremacy. At a time when, as
Swisher says, "the commerce clause is being interpreted as a source of power
almost without limit, when the power to tax and spend for the public welfare
is coming into its own as an independent source of authority . . . and when
conventional restrictions upon the exercise of power over property such as
that of substantive due process are fading into the limbo of lost things,"[2] the

73

Roosevelt Court has found previously unrealized restrictions and limitations on legislative powers in the Bill of Rights. And legislative judgments, impregnable as they may seem in other fields, can be demolished with comparative ease by the explosive charge that civil liberties have been infringed.

The truth is that the Roosevelt Court has developed a double standard for guiding judicial review. The extent to which judges may question legislative action varies according to the position which the value threatened by legislation occupies in the Court's scale of deference. The liberties guaranteed by the First Amendment stand unchallenged at the apex of the Court's value system. These civil rights—free speech, free press, freedom of religion and assembly—are the fundamental freedoms which are a condition of all the others. Justice Black has put this view most forcefully:

> I view the guaranties of the First Amendment as the foundation up-on which our governmental system rests and without which it could not continue to endure as conceived and planned. Freedom to speak and write about public questions is as important to the life of our government as is the heart to the human body. In fact, this privilege is the heart of our government. If that heart be weakened, the result is debilitation; if it be stilled, the result is death.[3]

While no one on the Roosevelt Court would quarrel with this sentiment, there has been disagreement as to its implications for judicial {93} review. Out of the disputations on this point a clear majority conviction emerged about 1943 which holds that the primacy of these liberties requires the denial of any presumption of validity to legislation which on its face appears to infringe these guaranties. Justice Rutledge stated this position for the Court majority in the following words:

> Any attempt to restrict those liberties must be justified by a clear public interest, threatened not doubtfully or remotely, but by clear and present danger. The rational connection between the remedy provided and the evil to be curbed, which in other contexts might support legislation against attack on due process grounds, will not suffice. These rights rest on firmer foundation. Accordingly, whatever occasion would restrain orderly discussion and persuasion, at appropriate time and place, must have clear support in public danger, actual or impending. Only the gravest abuses, endangering paramount interests, give occasion for permissible limitation.[4]

A contrary view, usually in the minority, with Justice Frankfurter for its spokesman, feels that the canons of judicial review must be consistently applied, and that in civil liberties cases as in problems of economic regulation the role of the Court is limited to inquiring whether there is reasonable justification for the legislative judgment. But the development of these positions becomes more meaningful when considered in terms of the actual controversies in which they have been hammered out.

Jehovah's Witnesses et al.

Most of the religious liberty questions coming before the Roosevelt Court have arisen out of the determined and fanatic efforts of Jehovah's Witnesses to preach their doctrines to unbelieving and often unwilling listeners. Their unorthodox methods of evangelism, their phonograph playing, their door-to-door peddling of literature, together with their bitter attacks on other religious groups, particularly the Catholic Church, have brought them into constant conflict with law enforcement officers and local and state regulations. While there has been some deliberate and organized persecution of the sect, in many {94} instances the regulations of which they ran afoul had not been adopted to hamper the work of the group, but were general police or safety or revenue provisions which had seldom before been challenged.[5]

Some explanation is required of the course of constitutional development which has made it possible for the Witnesses to bring their complaints before the Supreme Court. The guaranty of "free exercise" of religion in the First Amendment is by its terms applicable only against abridgement by Congress, and attempts to make the protections of the Bill of Rights available as against state action were defeated early in American constitutional history. It was not until 1925 in the case of *Gitlow* v. *New York* that the Supreme Court conceded that the "liberty" protected by the due process clause of the Fourteenth Amendment against state action was broad enough to encompass the basic civil liberties of the First Amendment. Acting on this theory, the Supreme Court in 1931 for the first time invalidated a state statute on the ground that it was incompatible with the protections of the First Amendment as brought into play by the Fourteenth.[6] Since 1931 a steadily increasing stream of state civil liberties cases has poured in upon the Supreme Court.

The adventures of the Roosevelt Court with Jehovah's Witnesses began rather quietly in 1938, when the sect brought before the Court a Georgia municipal ordinance prohibiting the distribution of all literature or circulars without the consent of the city manager. Chief Justice Hughes for a unanimous Court held that "the ordinance was invalid on its face and established a censorship of the press."[7] The following year this principle was extended in invalidating an ordinance which forbade canvassing or the distribution of literature from house to house without permission of the police.[8]

The group's next appearance before the Supreme Court was in 1940 in connection with a Connecticut statute which made it a crime for any person to solicit or canvass from house to house for any religious or philanthropic cause without securing the prior approval of the secretary of the public welfare council, who was authorized to determine whether the cause was a bona fide religious one, conforming to reasonable standards of efficiency and integrity. The Court unanimously held {95} this statute to abridge freedom of religion.

The state, Justice Roberts said for the Court, may surround the solicitation of funds for religious and charitable purposes with reasonable regulations, but a requirement of prior approval by a public official, which may be refused in his discretion, constitutes "a censorship of religion as a means of determining its right to survive."[9]

Up to this point the Witnesses had been uniformly successful and the Court had been unanimous in its rulings, except for one dissenting vote by McReynolds. Then came the *Gobitis* case, which they lost, but which saw the Court still practically a unit, with only Justice Stone in dissent. It is not irrelevant to note that this decision came in June, 1940, at a time when the Germans were overrunning France and the Low Countries, and American security was challenged as it had not been for 125 years. The consequent upsurge of national feeling and the intensification of patriotic fervor had its effect even on the Supreme Court. Justice Frankfurter, who wrote the majority opinion, stressed that "national unity is the basis of national security," and such unity

is fostered by all those agencies of the mind and spirit which may serve to gather up the traditions of a people and transmit them from generation to generation, and thereby create that continuity of a treasured common life which constitutes a civilization. "We live by symbols." The flag is the symbol of our national unity, transcending all internal differences, however large, within the framework of the Constitution.

Frankfurter's second principal contention was that the rule of the local school board must be viewed as though it were the action of the state legislature, and that a legislative judgment as to what means would best promote an attachment to the institutions of the country was entitled to great respect. For the Court to hold the flag salute requirement void "would amount to no less than the pronouncement of a pedagogical and psychological dogma in a field where courts possess no marked and certainly no controlling competence."

Justice Stone completely disagreed with these views. In his opinion the flag salute requirement not only suppressed freedom of speech and the free exercise of religion, but actually sought to coerce children to express a sentiment violative of their deepest religious convictions. {96} Of greater concern to us at this point, however, is his difference with Frankfurter over the nature of judicial responsibility in civil liberties cases. Two years earlier, Stone had buried in the footnotes of a decision involving economic regulation his view that while the Court should be tolerant of legislative judgments in the commercial field, it should be less ready to presume that the legislature knows what it is doing when it seeks to limit rights and conduct lying outside that area.[10] Now that argument leaped from the footnotes to become the keystone in his denial of Frankfurter's contention that "so long as the remedial channels of the democratic process remain open and unobstructed," personal liberty is most secure "when it is ingrained in a people's habits and not enforced against popular policy by the coercion of adjudicated law." Stone replied that, when confronted with legislation which stifles the freedom of helpless minorities, the Supreme Court should not hesitate to assume the role of protector, even if in doing so it supplants the legislative judgment with its own conception of what is appropriate.

> The Constitution expresses more than the conviction of the people that democratic processes must be preserved at all costs. It is also an expression of faith and a command that freedom of mind and spirit must be preserved, which government must obey, if it is to adhere to that justice and moderation without which no free government can exist.

The *Gobitis* case ushered in a bad period for the Witnesses. In 1941 the Court unanimously upheld the conviction of a group of the sect's members who had marched single-file through the streets of Manchester, New Hampshire, carrying placards to advertise a meeting, without securing the special license required by state statute for "parades or processions" upon a public street. The act was upheld as a reasonable police regulation designed to keep order and promote the safe and orderly use of the streets.[11]

In 1942 the Court was not impressed by the case of Walter Chaplinsky who, threatened with arrest after creating a public disturbance by his open denunciations of all religion as a "racket," had told a city marshal of Rochester, New Hampshire, that "you are a God damned racketeer" and "a damned Fascist and the whole government of {97} Rochester are Fascists or agents of Fascists." The Court unanimously upheld Chaplinsky's conviction of violating a state statute against calling anyone "offensive or derisive" names in public. Justice Murphy cogently observed that insults and "fighting" words "are no essential part of any exposition of ideas, and are of such slight social value as a step to truth that any benefit that may be derived from them is clearly outweighed by the social interest in order and morality." The justice thought it unnecessary to demonstrate that "the appellations 'damn racketeer' and 'damn Fascist' are epithets likely to provoke the average person to retaliation, and thereby cause a breach of the peace."[12]

Three months later, in the case of *Jones* v. *Opelika,* the Court supported the validity of municipal license fees on transient merchants or book agents as applied in three different cities to Witnesses engaged in door-to-door peddling of religious tracts. None of these ordinances discriminated against the sale of religious literature, nor were they drafted with the Witnesses in mind. They were ordinary taxes on the privilege of peddling. The Court assumed that the taxes imposed were not unduly burdensome, since they had not been attacked on that ground, and treated them simply as non-discriminatory license fees. When religious advocates resort to commercial methods to raise funds for religious propaganda, the Court said, it is natural and proper to subject them to the payment of a fee. "The First Amendment does not require a subsidy in the form of fiscal exemption."

This decision was by a bare 5 to 4 majority, the first such vote to appear in the Witnesses' cases. Chief Justice Stone attacked the conclusions of the Court, but the most interesting development was that Black, Douglas, and Murphy not only joined with Stone in dissent, but appended an unprecedented and gratuitous statement confessing repentance for their part in the flag salute decision of two years previous. They wrote:

> This is but another step in the direction which *Minersville School District* v. *Gobitis* took against the same religious minority and is a logical extension of the principles upon which that decision rested. Since we joined in that opinion in the *Gobitis* case, we think this is an appropriate occasion to state that we now believe that it was also wrongly decided. {98}

Thus the safe majority of the *Gobitis* case was whittled down to a bare 5 to 4 margin, and when Justice Rutledge came on the Court in the fall of 1942 the stage was set for a new deal for the Witnesses. *Jones* v. *Opelika* was put down for rehearing, and certiorari was granted in another case, *Murdock* v. *Pennsylvania*, which raised the same question. In May, 1943, a 5 to 4 decision ruled such license fees to be a tax on the free exercise of religion. The pamphlet peddling of Jehovah's Witnesses was held not to be a mere commercial enterprise. The incidental collection of small sums for books and tracts to help finance the spread of religion was not regarded by the Court as making this evangelism commercial, any more than passing the collection plate makes a church service commercial. The Court did indicate that ordinances carefully drawn to protect people in their homes against solicitation evils, and imposing nominal charges to defray a city's expenses in protecting against the abuses of solicitors, would not be regarded as unconstitutional.

One month later the flag salute decision of 1940 succumbed to the new Court majority, but this time the decision was by a 6 to 3 vote, Justice Jackson leaving his colleagues of the *Murdock* minority to write the majority opinion in *West Virginia State Board of Education* v. *Barnette*. While building upon Stone's dissent in the *Gobitis* case, Jackson added some telling blows of his own against this type of compulsion. The refusal to salute the flag, he pointed out, did not involve any

> collision with the rights asserted by any other individual, nor was it accompanied by any conduct which was not peaceable and orderly. It is now a commonplace that censorship or suppression of expression of opinion is tolerated by our Constitution only when the expression presents a clear and present danger of action of a kind the State is empowered to prevent and punish.

He attacked vigorously Frankfurter's argument that the legislative judgment should be permitted to prevail, saying that the purpose of the Bill of Rights was to withdraw freedom of speech, press, religion and other basic rights from the reach of legislatures and popular majorities. Finally, his opinion challenged the notion that {99} "uniformity of sentiment" can be produced by coercion. "Compulsory unification of opinion achieves only the unanimity of the graveyard."

Justice Frankfurter, dissenting along with Reed and Roberts, sought to add new weight to his earlier opinion. The only issue as he saw it was "whether legislators could in reason have enacted such a law, and it would require more daring than I possess to deny that reasonable legislators could have taken the action which is before us for review." The "clear and present danger" test originated by Justice Holmes and here used to support the majority conclusions was, he felt, quite inappropriate as applied to this type of legislation.

The Witnesses won other victories in the same term,[13] the Court even going so far as to hold invalid a city ordinance making it unlawful to ring doorbells or knock on doors for the purpose of summoning the occupants to the door to give them handbills, circulars, or other advertisements. The regular procedures of Jehovah's Witnesses of course violated this ordinance. Justice Black, speaking for the Court, took the position that door-to-door visitation to circulate pamphlets had long been an accepted method of communication, and that forbidding it altogether violated freedom of speech and press.[14]

The principles established by the Roosevelt Court in 1943 have apparently given answers to the more pressing problems arising out of the Witnesses' activities, for since then the cases have dwindled rapidly, only four being decided in the next three terms.[15] The only one of the four that the Witnesses lost involved a nine-year-old girl who, accompanied by her aunt, sold literature of the Witnesses on a downtown street corner at night. A Massachusetts statute forbids boys under 12 and girls under 18 to sell newspapers or other merchandise on the streets, and punishes parents or guardians who permit children to do so. The Court by a 5 to 4 vote held this statute to be a reasonable police regulation designed to protect the welfare of children, taking precedence over the competing claims of religious freedom.[16] Two 1946 decisions upheld the right of Witnesses to distribute literature on the premises of a federal housing authority project in Texas and a "company town" in Alabama, without becoming liable to the penalty provided by state laws for remaining on the premises of another after being warned not to do so.[17] It is interesting to note {100} that on these two most recent decisions Justice Frankfurter gave up his losing battle and bowed to the pro-Witnesses Court majority, while Chief Justice Stone, who had begun this line of thought with his *Gobitis* dissent, felt that the Court was going too far in protecting civil liberties and seceded from the majority to vote with Reed and Burton.

What has been the net result of these Jehovah's Witnesses cases for American constitutional law? First of all, it is clear that some principles of major importance in the general field of civil liberties have been established. The

Witnesses have been largely responsible for the constitutional protection now covering the distribution of handbills. The overriding of the claims of conscience for which the compulsory flag salute was responsible cannot easily be condoned. The taxing power was rather clearly being used in a discriminatory and burdensome fashion for the elimination of this unpopular religious group, until the Court stepped in with its *Murdock* ruling. The power of the owner of a company town to bar distribution of literature was properly challenged. These and other gains have resulted from this litigation.

But it is at least open to question whether the Court majority has not tended to follow its zeal for civil liberties a little too blindly, without taking into full account the uncivil liberties with the rights of others characteristically taken by this particular religious group. The management and control of the Jehovah's Witnesses sect are shrouded in secrecy. Its operation is thought to be a tremendously profitable business. Its method, according to the instructions given its adherents, is to invade the privacy of homes, to force its doctrine upon people who do not want to receive it (referred to in their literature as "sourpusses").[18] The nature of its attacks on other religions go far beyond the bounds of good taste, and its leaders have at least on occasions deliberately sought to cause commotion and disturbance, as by the large-scale invasion of a predominantly Catholic community on Palm Sunday.

Considerations of this sort were ably stated by Justice Jackson in his remarkable dissent from the Court's decisions in the *Murdock* and *Struthers* cases, which concluded: "Civil government cannot let any group ride rough-shod over others simply because their 'consciences' tell them to do so." What would be the result, he asks, "if the right {101} given to these Witnesses should be exercised by all sects and denominations"? Corwin suggests that the Court's handling of these cases shows that it has not "thought its problem quite through." Otherwise it would not have acted on the assumption that

> the right of people to resort to their own places of worship and listen to their chosen teachers stands on a constitutional level with the right of religious enthusiasts to solicit funds and peddle their doctrinal wares in the street, to ring doorbells and disturb householders, and to accost passersby and insult them in *their* religious beliefs.[19]

Issues of religious freedom have been raised in a few cases where the Witnesses were not the injured parties. *United States* v. *Ballard* was a proceeding against the Ballard family, promoters of the "I Am" cult, for using the mails to defraud. Ballard had presented himself as a divine messenger, with supernatural healing powers, and solicited money and membership in the movement on the basis of these claims. At the trial the judge, scenting the possibility that religious persecution might be charged, refused to submit to the jury the question of the truth or falsity of the religious beliefs of the defendants, and confined the issue of guilt to the sole question whether they honestly and in good faith believed the statements they had made. The jury found them guilty on this basis.

Eight members of the Supreme Court agreed that the district judge had rightly withheld the matter of the truth of the doctrines from the jury, but five justices were so sensitive to possible claims of religious persecution that they sent the case back to the lower court for argument on other constitutional issues which they felt had not been adequately covered. Stone, Roberts, and Frankfurter thought this an excess of caution. Justice Jackson, on the other hand, would have declared the whole proceeding invalid as a judicial examination of other people's faiths, a position characterized by Corwin as taking "leave of common sense to indulge some high-flown doubts that were evidently suggested to him by a perusal of William James's *The Will to Believe.*"[20]

The Court's record on civil liberties was badly, but perhaps only temporarily, marred in 1945 by its handling of *In re Summers.* Summers, {102} a conscientious objector to war, was refused admission to the bar in Illinois because the examiners concluded that his religious scruples "seem inconsistent with the obligation of an attorney at law." Specifically, this conclusion was based on the fact that Illinois lawyers must take oath to support the state constitution, which requires that the state militia consist of all "able-bodied male persons resident in the state," except those exempted by the laws of the United States or of Illinois. Incidentally, Illinois law provides no exemptions, but men have not been drafted into the state militia since 1864. Summers was willing to take the oath, but the examiners ruled he could not do so in good faith.

Five justices of the Court held that Summers had not been denied due process by infringement of his religious freedom. Admittedly the state could not exclude members of a particular religious group from the bar, but that was not the ground for the action taken here. A principal reliance of the majority was upon the Court's earlier decisions in the cases of *United States* v. *Macintosh* and *United States* v. *Schwimmer,* in which conscientious objectors had been refused admission to American citizenship. A biting dissent by Black, Douglas, Murphy, and Rutledge attacked the exclusion of Summers from the bar as a direct assault on his freedom of religion, and held the *Schwimmer* and *Macintosh* cases to have been wrongly decided.

A year later these two decisions were in fact overruled by the Court in *Girouard* v. *United States.* The *Schwimmer* case had been decided in 1929 over the protest of Holmes, Brandeis, and Sanford, and the Macintosh decision (1931) had been objected to by the truly impressive lineup of Holmes, Brandeis, Stone, and Hughes. It was in the *Schwimmer* dissent that Justice Holmes wrote this often-quoted passage:

> If there is any principle of the Constitution that more imperatively calls for attachment than any other it is the principle of free thought—not free thought for those who agree with us but freedom for the thought that we hate. I think that we should adhere to that

principle with regard to admission into, as well as to life within this country.

The Holmes philosophy became the law in the *Girouard* decision. Girouard was a Seventh Day Adventist who was willing to serve in {103} the army as a non-combatant, but refused to bear arms. The majority opinion noted that his religious scruples would not disqualify him from becoming a member of Congress or holding other public offices, and refused to believe that Congress had "set a stricter standard for aliens seeking admission to citizenship than it did for officials who make and enforce the laws of the nation." The Court also refused to conclude that Congress had adopted the rule announced in the earlier decisions by refusing to amend the statutory provisions interpreted by them.

Chief Justice Stone dissented from the *Girouard* decision on the last day of his long and useful life. Although he had himself objected to the *Macintosh* decision, he was convinced that Congress had since that time "adopted and confirmed" the construction of the naturalization laws given by the Court majority in that case, and so he felt constrained to stick by the principle of the earlier decisions, even though it was personally obnoxious to him. Justices Reed and Frankfurter joined him in this position. It is scarcely necessary to point out that the principle of the *Summers* case is weakened by the overruling of the decisions on which it was largely based.

In all of these cases the constitutional question raised pertained to the guaranty of the First Amendment for "free exercise" of religion. But the Amendment also prohibits the making of any law "respecting an establishment of religion." The Roosevelt Court finally encountered a problem of this sort in a 1947 case, *Everson* v. *Board of Education of Ewing Township.* The state of New Jersey had authorized local boards of education to make rules and contracts for transportation of children to and from schools, whether public or private, "except such school as is operated for profit in whole or in part." Under this statute the Ewing township board arranged to reimburse parents for money expended by them for transportation of their children on the regular public transportation system. The resolution adopted by the board authorized reimbursement only for parents of public and Catholic school pupils.

A taxpayer brought suit challenging on constitutional grounds the right of the board to reimburse parents of parochial school students, but lost in the Supreme Court by a 5 to 4 vote. Justice Black's opinion {104} for the majority (including Douglas, Murphy, Vinson, and Reed) considered two constitutional objections. First, there was the due process argument, which contended that since children were sent to Catholic schools to satisfy the personal desires of their parents, using tax money to facilitate this purpose would be spending public money for private ends. Black noted that the Court had always been very cautious in using this power to invalidate public expenditures as not furthering a public purpose, preferring to leave the determination of that question to the legislatures, and adding that in any case "it is much too late to argue that legislation intended to facilitate the opportunity of children to get a secular education serves no public purpose."

The second and principal objection was that the statute amounted to an "establishment of religion." To assist in securing an understanding of the meaning of this provision, Black reviewed the European and American colonial history of government-established and -supported churches, which finally brought the demand for separation of church and state as expressed in Jefferson's and Madison's famous Virginia Bill for Religious Liberty and ultimately the First Amendment itself. From this review and subsequent interpretations Black concluded that the First Amendment means at least this:

Neither a state nor the Federal Government can set up a church. Neither can pass laws which aid one religion, aid all religions, or prefer one religion over another. Neither can force nor influence a person to go to or to remain away from church against his will or force him to profess a belief or disbelief in any religion. No person can be punished for entertaining or professing religious beliefs or disbeliefs, for church attendance or non-attendance. No tax in any amount, large or small, can be levied to support any religious activities or institutions, whatever they may be called, or whatever form they may adopt to teach or practice religion.

On the basis of these principles Black acknowledged that the New Jersey statute approached "the verge" of constitutional power. Indeed, looking at the establishment of religion clause as forbidding the contribution of "tax-raised funds to the support of an institution which teaches the tenets and faith of any church"—and Black admitted this is what the provision means—it would be hard to support the statute. {105} But Black escaped from the necessity of reaching this conclusion by moving over to the "free exercise" of religion clause, which he interpreted as commanding New Jersey not to "hamper its citizens in the free exercise of their own religion." The state must not exclude any individuals, *because of their faith, or lack of it,* from receiving the benefits of public welfare legislation."

Fearful that this argument might prove too much, Black hurried on to say that of course a state could limit its provision of transportation assistance to public school children only. But in fact, he added, the states have generally not taken this line. They already furnish many services to church schools with general approval, such as fire and police protection, sidewalks and public highways. The First Amendment "requires the state to be a neutral in its relations with groups of religious believers and non-believers; it does not require the state to be their adversary. State power is no more to be used so as to handicap religions, than it is to favor them." His argument closed with the contention that this New Jersey action did not constitute "the slightest breach" in the wall between church and state, which "must be kept high and impregnable."

These protestations reminded Justice Jackson of the case of Julia "who, according to Byron's reports, 'whispering "I will ne'er consent,"—consented.'" He was convinced that the Court's decision approved the commingling of church and state in educational matters. Black's effort to prove that the township was merely providing another type of public service he rejected, pointing out that no service at all was being rendered by the township; it was merely paying bus fare on the public transportation system. But his main objection was that the statute as applied in this particular township authorized paying the cost of carrying pupils to church schools of one specified denomination. Police and fire protection are given to all men because they are members of society, and to all property because it is part of society's assets. But under this law, as applied in Ewing Township, any pupil who did not attend a public school could be given aid only if he was attending a Catholic school.

Justice Rutledge's dissenting opinion in which all the other dissenting judges (Jackson, Frankfurter and Burton) also joined, was a {106} longer and more scholarly attack on the majority case. The basic question, Rutledge contended, was a simple one: "Does New Jersey's action furnish support for religion by use of the taxing power?" No one denies that the Catholic schools give religious instruction, and transportation, Rutledge argues, "is as essential to education as any other element." And if providing transportation is merely "public welfare legislation," then there can be "no possible objection to more extensive support of religious education by New Jersey." If the smaller items may be paid by the state, why not the larger ones also? Both Jackson and Rutledge stressed the fact that if the public can aid religions, it can also regulate them. This is the first step in the direction of an establishment of religion, Rutledge concludes.

While the Court upheld the questioned state assistance to religious schools in the *Everson* case, the narrow margin by which it did so, and the fact that the entire Court agreed that the establishment provision had a much wider scope than merely to prohibit an established church, obviously opened the way to more litigation in this general area. The second gun was fired in March, 1948, as the Court decided in the *McCullom* case that a "released time" program of religious education in the public schools of Champaign, Illinois, violated the establishment of religion clause. Under this program public school children, on consent of their parents, attended classes in Protestant, Catholic, or Jewish religious instruction during school hours and in the school building. The religious teachers were not paid by the schools, but were under the supervision of the school superintendents, and attendance was compulsory for participants in the program.

Justice Black, speaking for six justices, held that under this plan tax-supported school buildings were being used in disseminating religious doctrines, and the state's public school machinery was being employed to provide pupils for religious classes—a clear violation of the *Everson* principle that the "wall between Church and State . . . must be kept high and impregnable." Justices Frankfurter and Jackson concurred in separate opinions. Jackson agreed that the Champaign religious classes went beyond permissible limits, but he was worried over the prospect of the Supreme Court becoming "a super board of education for every school district in the nation." Without a clearer {107} statement of legal principles to provide guidance to both educators and judges than Black's opinion provided, he feared that the wall of separation between church and state was likely to become "as winding as the famous serpentine wall designed by Mr. Jefferson for the University he founded." Only Justice Reed would have held the Champaign plan constitutional.[21]

Freedom of the Press

American traditions of a press free from government interference or control have been so strong and so well observed that very few freedom of the press cases have come to the Supreme Court. There were two principal decisions prior to 1937. One was *Near* v. *Minnesota,* where a state statute authorizing the enjoining, as a public nuisance, of "malicious, scandalous and defamatory" publications was declared unconstitutional, over the protest of the Court's conservative old guard. The other was the Court's unanimous invalidation of a discriminatory Louisiana tax adopted by the Huey Long-controlled legislature as a blow at the large New Orleans newspapers which were opposing his regime.[22]

The Roosevelt Court has had three kinds of questions to consider in connection with application of the First Amendment to newspapers and periodicals. It has, first of all, substantially freed newspapers from the threat of contempt action for published comments on judicial proceedings, overruling one earlier decision in the process—the case of *Toledo Newspaper Co.* v. *United States*, dating from 1918. A federal statute adopted in 1831 to curb abuse of the judicial contempt power had forbidden "summary punishments for contempts of court" (i.e., without jury) except in the case of misbehavior "in the presence of said courts, or so near thereto as to obstruct the administration of justice." The *Toledo* case held, over the protest of Holmes and Brandeis, that a newspaper publishing objectionable comments about a judge and his conduct of pending litigation was "so near thereto" as to justify summary punishment. When the 1941 case of *Nye* v. *United States* offered an opportunity to overrule the *Toledo* decision, the Court was quick to do so by a 5 to 3 vote. {108}

A series of three cases involving contempt actions against editors by state judges has been decided by the Roosevelt Court. The first, in 1941, involved the *Los Angeles Times*, which had been adjudged guilty of contempt because of three editorials it had published on a labor case involving assault by labor union members on non-union truck drivers. At a time when the defendants had been found guilty, but not yet sentenced, the anti-labor *Times* said editorially: "Judge A. A. Scott will make a serious mistake if he grants probation to Matthew Shannon and Kennan Holmes. This community needs the example of their assignment to the jute-mill." By a 5 to 4 vote the Supreme

Court ruled that a contempt conviction on the basis of this statement abridged freedom of the press. Since no California statute held this type of publication unlawful, there would have to be "a clear and present danger" that the publication would obstruct justice if the contempt action was to be justified. The majority of Black, Douglas, Murphy, Jackson, and Reed found no such threat. The anti-labor position of the paper was well known in the community; to regard the publication "as in itself of substantial influence upon the course of justice would be to impute to judges a lack of firmness, wisdom, or honor which we cannot accept as a major premise.[23]

A vigorous dissent was filed by Justice Frankfurter for himself, Stone, Roberts, and Byrnes, declaring that the Court was leaving the administration of justice without protection from outside pressure and coercion. In the light of this narrow division in 1941, it is interesting to note that when the next contempt case came up in 1946, the Court unanimously upheld the newspaper involved against the charge. Two editorials and a cartoon published by the *Miami Herald,* criticizing the handling of cases in the local county courts, were the basis for the contempt action reviewed in *Pennekamp* v. *Florida.* The Court applied the "clear and present" danger rule used in the *Los Angeles Times* decision and concluded that "the danger under this record of fair judicial administration has not the clearness and immediacy necessary to close the door of permissible public comment. When that door is closed, it closes all doors behind it."[24]

Justice Frankfurter, who had been the principal dissenter in the *Times* case, wrote a critical concurring opinion. He again objected to {109} the use of the "clear and present danger" rule which he contended had never been intended by Holmes "to express a technical legal doctrine or to convey a formula for adjudicating cases. It was a literary phrase not to be distorted by being taken from its context." He went on to argue the need for protection of the courts, especially in their handling of criminal cases, such as were involved in the Miami situation. However, he eventually wound up in agreement with the majority on the ground that the judges had already made their decision in these cases at the time the Miami paper published its comments, and that consequently the editors "could not have disturbed the trial court in its sense of fairness but only in its sense of perspective."

The unanimity thus achieved on this issue proved transitory. In 1947 another contempt proceeding against a Texas editor arising out of an insignificant local dispute came up for review in the case of *Craig* v. *Harney.* Justice Douglas held that the newspaper accounts, while inaccurate and not in "good taste," still fell "far short of meeting the clear and present danger test." Murphy in a concurring opinion appeared to take the position that summary contempt procedures are flatly forbidden by the First Amendment.

Frankfurter, who dissented along with Jackson and Vinson, contended that the decision, "in effect though not in terms, holds unconstitutional a power the possession of which by the States this Court has heretofore deemed axiomatic." Frankfurter was at particular pains to point out that Justice Holmes, whose views as expressed in his *Toledo Newspaper Co.* dissent had been so heavily relied on by the majority, was there concerned only with the proper interpretation of a federal statutory limitation on punishments for contempt, and that he had expressed no opinion at all concerning "the Constitutional power of the States to enforce a broader contempt policy." As for Holmes' remark in the same case that "a judge of the United States is expected to be a man of ordinary firmness of character," Frankfurter made the curious comment: "It is pertinent to observe that that was said by an Olympian who was so remote from the common currents of life that he did not read newspapers." Jackson wound up his dissent with an argument similarly ad hominem in character: {110}

> Of course, the blasts of these little papers in this small community do not jolt us, but I am not so confident that we would be indifferent if a news monopoly in our entire jurisdiction should perpetrate this kind of an attack on us.

A second type of threat to freedom of the press which has considerably worried persons concerned about civil liberties is the possibility that the Post Office Department might use the denial of second-class mailing privileges as a form of censorship. Second-class mail is carried at substantially less than cost, and the classification is consequently a matter of great financial importance for publications. The discretion of the Postmaster General in denying second-class privileges has been very broad, and opportunities for judicial review have been quite limited under judicial decisions dating from the First World War. Refusal of such classification has consequently been an easy and a deadly device to use when the Post Office felt that the occasion warranted.

During the first year of World War II, 70 newspapers and other publications were barred from the mails at the request of the Department of Justice by the Postmaster General under authority conferred by the revived Espionage Act of 1917. The method ordinarily followed was to bar a single issue as objectionable under the law, and then to withdraw second-class mailing privileges from future issues, thus providing a formula for total suppression.[25] While most of these publications no doubt deserved their fate, the procedure employed was a serious potential threat to press freedom.

The small, insignificant, and generally vicious publications disposed of in this manner under wartime conditions yielded no tests of Post Office authority. But when Postmaster General Walker sought in 1943 to withdraw second-class mailing privileges from *Esquire* magazine, it was a different matter. Walker's action, taken after a hearing board appointed by him had recommended against revocation, was based on the contention that the publication did not meet one of the statutory conditions for second-class mail, to wit: "It must be originated and published for the dissemination of information of a public character, or devoted to literature, the sciences, arts, or some special industry, and having a legitimate list of subscribers." Walker argued that the {111} material in *Esquire,* while not obscene in a technical sense, was so close to it that it was "morally improper and not for the public welfare and the public good." On review of this decision in *Hannegan* v. *Esquire*, a unanimous Court held that Congress had not meant to grant the Postmaster General rights of censorship when it attached this condition to the second-class privilege. Under the statute the Postmaster General was limited to determining whether a publication "contains information of a public character, literature or art"; he was not granted "the further power to determine whether the contents meet some standard of the public good or welfare."

While the Roosevelt Court has thus been eager and willing to protect the press against what it felt to be genuine limitations on its freedom of expression, it has been cold to complaints by the publishing industry that government regulation of its business or labor relations is a threat to true freedom of the press. In 1937, before any Roosevelt appointees were on the Court, it had upheld a National Labor Relations Board order requiring the Associated Press to reinstate one of its news editors allegedly discharged because of his activities in organizing and furthering the American Newspaper Guild, denying the validity of the A.P. claim that the rights of a free press were being invaded.[26]

The Roosevelt Court has had occasion to apply a similar philosophy in two decisions. In a 1945 decision the Court held that certain by-laws of the Associated Press operated to restrain trade contrary to the Sherman Act. The A.P. is a non-profit cooperative association financed by assessment on its some 1200 newspaper members. The organization's by-laws have in the past prohibited members from selling news to non-members, and set up rules for admission to membership which made it very difficult for an applicant who would compete with an old A.P. member to be admitted. Specifically, the by-laws gave the competing member the right to object to the admission of the applicant, and this objection could be overridden only by a majority vote of all A.P. members, by relinquishing to the A.P. competitor any exclusive news or news features rights the applicant might have, and paying to A.P. ten per cent of "the total amount of the regular assessments received by it from old members in the same {112} competitive field during the entire period from October 1, 1900." This sum would have amounted in the Chicago morning field at the time of the suit to $416,631.90.

The government, stimulated by the refusal of the A.P. to admit the *Chicago Sun* to membership, brought proceedings against the A.P. for violation of the Sherman Act. The Supreme Court, by a divided vote (Black, Douglas, Frankfurter, Rutledge, and Reed constituting the majority), upheld the conviction against the contention, among others, that freedom of the press was being violated. Justice Black's answer was that "freedom to publish is guaranteed by the Constitution, but freedom to combine to keep others from publishing is not."[27]

The second problem came in 1946 when the Court, with only Murphy dissenting, upheld the application of the Fair Labor Standards Act to newspapers in two cases.[28] In neither instance did the Court feel that much argument was required to establish that the Act as applied to newspapers did not abridge the freedom of the press or burden or discriminate against the press.

The contention that investigation of newspaper wage payments by subpoena amounted to unconstitutional search and seizure was also rejected.

The Right to Go Left

Apart from wartime situations, it has characteristically been the states rather than the federal government that have acted, by legislation and prosecution, against radicals and unpopular minorities. Charges that state action in these categories abridges freedom of speech, press, or assembly have been coming to the Supreme Court in considerable numbers since 1925, when in the case of *Gitlow* v. *New York,* as already pointed out, the Court held for the first time that the freedoms protected by the First Amendment against abridgement by Congress are also included among the fundamental personal rights and liberties protected by the Fourteenth Amendment from impairment by the states. The Court was not originally inclined to strike down state legislation on this newly available ground. Gitlow's conviction under the New York Criminal Anarchy Act for circulating {113} writings advocating violent measures against the government was upheld, even though his action had resulted in no "clear and present danger" to the established order. Two years later the Court upheld a conviction under the California Criminal Syndicalism Act based on an individual's participation in the work of the Communist Labor Party.[29]

In the 1930s, however, the Court began to view radical activities with more equanimity and perspective. In 1931 it reversed the conviction of Yelta Stromberg for violating a California statute prohibiting the display of a red flag as a symbol of opposition to organized government, Chief Justice Hughes holding that the statute was so vague and indefinite as to menace the opportunity for free political discussion.[30] In 1937 the Court by a 5 to 4 vote reversed the Georgia conviction of an admitted Communist charged with "incitement to insurrection," by applying the clear and present danger test.[31] The same year it voided the conviction of a Communist who had been prosecuted in Oregon under that state's criminal syndicalism act, his offense being that he had spoken at a meeting of the Communist Party.[32]

By these decisions from the pre-Roosevelt Court the right of radical groups or parties to protection of the Constitution in their political activities was recognized, so long as they did not engage in overt action constituting a clear and present danger to the government. The Roosevelt Court has had no occasion to pass on further cases of this sort coming up from the states, but it has been confronted with several instances of congressional action aimed at or used against radicals or Communists.

One well-known case of this sort originated in 1943 when Congress, in one of its most unlovely moods, adopted an appropriation act rider removing three federal employees—Robert M. Lovett, Goodwin B. Watson, and William E. Dodd, Jr.—from the federal payroll.[33] Congressman Martin Dies had set these proceedings in motion when in a House speech on February 1, 1943, he named

39 federal employees as Communists or fellow travelers, as well as "irresponsible, crackpot, radical bureaucrats." Since one of the 39 was employed by the Treasury Department, whose appropriation was then under consideration, {114} the House voted immediately to withhold money for his salary. Then came the belated discovery that the employee in question was a Negro. Northern Republicans, fearful of the effect on the Negro vote, quickly beat a retreat, and a measure was adopted setting up a committee to examine the charges against the 39. Headed by Representative Kerr, this committee heard 9 of the 39 in secret session, and cleared 6 of them. Lovett, Watson and Dodd, however, were reported as "unfit" to continue in government service, and the two latter were specifically found "guilty" of "subversive activity."

When the two agencies employing these men (the Department of the Interior and the Federal Communications Commission) refused to discharge them and strongly defended their patriotism and integrity, the House adopted a rider to the current deficiency appropriation act forbidding the use of money appropriated in the statute to pay their salaries. Six times the Senate refused to adopt this rider and bitterly denounced it, but eventually under pressure of close of the fiscal year concurred in a compromise providing that no money would be available from the appropriation for their services after November 15, 1943, unless the President gave them appointments and the Senate confirmed them. President Roosevelt, unable to veto the rider without killing the whole act, signed it with a stinging rebuke to Congress for what he declared was an unconstitutional usurpation by Congress of executive and judicial functions, and announced that he did not regard the provision, which he characterized as a "bill of attainder," as binding on the executive.

The three employees named continued to work for their agencies after the November 15 deadline, but they were not paid after that date. They then proceeded to bring suit in the U.S. Court of Claims to recover compensation for the services rendered. They were victorious both in the Court of Claims and in the Supreme Court.[34] Five justices, led by Black, held the rider to be an unconstitutional bill of attainder, defined as "a legislative act which inflicts punishment without a judicial trial." They concluded that "permanent proscription from any opportunity to serve the Government is punishment. and of a most severe type," and added: "Much as we regret {115} to declare that an Act of Congress violates the Constitution, we have no alternative here." The other two justices participating, Frankfurter and Reed, while also upholding the claim, were unwilling to join in this declaration of unconstitutionality, arguing that constitutional questions should be avoided if at all possible. They preferred to consider the statute as merely preventing the ordinary disbursement of money to pay salaries of the three, but still leaving unimpaired the obligation of the government to pay them for services actually rendered.

A somewhat less sensational case which got to the Supreme Court involved the denaturalization of a naturalized citizen named Schneiderman who belonged to the Communist Party. A 1906 statute authorizes "cancelling the certificate of citizenship on the ground of fraud or on the ground that such a certificate of citizenship was illegally procured." Schneiderman was alleged to have secured his certificate illegally on the theory that no Communist could meet the required statutory test—namely, that during the five years immediately preceding his application he must have "behaved as a man of good moral character, attached to the principles of the United States, and well disposed to the good order and happiness of the same."

The Supreme Court rejected the government's contention.[35] Justice Murphy reasoned that since this was a proceeding to revoke the privilege of citizenship after it had been enjoyed for twelve years, the burden of proof was on the government to show that citizenship had been illegally acquired. This the government had failed to do. It had presented no evidence that Scheiderman was not a man of good moral character, nor that he believed in overthrow of the government by violence. The charges against him were based solely on his Communist Party membership and activity. The program of that party, the Court concluded, was not necessarily incompatible with the principles of the Constitution, so long as it was supported by peaceful and constitutional means. Chief Justice Stone, along with Roberts and Frankfurter, dissented.

Then there was the well-known deportation proceeding against Harry Bridges, Australian-born labor leader of the West Coast. {116} By his activity in the longshoremen's union and his leadership of the Pacific Coast maritime workers' strike in 1934, he had earned the enmity of powerful business interests. He was investigated as to liability for deportation as early as 1934 and 1935, but no grounds for action were found. In 1938, deportation proceedings were initiated on the charge that Bridges had been and then was a member of or affiliated with the Communist Party of the United States, and was consequently liable to deportation because that party advocated the violent overthrow of the government. The deportation statute in effect at that time had been construed by the Supreme Court as requiring proof of present membership in the Communist Party to justify deportation.[36] Dean Landis of the Harvard Law School acted as special examiner for the government in the case, and concluded that the evidence failed to prove Bridges a member of or affiliated with the party. The Secretary of Labor, who then had jurisdiction over deportation matters, agreed and the charges were dismissed in January, 1940.

The interests opposed to Bridges did not take this defeat as final. The House of Representatives proceeded to adopt an extraordinary and clearly unconstitutional special bill directing the Attorney General, "notwithstanding any other provisions of law," immediately to deport Harry Bridges, "whose presence in this country the Congress deems hurtful."[37] This shabby maneuver failed when the bill died in a Senate committee. Congress then proceeded in more proper fashion to amend the deportation statute so as to permit the deportation of aliens who at any time since entering the country had been members of or affiliated with an organization believing in the overthrow of the government by force and violence.

Action to deport Bridges was again begun under the amended statute. A special examiner held that the Communist Party did advocate the overthrow of the government by force and violence, and that Bridges had been affiliated with and a member of the party. The board of immigration appeals reversed the examiner, but Attorney General Biddle, who had succeeded the Secretary of Labor in control of deportation proceedings, in turn reversed the appeals board and ordered deportation. Bridges lost in two lower courts, but won {117} a 5 to 3 verdict in the Supreme Court.[38] Justice Douglas said that there was no evidence proving Bridges' cooperation with the party except in its "wholly lawful activities," such as seeking to organize labor and raise wages. Bridges had accepted the aid of revolutionary groups in order "to improve the lot of the workingmen on the waterfront." This cooperation in the securing of lawful objectives did not constitute "affiliation" with the party in the statutory sense. The finding that Bridges had actually been a member of the party was rejected because it was supported only by unsworn and unsigned statements. Justice Murphy, who concurred with the majority, would have gone further to declare the deportation statute unconstitutional as denying due process and abridging the liberties of the First Amendment. Stone, Roberts, and Frankfurter dissented.

Freedom in Wartime

The strong bias of the Roosevelt Court toward the maintenance of civil liberties was responsible to a large degree for the serious and on the whole successful effort made to prevent the development of intolerance and witch-hunts during World War II on the scale which had marred American participation in the preceding war. The Espionage Act of 1917, a convenient weapon of oppression in the first war, was strictly construed by the Court to prevent any such result the second time. The principal case involved an American citizen named Hartzel who had expressed hope for a German victory before this country entered the war, and who wrote articles in 1942 describing American participation in the war as a betrayal of America and attacking the English, the Jews, and the integrity and patriotism of President Roosevelt. He urged conversion of the war into a race struggle and occupation of this country by foreign troops until we "are able to stand alone." He mailed out some 600 copies of these articles, some going to Army officers and others to persons registered under selective service. He was convicted under the Espionage Act for seeking "willfully" to cause insubordination or disloyalty in the military forces and to obstruct enlistment. In a 5 to 4 decision the Supreme Court set aside the conviction, ruling that the word "willfully" {118} required proof of a specific intent or evil purpose to accomplish the purposes punished by the statute, and that it had not been proved beyond a reasonable doubt that Hartzel mailed these articles with such a specific intent in mind.[39]

The same urge to lean over backwards in applying wartime penalties was evident in the first of the treason cases which arose out of the famous German sabotage attempt on the United States. The case concerned Anthony Cramer, a naturalized citizen of German birth, who was a close friend of Werner Thiel, one of the saboteurs. Thiel, an ardent Nazi, had returned to Germany from the

United States in 1941. When Thiel landed in this country in June, 1942, on his mission of sabotage, he got in touch with Cramer in New York. Cramer met Thiel and another of the saboteurs at a tavern and agreed to keep Thiel's money. Cramer admitted that he assumed Thiel had come to the United States by submarine, and that he supposed Thiel was probably on a propaganda mission for Germany. Cramer was convicted of treason by a federal district court.

The Constitution states: "Treason against the United States shall consist only in levying war against them, or in adhering to their enemies, giving them aid and comfort. No person shall be convicted of treason unless on the testimony of two witnesses to the same overt act, or on confession in open court." These limiting provisions were included in the Constitution because of experience with the misuse of the treason charge in England. The Supreme Court concluded that the overt acts proved against Cramer were simply his meetings with Thiel and an associate, and their drinking and talking together, and that these acts were not sufficient to constitute giving aid and comfort to the enemy. Cramer's action in keeping Thiel's money, which clearly did give aid and comfort, had not been presented to the jury, and so could not be relied on to support the conviction. While striking down the treason charge, the Court noted that other and lesser charges might well have been made and sustained against Cramer.[40]

A four-judge minority, composed of Douglas, Stone, Black, and Reed, attacked the ultra-rigid test applied by the Court in determining overt acts, a test which Corwin said "just about gives the coup de grace {119} to the 'treason' clause." The provision, however, was harder to dispose of than Corwin thought. Two years later the Court, with only Murphy dissenting, upheld the treason conviction of the father of one of the same saboteurs in *Haupt* v. *United States.* Justice Douglas felt that the Haupt decision vindicated the stand of the dissenters in the Cramer case, and was "truer to the constitutional definition of treason . . ."

Another wartime case saw the Court, with Black and Douglas dissenting, reverse the conviction of George Sylvester Viereck for violation of the Foreign Agents Registration Act. The majority held that Viereck was required under the statute merely to report to the Secretary of State propaganda activities undertaken as the agent of a foreign principal, and was under no obligation to report similar activities undertaken on his own initiative. In a similar fashion the Court reversed the conviction of twenty-four leaders of the German-American Bund on the ground that the evidence offered was not sufficient to convict them of conspiring to counsel evasion of or resistance to the draft. This decision drew a dissent from the oddly assorted group of Stone, Reed, Douglas, and Jackson.[41]

The denaturalization procedure already discussed is another tempting device to apply during wartime against naturalized citizens whose loyalty is suspect. Considerable use was made of it during World War I, and by the end of 1942 the World War II record was 42 denaturalizations accomplished, 300 suits pending in the courts, and 2500 cases being actively investigated.[42] This drive ran into difficulties in 1943, however, when the Supreme Court laid down the strict rule in the Schneiderman case that the evidence to support denaturalization must be "clear, unequivocal, and convincing."

The principle of this decision was applied when the first of the disloyalty cases arising out of the war reached the Court. It concerned an electrical engineer named Baumgartner who had been born and educated in Germany, and had served as a German officer during the first war. He came to this country in 1927, and was naturalized in 1932. Beginning in 1933 he publicly supported Hitler and spoke contemptuously of American democracy. He belonged to the Bund, and attended meetings at which the Nazi salute was given. He {120} was violently anti-Semitic. The Supreme Court, however, unanimously held that the government had failed to prove that Baumgartner had mental reservations when he swore allegiance to this country in 1932, at a time when Hitler had not yet come to power. His subsequent admiration for Nazism did not prove he was dishonest in the oath he had taken in 1932. "One of the prerogatives of American citizenship is the right to criticize public men and measures—and that means not only informed and responsible criticism but the freedom to speak foolishly and without moderation." Justice Murphy added that "the naturalized citizen has as much right as the natural born citizen to exercise the cherished freedoms of speech, press and religion."[43]

Two years later, however, a second proceeding of this type reached the Court involving one Knauer, who had come to this country in 1925 at the age of 30, and had become a citizen in 1937. Unlike the Baumgartner case, the evidence against Knauer showed that before his naturalization, at the time of his naturalization, and after naturalization he had followed "a clear course of conduct . . . designed to promote the Nazi cause in this country." He was not, the Court concluded, "an underling caught up in the enthusiasm of a movement, driven by ties of blood and old associations to extreme attitudes, and perhaps unaware of the conflict of allegiance implicit in his actions. Knauer is an astute person. He is a leader. . . . His activities portray a shrewd, calculating, and vigilant promotion of an alien cause." The Court majority thus distinguished Knauer's situation from that of Baumgartner, and concluded that "when Knauer forswore allegiance to Hitler and the German Reich he swore falsely."[44]

Justices Rutledge and Murphy agreed that if any man ever deserved denaturalization, Knauer did. But they could not bring themselves to admit that the power to denaturalize exists in the hands of the federal government. If it does, they contended, then all naturalized citizens are second-class citizens. "Any process which takes away their citizenship for causes and by procedures not applicable to native-born citizens places them in a separate and an inferior class." It sets up "two classes of citizens, one free and secure except for acts amounting {121} to forfeiture within our tradition; the other conditional, timorous and insecure because blanketed with the threat that some act or conduct, not amounting to forfeiture for others, will be taken retroactively to show that some prescribed condition had not been fulfilled and be so adjudged."

94

From the point of view of the number of persons affected, the threat to civil liberties from the denaturalization program did not begin to compare with that resulting from the evacuation of Japanese and Japanese-Americans from the West Coast, a program which has been called "our worst wartime mistake." The Roosevelt Court, devoted as it has generally proved itself to be to the principle of freedom, did not undertake to invalidate that policy. The Court moved cautiously, not boldly, in this matter, and sought to avoid or postpone a decision on the issues as long as possible.

Army regulations for the West Coast, adopted on the authority of a Presidential order and subsequent supporting legislation, included a curfew regulation applicable to all aliens and to all persons of Japanese ancestry, requiring them to be in their residences between 8:00 P.M. and 6:00 A.M. Shortly after the curfew was adopted, the program of complete evacuation was undertaken. Hirabayashi, an American-born citizen of alien Japanese parents, and a student at the University of Washington, was convicted of failure both to obey the curfew and to report for registration for evacuation. Sentence for the two offenses was made to run concurrently.

The Supreme Court took advantage of this fact to limit its review to the question of the curfew, clearly a less drastic interference with liberty than the enforced evacuation, and unanimously upheld it as a temporary emergency war measure. Under the circumstances that existed at the time, the Court concluded that it was not unreasonable for those charged with the national defense to feel that the Japanese constituted a peculiar danger to national security. Racial discriminations are odious and usually unconstitutional, because justified by no proper legislative purpose. But "in time of war residents having ethnic affiliations with an invading enemy may be a greater source of danger than those of a different ancestry." Concurring opinions by Douglas and Murphy indicated that the justices {122} found it uncomfortable to have to approve the curfew, and stressed the need for restoring normal freedoms as soon as possible.[45]

The decision in the *Hirabayashi* case was rendered in June, 1943, a year after the evacuation. It was another year and a half, in December, 1944, before a decision on the evacuation program itself was reached. Then the government action was upheld by a divided Court, in *Korematsu v. United States.* The majority opinion followed the lines of the earlier decision, holding that the military authorities were not unjustified in concluding that the Japanese residents of the coast area constituted a potentially grave danger to the public safety, a danger so great and pressing that there was no time to set up procedures for determining the loyalty or disloyalty of individual Japanese. Three justices—Roberts, Murphy, and Jackson—dissented. Murphy challenged the reasonableness of the military conclusion, which he charged was not based on any demonstrated public necessity, but upon "an accumulation of much of the misinformation, half-truths, and insinuations that for years have been directed against Japanese-Americans by people with racial and economic prejudices." Jackson suggested that even if the military decision was justified, the Court should refuse to enforce it, because Court approval would give constitutional sanction to "a military expedient that has no place in law under the Constitution."

In these cases, then, the Court abandoned its clear and present danger test, reverting to the principle of judicial acquiescence in legislative or executive action provided reasonable justification for the action can be shown. Even in examining into the reasonableness of and the alleged necessity for the evacuation program, the Court was exceeding superficial. The result is a dangerous precedent supporting the principle of military supremacy and threatening the status of minority groups.[46]

Civil Liberties and Political Rights

It is appropriate to note at this point the more important decisions in which the Roosevelt Court has considered civil liberties and rights in their political contexts, even though these cases may take us away {123} from the confines of the First Amendment. The Court has decided two significant cases concerning the right to participate in elections and have one's vote counted. In the 1941 decision of *United States* v. *Classic,* the Court overruled the doctrine established by the *Newberry* decision in 1921 that the federal government has no power to regulate the conduct of primary elections at which candidates for national offices are nominated.[47] Classic, a commissioner of elections in New Orleans, was indicted in a federal district court for willfully altering and falsely counting ballots cast in a congressional primary election. It was charged that Classic had violated two sections of the Criminal Code, which in very general language provide punishment for anyone depriving persons of "any rights, privileges or immunities secured or protected by the Constitution and laws of the United States." The Court, speaking through Justice Stone, ruled that the right of a qualified voter to have his vote for congressional offices honestly and correctly counted is a right secured by the Constitution and laws of the United States. Because the primary election is a vital part of the congressional election system in Louisiana, the constitutional right of the voter to "choose" a congressman includes the right to cast a ballot in a congressional primary election and have it counted.

Hidden away in the *Classic* decision was a delayed-action bomb which exploded four years later, wrecking the South's Democratic "white primary" system. Specifically involved was the state of Texas, which had exhibited a remarkable fertility in devising means for excluding Negroes 'legally" from that state's Democratic primaries. Apparently relying upon the *Newberry* decision the Texas legislature in 1923 flatly prohibited Negroes from voting in the Democratic primaries. The Supreme Court promptly invalidated the statute as a denial of equal protection of the laws.[48] The Texas legislature, nothing daunted, passed a new law authorizing each political party in the state through its state executive committee to prescribe the qualifications for voting in its primaries, their theory being that what the state was forbidden to do directly by the Fourteenth Amendment could be done indirectly under state authorization. The Democratic state executive committee then excluded Negroes from primary elections, but the Supreme Court held that the party committee had acted as the {124} agent of the state legislature, which made the action equivalent to that by the state itself and so unconstitutional.[49]

This latter decision left open the possibility that if Negroes were excluded from primaries solely by party organs acting on their own initiative and without authority of state law, the constitutional problem might be solved. Accordingly, the state Democratic convention adopted a resolution in 1932 confining membership in the party to white citizens. This formula proved, for the time being, a successful one, the Supreme Court concluding unanimously in the 1935 decision of *Grovey* v. *Townsend* that the discrimination was an act of the party and not of the state, and so not covered by the Fourteenth Amendment.

There the matter rested until 1941 when the *Classic* decision held primaries to be an integral part of the machinery of elections, protected by the constitutional right to "choose" members of Congress. Encouraged by this decision, another test case came up from Texas in 1945, *Smith* v. *Allwright*. By an 8 to 1 vote, the Supreme Court reversed *Grovey* v. *Townsend*. Since the *Classic* case, the Court held, party primaries could no longer be regarded as private affairs nor the parties conducting them as unaffected with public responsibilities. Noting that parties and party primaries in Texas were in fact regulated at many points by state statutes, the Court reasoned that a party required to follow these directions was "an agency of the state," and if it practiced discrimination against Negroes, that was "state action within the meaning of the Fifteenth Amendment." The only hope for a legal white primary after this decision was for a state to eliminate all regulations of primary elections from its statute books, a stratagem which South Carolina immediately tried. The lower federal courts, however, refused to concede that the Democratic party had by this device transformed itself into a "private voluntary association of individuals," which could exclude Negroes by "club rules," and in April, 1948, the Supreme Court upheld this position by denying certiorari in the case of *Rice* v. *Elmore*.

The Court's action safeguarding political rights in these cases is offset by three decisions where it revealed greater reluctance to interpose its authority, in spite of strong urging from the left wing. {125} *Colegrove* v. *Green,* decided in 1946, was an interesting action questioning the legality of Illinois' failure since 1901 to redistrict the state for purposes of representation in the House of Representatives. As a result of this failure a great inequality had developed among the various congressional districts, with some almost nine times as populous as others. This situation, it was here contended, was contrary to the Constitution and to congressional legislation, and the Court was asked to declare the districting plan invalid. By a 4 to 3 vote, however, the Court refused to take this action, Justice Frankfurter holding for the majority that it was the responsibility of Congress to secure fair representation from the states, and that "courts ought not to enter this political thicket."

Justices Black, Douglas, and Murphy would have granted the petition. The gross inequality of voting power resulting from the failure to reapportion the districts constituted in their view a denial of equal protection of the laws. The fact that a political question was involved did not mean that the Court was rendered powerless to intervene, they held, citing the *Classic* case among others as a precedent. The fact that the decision was made by less than a clear majority of the Court, and that Rutledge's concurring opinion was somewhat equivocal, led to the request for a rehearing of the case, which was denied in October, 1946. On the same day the Court, with Black, Murphy, and Rutledge dissenting, refused to pass on the validity of Georgia's county unit system for selecting candidates for election to public office.[50]

In *United Public Workers* v. *Mitchell*, a 1947 decision, the Court rejected by a 4 to 3 vote a claim of unconstitutionality brought against the Hatch Act, which limits the political activity of government employees. One Poole, a skilled laborer in the mint at Philadelphia, had served as a ward committeeman of the Democratic Party, and was politically active on election day as a worker at the polls. As required by the Hatch Act, he was removed from his position by the Civil Service Commission for having taken an "active part in political management or in political campaigns."

Justice Reed, speaking for Frankfurter, Vinson, and Burton as well, held the statute not to be an unconstitutional invasion of the rights {126} of free speech or of the Fifth, Ninth, or Tenth Amendments. Congress had concluded that it is in the best interests of an efficient public service for classified employees to be prohibited from active participation in politics.

> To declare that the present supposed evils of political activity are beyond the power of Congress to redress would leave the nation impotent to deal with what many sincere men believe is a material threat to the democratic system.

It may be, Reed continued, that political neutrality is not indispensable to a merit system, but "because it is not indispensable does not mean that it is not desirable or permissible." As for the argument that such limitations ought not to be imposed on employees in the lower ranks who have no chance to influence policy determination, the reply was that there are hundreds of thousands in such capacities, and it was not unreasonable for Congress to fear that political influence would be used to build them into a political machine. Congress has the right to forestall dangers to the integrity and competency of the civil service, Reed concluded, so long as it remains within "the general existing conception of governmental power."[51]

Justices Black, Douglas, and Rutledge (Murphy not participating) would have held the statute unconstitutional. Douglas contended that if political influences needed to be limited, the legislation should be more narrowly and selectively drawn to get at the specific conduct constituting a clear and present danger. He suggested the possibility of drawing a line between the administrative class of government employees—who prepare the basic data on which policy decisions are made—and industrial employees, such as Poole. Suppose the United States should at some future time undertake a nationalization program such as England's, Douglas suggested. The Hatch Act rule would bar the hundreds of thousands of workers in nationalized industries from "the normal political activity which is one of our valued traditions."

Justice Black's argument was in more general terms and more ringing language. He unsparingly castigated a policy which muzzles several million citizens and deprives the body politic of their political {127} participation and interest. "I think the Constitution prohibits legislation which prevents millions of citizens from contributing their arguments, complaints, and suggestions to the political debates which are the essence of our democracy." Moreover, the statute endows the Civil Service Commission "with the awesome power to censor the thoughts, expressions, and activities of law-abiding citizens in the field of free expression from which no person should be barred by a government which boasts that it is a government of, for, and by the people—all the people."

The Court's latter-day hesitancy to be too adventuresome in protection of political rights was also manifested in 1947 when it refused certiorari in the case of *Friedman* v. *Schwellenbach*. Friedman, a non-civil service federal employee, had been given a war service appointment in 1942, conditional upon a character examination which included a check on his loyalty. In Friedman's case investigation disclosed that he had been an active member of American Peace Mobilization, an organization which at first bitterly fought American participation in the war on Germany, but experienced a remarkable conversion to all-out support of the war as soon as Russia was attacked. The Civil Service Commission concluded that his record indicated Friedman was not eligible for retention in the federal service, directed the War Manpower Commission to dismiss him, and cancelled all his pending eligibilities for civil service employment.

The district court denied that this action constituted any abridgement of the plaintiff's constitutional rights under the First and Fifth Amendments, holding that the right of the government to disqualify federal employees because of a "reasonable doubt" of their loyalty "would seem obvious enough in time of war." The wartime character of the case, and the fact that it was technically not a question of removal but merely a decision that a conditional appointee had not met the character standards required, may have buttressed the Supreme Court in its refusal to hear it; but the Court is unlikely to escape so easily from peacetime tests of the "loyalty" investigation of federal employees required by President Truman's executive order of March 21, 1947. The summary removal procedure established by this order raises problems not settled by the *Friedman* decision. {128}

Also looming on the horizon are constitutional problems raised by the anti-Communist investigative tactics of the House Committee on Un-American Activities. In February, 1948, the Court refused to review Leon Josephson's conviction for refusal to be sworn and to testify before the Committee, although Douglas, Murphy, and Rutledge voted to grant certiorari in the case.[52] But the more celebrated controversy involving ten Hollywood writers and directors who refused to answer the Committee's questions as to their present or past membership in the Communist party, and who were consequently cited for contempt of Congress in November, 1947, will bring before the Court the considerably more difficult problem as to the constitutional status of congressional inquiries into individual political affiliations.

Anti-Okie and Jim Crow

Finally, it is relevant to note two situations where the Court has employed the commerce clause to vindicate personal liberties challenged by state legislation. As pointed out in the preceding chapter, the Roosevelt Court has been rather reluctant to make the commerce clause a barrier to state business regulation, but when it is available as a check on state limitation of individual liberties, the reluctance changes into alacrity. In 1941 the Court invalidated California's "Anti-Okie" law, which made it a misdemeanor for anyone to bring an "indigent person" into the state, on the ground that it was an unconstitutional barrier to commerce. Four members of the Court would have preferred to rest the case on the "privileges and immunities" clause of the Fourteenth Amendment, but the justices were unanimous that the statute was invalid.[53]

Then, in 1946, the commerce clause was employed to invalidate a state Jim Crow statute in the case of *Morgan* v. *Virginia*. The law in question related to the segregation of passengers on all public motor carriers according to color, and made it a misdemeanor for any passenger to refuse to change seats as required by the driver, who was to see that contiguous seats were not occupied by persons of different races at the same time. This case arose when a Negro woman passenger on an interstate bus traveling through Virginia {129} refused to move to a back seat as requested by the driver. Balancing the claims of local police power against the need for national uniformity in the regulation of interstate travel, the Court, with only Justice Burton dissenting, concluded that "seating arrangements for the different races in interstate motor travel require a single uniform rule to promote and protect national travel," and consequently the statute was invalid.

Perhaps the most interesting part of the *Morgan* case was Black's concurring opinion. He had expressed his belief in such preceding decisions as *Nippert* v. *Richmond* and the Arizona train-limit case that the commerce clause "means that Congress can regulate commerce and that the courts cannot . . . whether state legislation imposes an 'undue burden' on interstate commerce raises pure questions of policy, which the Constitution intended should be resolved by the Congress." But since this view had not prevailed in the two cases mentioned, and since the Court had adopted the "undue burden on commerce formula," Black announced that "I must make decisions under it." Thus he was "forced" into a result which was extremely satisfactory to him.

100

The *Morgan* situation was reversed in *Bob-Lo Excursion Co.* v. *Michigan,* decided in February, 1948, where a state civil rights act was applied against racial discrimination by a Detroit boat company on excursions to a nearby island on the Canadian side of the boundary, but in this case the Court upheld the state law by a 7 to 2 vote. Justice Jackson, with Vinson concurring, alleged the inconsistency of considering that a state Jim Crow law was a burden on commerce while a state civil rights act was not. But two months later the Court was unanimous in denying judicial enforcement to racial restrictive covenants covering sale of real estate, with Vinson writing the opinion in *Shelley* v. *Kraemer.*

The Court as Super-Legislature

Civil liberties problems have given the Roosevelt Court one of its most controversial groups of cases. Some 34 nonunanimous decisions have been recorded in this field between 1939 and 1947, with 12 of {130} them yielding 5 to 4 or 4 to 3 splits. The divisions among the justices are strikingly revealed when the data of these 34 decisions are put in tabular form. The left-wing grouping of Murphy, Rutledge, Black, and Douglas is clearly marked off from the rest of the Court by their votes on civil liberties issues, but the split within that bloc is no less striking. Justice Murphy, the Court's outstanding protagonist of civil rights, cast only one vote against the claims of freedom in the 32 nonunanimous decisions where he was a participant, and that was in the first flag salute case, a vote he subsequently announced had been mistaken. Rutledge's zeal was considerably less intense than that of Murphy, and on several occasions he was willing to support a restriction that was objectionable to Murphy. Specifically, he approved the application of the Fair Labor Standards Act to newspapers, the Sherman Act as a restriction on the Associated Press, the Massachusetts child labor, law as a limitation on the right of children to sell Jehovah's Witnesses publications, and the Japanese evacuation program.

Black and Douglas differed from Rutledge, so far as cases in which all three participated are concerned, principally in their views on wartime problems. Both Black and Douglas opposed Rutledge's position in the first treason decision, where they would have held Cramer guilty, and in the Knauer case, where they were part of the majority approving the denaturalization of this Nazi sympathizer. In addition, Douglas opposed both Rutledge and Black in the *Hartzel* Espionage Act case, and was one of the minority convinced that Hartzel's guilt under the act had been sufficiently proved. It is worth noting that Douglas was the only justice on the Court who supported the government in every one of the nonunanimous wartime freedom decisions.

The remaining members of the Court fall far below its average position on civil liberties problems. The late Chief Justice Stone presents an interesting case. His lone dissent in the first flag salute decision might have seemed to mark him as the most ardent of the Court's members in his concern for the protection of individual liberties of conscience and action, but his record reveals only 44 per cent support for these claims. He did maintain rather consistently {131} his support for Jehovah's Witnesses, his only votes against this sect being registered in the Massachusetts child labor case and the two 1946 decisions involving the right to circulate literature on the premises of a company town and a federal housing project. But in the other categories his vote was usually in favor of the challenged federal or state restriction.

TABLE XVI

ALIGNMENTS OF JUSTICES IN NONUNANIMOUS CIVIL LIBERTIES CASES, 1939-1946 TERMS

	No. Cases	Decisions in Favor of					Total
		Freedom of Religion	Free Press	Radicals	Wartime Freedom	Political Rights	
No. Cases		15	6	2	7	3	34*
Majority	34	67%	50%	100%	57%	33%	62%
Murphy	32	93	100	100	100	100	97
Rutledge	28	83	25	100	67	67	71
Black	34	80	50	100	29	100	68
Douglas	34	87	50	100	0	100	65
Stone	27	57	20	0	40	100	44
Jackson	18	20	50	..	40	100	33
Reed	34	20	50	100	14	33	32
Roberts	22	9	33	0	100	0	32
Frankfurter	34	27	17	0	43	33	29
Burton	12	25	33	..	0	0	17
Vinson	4	0	0	..	0	0	0

*Total includes one additional case, Morgan v. Virginia.

Justice Jackson, who participated in fewer cases, generally was not receptive to libertarian arguments, in spite of his decision in the second flag salute case. Justice Reed was a confirmed supporter of the state regulations protested by Jehovah's Witnesses and of the federal government's position in the wartime freedom cases. He did, however, vote against the government in the two radical cases involving the Schneiderman denaturalization proceeding and the Bridges deportation case. Justice Roberts voted for Jehovah's Witnesses in a contested decision only once, and that was in the 1939 case upholding their right to distribute handbills where only Justice McReynolds was in dissent. It is comparatively easy to understand {132} Roberts' vote to exempt the Associated Press from Sherman Act control, but it is more difficult to understand the sudden zeal he showed for individual protection in the wartime cases.

The Court's two post-Roosevelt appointees, Burton and Vinson, stand at the bottom of the table. While they have not participated in a large number of cases, it is obvious that the net effect of their substitution for Roberts and Stone has been to shift the balance of the Court toward the right on civil liberties matters, so that in an increasing number of instances Black, Douglas, Murphy, and Rutledge find it impossible to pick up the one additional justice necessary to maintain the activist attitude toward judicial protection of civil liberties generally characteristic of the Roosevelt Court.

Justice Frankfurter offers by far the most interesting case for examination in his reaction to civil liberties issues. In view of his very active interest in this field before his appointment to the Court, it seems paradoxical to find him giving less support to individual claims for freedom of action or conscience than any other Roosevelt appointed justice. Frankfurter supported Jehovah's Witnesses in 4 of the 11 proceedings considered here, but 2 of those were the 1946 company town and federal housing project decisions in which he concurred only on the ground that he was obliged to accept the past rulings of the Court as binding, and the third was the handbill case in which every justice except McReynolds joined. Apart from these Jehovah's Witnesses cases, Frankfurter voted for the individual claims in only 6 of the 23 cases, 3 of his favorable votes being on wartime freedom problems.

Justice Frankfurter's own explanation of his votes has been almost entirely in terms of the respect which he believes that courts must give to legislative judgments. Justice Holmes once wrote: "It must be remembered that legislatures are ultimate guardians of the liberty and welfare of the people in quite as great a degree as the courts."[54] Frankfurter, who undertakes to serve as the interpreter of Holmes to the present Court, said in the second flag salute case that he regarded this statement as going "to the very essense of our constitutional system and the democratic conception of our society," and he continued: {133}

> He [Holmes] was stating the comprehensive judicial duty and role of this Court in our constitutional scheme whenever legislation is sought to be nullified on any ground, namely, that responsibility for legislation lies with legislatures, answerable as they are directly to the people, and this Court's only and very narrow function is to determine whether within the broad grant of authority vested in legislatures they have exercised a judgment for which reasonable justification can be offered.

The Roosevelt Court has, as noted in the preceding chapter, accepted this philosophy so far as general economic and social regulations are concerned, but in Bill of Rights cases it has contended that the Court must subject legislative action to more rigorous tests, or, as Chief Justice Stone put it, to a "more searching judicial inquiry." The Court majority which has developed and enforced this rule has denied that there is any inconsistency in the different treatment accorded these two fields. They have pointed out that the due process clause standing alone states a vague concept, and that consequently when it is invoked in economic regulation cases it affords a slender reed for a reviewing court to lean upon. But in civil liberties cases the due process clause becomes much more definite by reason of its incorporation of the specific freedoms guaranteed by the Bill of Rights, and the courts are supplied with a much more tangible standard against which to measure legislative judgments. As Justice Jackson wrote in defense of the second flag salute decision:

> Much of the vagueness of the due process clause disappears when the specific prohibitions of the First [Amendment] become its standard. The right of a State to regulate, for example, a public utility may well include, so far as the due process test is concerned, power to impose all of the restrictions which a legislature may have a "rational basis" for adopting. But freedoms of speech and of press, of assembly, and of worship may not be infringed on such slender grounds. They are susceptible of restriction only to prevent grave and immediate danger to interests which the state may lawfully protect.

Justices Black, Douglas, and Murphy have expressed a similar view justifying this double standard in interpreting the due process clause.

> To hold that the Fourteenth Amendment was intended to and did provide protection from state invasions of the right of free speech {134} and other clearly defined protections contained in the Bill of Rights . . . is quite different from holding that "due process," an historical expression relating to procedure . . . confers a broad judicial power to invalidate all legislation which seems "unreasonable" to courts. In the one instance, courts proceeding within clearly marked constitutional boundaries seek to execute policies written into the Constitution; in the other, they roam at will in the limitless area of their own beliefs as to reasonableness and actually select policies, a responsibility which the Constitution entrusts to the legislative representatives of the people.[55]

All this is unconvincing to Justice Frankfurter. He believes that the Court has no greater jurisdiction or authority in reviewing legislation touching civil liberties and personal rights than in handling legislation affecting economic liberties and property rights. Shortly before his appointment to the Court he wrote:

> There is truth behind the familiar contrast between rights of property and rights of man. But certainly in some of its aspects property is a function of personality, and conversely the free range of the human spirit becomes shrivelled and constrained under economic dependence. Especially in a civilization like ours where the economic

interdependence of society is so pervasive, a sharp division between property rights and human rights largely falsifies reality.[56]

And in the second flag salute decision he sought specifically to refute the concept of a dual approach to the due process clause.

> The Constitution does not give us greater veto power when dealing with one phase of "liberty" than with another. . . . In neither situation is our function comparable to that of a legislature or are we free to act as though we were a super-legislature. Judicial self-restraint is equally necessary whenever an exercise of political or legislative power is challenged. There is no warrant in the constitutional basis of this Court's authority for attributing different roles to it depending upon the nature of the challenge to the legislation. Our power does not vary according to the particular provision of the Bill of Rights which is invoked. The right not to have property taken without just compensation has, so far as the scope of judicial review is concerned, the same constitutional dignity as the right to be protected against unreasonable searches and seizures, and the latter has no less claim than {135} freedom of the press or freedom of speech or religious freedom. In no instance is this Court the primary protector of the particular liberty that is invoked.

Thus the man who felt it necessary to deny that he was a Communist when he was appointed to the Supreme Court protests the inferior status to which the Court majority has relegated property rights. Another paradox in the Frankfurter position is that, while following rigorously what he conceives to be the Holmes doctrine, he sometimes finds Holmes on the other side of the Court. When the majority in the second flag salute case relied upon the Holmes "clear and present danger" test in striking down this compulsory school exercise, Frankfurter replied that the Court was not playing fair.

> To talk about "clear and present danger" as the touchstone of allowable educational policy by the states whenever school curricula may impinge upon the boundaries of individual conscience, is to take a felicitous phrase out of the context of the particular situation where it arose and for which it was adapted.

And when, in *Girouard* v. *United States*, the Court majority upheld the right of an alien conscientious objector to become an American citizen and thus vindicated two of Holmes' finest dissents, Frankfurter was not with them. Instead, he went along with Chief Justice Stone in concluding that since Congress had failed to amend the naturalization laws after the Court's earlier opinions, it must be considered to have ratified the judicial interpretation contained therein.

Finally, there is Frankfurter's charge that the Court in its civil liberties decisions has been acting like a "super-legislature." The last time that phrase was heard, it will be recalled, was at the conclusion of the preceding chapter when Justices Black and Douglas used it to refer to the action of the Court majority in invalidating the Arizona train-limit law and the Richmond drummers' tax. The majority in each of those two cases included Justice Frankfurter. Truly, constitutional interpretation grows "curioser and curioser." {136}

* * *

What it all adds up to is simply that the Roosevelt Court no more than its predecessors has been willing to yield to legislative judgments which challenge its primary values. When the old Court saw property rights being kicked around by progressive legislatures, it could not resist using the due process or commerce clauses to cut short the experiments. The Roosevelt Court can view most such essays with equanimity, but it can react sharply enough when civil liberties are molested, being willing even to invalidate an act of Congress which invades those precincts.

In recent terms, it is true, the enthusiasm of the Court's challenge to legislative supremacy has waned with the strengthening of the Court's right wing. The best illustration of this development is the decision on the last day of the term in June, 1948, in which the Court by a 5 to 4 vote avoided a constitutional test of the Taft-Hartley Act's prohibition on expenditures by labor organizations in connection with federal elections by holding that Congress had not intended to include expenditures in publishing union newspapers within this ban. Rutledge for the left accused the Court of "abdicating its function in the guise of applying the policy against deciding questions of constitutionality unnecessarily," but the Court's opinion left no doubt that the section would be held unconstitutional if its language were interpreted more broadly. The post-Roosevelt Court may thus demand somewhat more in the way of provocation to assert its supremacy, but judicial primacy in protection of civil liberties remains well established.

CHAPTER SIX

Crime and Punishment

THE ROOSEVELT COURT is clearly a Bill of Rights court. But the rights discussed in the preceding chapter—freedom of speech, press, assembly, and religion—take us no farther into the Bill of Rights than the first of its ten amendments. The bulk of that charter of liberties—specifically the Fourth through the Eighth Amendments—is concerned with stating limitations on the powers exercised by federal law enforcement agencies and with laying down procedures to be followed by federal courts, particularly in criminal prosecutions. There are specific guaranties covering indictment by grand jury, trial by jury, and speedy and public trial, as well as protection against self-incrimination, unreasonable searches and seizures, double jeopardy, and cruel and unusual punishments. The values enshrined in these provisions are closely related to the freedoms of the First Amendment, and the Roosevelt Court has to a considerable degree exhibited the same kind of concern for protection of the procedural rights of defendants in criminal cases that it has shown for the protection of civil liberties.

A preliminary word is required concerning the jurisdiction of the Supreme Court in this field. So far as federal justice is involved, the Court is of course responsible for seeing that the provisions of the Fourth, Fifth, Sixth, Seventh and Eighth Amendments are enforced. In addition to these relatively specific guaranties, moreover, the {138} Supreme Court has ruled that it has a general responsibility for supervision of the administration of justice in the federal courts which "implies the duty of establishing and maintaining civilized standards of procedure and evidence."[1]

With respect to the state courts, the Supreme Court's authority has historically been less extensive. It was held long ago that the specific provisions of the Bill of Rights dealing with judicial procedure do not apply to the states. They are, however, bound by the Fourteenth Amendment, and under the due process requirement state judicial proceedings in criminal cases have been reviewed by the Supreme Court to determine the extent of their conformance with two fundamental requisites—that the court have jurisdiction over the defendant, and that the defendant receive trial in an orderly manner before an impartial tribunal. The Roosevelt Court has been the scene of a spirited battle to determine whether an increased measure of control over state criminal procedure is justified.[2]

The Right to Counsel

One of the principal aspects of criminal procedure to which the Court has devoted attention is the right of defendants to counsel, a right which is specifically protected in the federal courts by the Sixth Amendment. That this right may also be a fundamental element of due process in state prosecutions was first established in 1932 in the famous *Scottsboro* case.[3] There the Court, over the dissent of Justices Butler and McReynolds, held that

> in a capital case, where the defendant is unable to employ counsel, and is incapable adequately of making his own defense because of ignorance, feeble-mindedness, illiteracy, or the like, it is the duty of the court, whether requested or not, to assign counsel for him as a necessary requisite of due process of law. . . .

This, the Court added, is one of the immutable principles of justice which no state of the Union may disregard.

While the Roosevelt Court has been in general agreement with this rule, it has encountered some difficulty in determining how far its protective {139} force is to be carried. Two 1942 decisions illustrate this disagreement. In *Glasser v. United States,* a former assistant U.S. attorney on trial with other defendants in a federal court for fraud, was represented by an attorney of his choice. However, the presiding judge, over Glasser's protest, appointed Glasser's attorney to represent also a co-defendant, whose legal interests were not identical with those of Glasser. The Supreme Court ruled that this was an impairment of Glasser's constitutional right to counsel, because it denied him the undivided time and attention of his own lawyer. Frankfurter and Stone dissented on the ground that Glasser's legal experience made entirely frivolous his claim that he had been injured by having to share his lawyer.

But a few months later, in *Betts* v. *Brady,* the Court majority through Justice Roberts held that a defendant on trial for robbery in Maryland had had his interests adequately taken care of even though he had not been represented by counsel. The Scottsboro decision had held that each instance of denial of counsel must be judged in its own setting, and the majority in the *Betts* case considered that the right was not under all circumstances a fundamental one, since a number of state constitutions do not recognize it, nor is it required by the common law. Corwin surmises that this decision "may have been influenced in some measure by the known high character of the trial judge, who acted, as the state law permitted in the circumstances, without a jury."[4] Whether or not that was a factor, the decision was anathema to Black, Douglas, and Murphy, who contended that the right to counsel is a fundamental one whose denial is "shocking to the universal sense of justice."

This triumvirate gained additional support for their position when Rutledge joined the Court, and during the 1944 term all four of the nonunanimous decisions in which the absence of counsel was at issue went in favor of the defendant, the dissents being supplied by one or more of the Frankfurter-Roberts-Jackson group.[5] But since that term the pendulum has swung back toward *Betts* v. *Brady*. Particularly in the three counsel cases decided during the 1946 term, all of which were 5 to 4 decisions with Justice Frankfurter writing the majority opinions, were the issues bitterly contested.[6] {140}

In one of these cases, *Foster* v. *Illinois*, two prisoners sought to contest their conviction for burglary eleven years after the trial. The record showed that the defendants, who had been unrepresented by counsel and who had entered pleas of guilty, had been advised by the court "of their rights of trial and of the consequences of entering such pleas of guilty." The majority felt that this procedure met the standards of due process. It would not be proper, Frankfurter argued, to turn due process "into a destructive dogma in the administration of systems of criminal justice," and for the Court to make the provision of counsel mandatory in state cases would be "an abrupt innovation" which "would furnish opportunities hitherto uncontemplated for opening wide the prison doors of the land."

On the same day in June, 1947, the Court took a similar position with respect to a young second offender in *Gayes* v. *New York*. Gayes had been convicted of burglary and petty larceny (the amount stolen was $4.75) at the age of 16. Three years later he pleaded guilty on another burglary charge, and was sentenced as a second offender. He subsequently sought to have the first judgment vacated on the ground that he had not been informed of his rights to counsel, and that a boy of 16 could not intelligently waive such a right. This action also constituted a challenge to the second conviction because the length of the second sentence was based partly on the earlier conviction. The Court majority denied the claim, however, contending that any infirmity in the first sentence should have been contested at the second trial, and not in a subsequent proceeding by what Frankfurter called "a flank attack."

Justices Black, Douglas, Murphy, and Rutledge seethed with indignation over both these decisions. The notion that Gayes had forfeited his constitutional rights was "shocking," Rutledge said, and the "presumption of regularity" in state judicial proceedings set up by the Court in the Foster case made "a mockery of judicial proceedings . . . and a snare and a delusion of constitutional rights for all unable to pay the cost of securing their observance." Black scornfully denounced Frankfurter's fear that the prison doors would swing open as not "even relevant to a determination that we should decline to enforce the Bill of Rights." The Foster opinion, he added, "is another example {141} of the consequences which can be produced by substitution of this Court's day-to-day opinion of what kind of trial is fair and decent for the kind of trial which the Bill of Rights guarantees."

The importance which the Black wing of the Court has attached to the protection of counsel in criminal cases is evident from Table XVII, which summarizes the Court's divisions in this field as well as the others discussed in the present chapter.

TABLE XVII

ALIGNMENTS OF JUSTICES IN NONUNANIMOUS CASES INVOLVING CERTAIN
CONSTITUTIONAL RIGHTS OF CRIMINAL DEFENDANTS, 1941-1946 TERMS

	No. CASES	Decisions for Defendants on					TOTAL
		Right to Counsel	Jury Trial	Third Degree	Search and Seizure	Martial Law	
No. CASES		10	4	6	6	3	29
Majority	29	50%	50%	50%	17%	33%	41%
Murphy	29	100	100	67	100	100	93
Rutledge	22	100	75	67	100	100	91
Black	29	90	100	100	17	33	72
Douglas	29	90	75	67	17	33	62
Stone	18	57	100	50	0	33	50
Jackson	18	44	0	20	100	..	33
Reed	29	50	25	17	17	33	31
Frankfurter	29	10	0	33	100	0	31
Roberts	15	17	0	33	0	..	20
Burton	14	0	33	..	0	0	7
Vinson	6	0	0	..	0	..	0

The Representative Character of Juries

A second procedural aspect of criminal justice which has received much attention from the Roosevelt Court is the representative character of juries, both grand and trial. Usually this question has been raised by the absence of Negroes from juries in state criminal prosecutions in the South. The equal protection clause of the Fourteenth Amendment was first applied in connection with the exclusion of Negroes from juries in 1880. In that year a Virginia judge charged with excluding Negroes from the jury lists because of their race and color was found guilty of denying equal protection,[7] and a {142} West Virginia statute requiring juries to be composed exclusively of white male citizens was likewise held unconstitutional.[8]

It was the "second Scottsboro case," however, which laid the basis for more recent extension of protection in this field. Following the decision in the first case, a second trial was held in another county and the defendants were again convicted. This second conviction was attacked on the ground that Negroes were systematically excluded from the grand jury in the county where the indictment was found, and from the trial jury in the county where the trial was held. The Supreme Court unanimously sustained this contention in 1935 in the case of *Norris* v. *Alabama,* finding that in each of the two counties no Negroes had ever been called for jury service within the memory of the oldest inhabitants or any officer of the courts. This was in spite of the fact that there were Negro citizens in each county well able to render jury service, and that Negro citizens had been called to serve on federal juries in that district. "For this long-continued, unvarying, and wholesale exclusion of Negroes from jury service," Chief Justice Hughes concluded, "we find no justification consistent with the constitutional mandate." The great advance of the *Norris* decision over earlier rulings was that previously it had been necessary to prove positive and intentional racial discrimination in concrete cases, whereas under the *Norris* doctrine discrimination was to be inferred from the general fact that Negroes, without specific justification, were denied equal treatment.

The Roosevelt Court has undertaken to enforce this rule. In a 1939 decision the Court made it clear that the doctrine applied to grand juries as well as petit juries.[9] In *Smith* v. *Texas,* a 1940 decision, the county jury commissioner in a county where the Negro population was over 20 per cent, denied that there was any discrimination against Negroes, and explained that the reason why only 5 of 384 grand jurors serving over a period of eight years were Negroes was because "he was not personally acquainted with any member of the Negro race." Assuming the truth of this unlikely story, the Court pointed out that for a jury commissioner to limit jurors to his personal acquaintance was in itself a discriminatory procedure.

In another Texas case, *Hill* v. *Texas,* decided in 1942, the state court {143} held that the Negro defendant had not sustained the burden of proof in demonstrating that Negroes had been kept off grand juries in his county for 16 years because they were Negroes. This ruling contravened the *Norris* decision, and the Supreme Court reversed the state court, holding that Hill was not obliged to prove actual personal discrimination, but simply to make out a prima facie case of the discriminatory exclusion of Negroes as a general policy.

The county where the *Hill* case arose was quick to develop a policy conforming with the letter, though hardly with the spirit, of these Supreme Court rulings. In 1943 a Negro named Akins was indicted in this county, and the jury commissioners carefully placed one Negro on the grand jury. The commissioners freely admitted that the limitation of Negro representation to one juror was intentional. The Supreme Court, in *Akins* v. *Texas,* was unable to find any loophole in this technical compliance with constitutional requirements. Mathematical exactitude or proportional representation of races or groups, the Court said, was not required to meet the equal protection guarantee. In this particular county 15 per cent of the population was Negro, so that an average representation of Negroes would be 1.85 on a jury of 12. "The mere fact of inequality in the number selected does not in itself show discrimination." There were dissents from Stone, Black, and Murphy, the latter writing a biting opinion to the effect that "racial limitation no less than racial exclusion in the formation of juries is an evil condemned by the equal protection clause. . . . Selections must in no way be limited or restricted by such irrelevant factors."

The Roosevelt Court's concern for the representative character of juries has also manifested itself in some federal cases where no question of racial

111

discrimination was present. In the *Glasser* case already mentioned, the defendants alleged that they had been denied an impartial jury trial because all the names of women from which the jury panel was drawn were taken from a list furnished the clerk of the court by the Illinois League of Women Voters, the list being made up exclusively from those of its members who had attended special "jury classes." The Court ruled that insufficient proof of this allegation was presented, but added that if it had been proved that women jurors {144} were selected by the method alleged, then a new trial would have to be granted. Officials charged with selecting federal jurors

> may exercise some discretion to the end that competent jurors may be called. But they must not allow the desire for competent jurors to lead them into selections which do not comport with the concept of the jury as a cross section of the community. Tendencies, no matter how slight, toward the selection of jurors by any method other than a process which will insure a trial by a representative group are undermining processes weakening the institution of jury trial, and should be sturdily resisted.

The Court later had occasion to give practical effect to this dictum when the case of *Thiel v. Southern Pacific Co.* came up for review in 1946. This was a personal injury action in which a jury trial was demanded, rather than a criminal proceeding. The plaintiff moved to strike out the entire jury panel, alleging that it was composed mostly of "business executives or those having the employer's viewpoint." The motion was denied. The Supreme Court, however, found that it was the practice in that judicial district "deliberately and intentionally" to exclude from the jury lists "all persons who work for a daily wage." This policy had been adopted, the clerk of the court testified, because it had been found by experience that persons drawing daily wages suffered a hardship in having to give up their regular wages for the $4 a day paid to jurors, and the judge always excused them from service on those grounds. Consequently the clerk simply left them off the list. The evidence showed that laborers receiving weekly or monthly wages were placed on the jury lists, as well as the wives of daily wage earners.

The Supreme Court, in an opinion by Justice Murphy, ordered a new trial on the ground that this policy of exclusion could not be justified. While a judge may excuse a daily worker on grounds of financial hardship, that is no reason for excluding all daily wage earners regardless of whether actual hardship is involved. Jury service is a duty as well as a privilege of citizenship, and only when the financial embarrassment is a real burden is there a valid excuse for non-service. Justices Reed and Frankfurter, dissenting, were disturbed at what they felt to be the too drastic intervention of the Court. The issue was {145} purely one of judicial administration which they believed could have been appropriately taken care of by an admonition or by action through the Conference of Senior Circuit Judges. "To reverse a judgment free from intrinsic infirmity and perhaps to put in question other judgments based on verdicts that resulted from the same method of selecting juries, reminds too much of burning the barn in order to roast the pig," concluded Justice Frankfurter.

The barn-burning process continued, however. When *Ballard v. United States* came up to the Supreme Court for a second time in 1946, this case, which had been argued on religious liberty grounds on its first appearance, was dismissed for the reason that women were intentionally and systematically excluded from the panel of grand jurors which returned the indictment, and from the panel of petit jurors before whom the case was tried. This practice had been consistently followed down to 1944 in the federal judicial district of Southern California where the *Ballard* case had originated, in spite of the fact that women were eligible for jury service under California law, and federal statutes provide that jurors in federal courts shall have the same qualifications as those of the highest state court. The federal practice of exclusion of women in this district was apparently adopted in recognition of the fact that women, while eligible for jury duty in state courts under California law, were practically never called.

Justices Douglas, Black, Murphy, Rutledge, and Reed held that the systematic and intentional exclusion of women from juries, when they were eligible to serve, was similar to the exclusion of racial groups or economic or social classes in depriving the jury system of "the broad base it was designed by Congress to have in our democratic society." Justices Frankfurter and Burton, with Vinson concurring, attacked the decision on a variety of grounds: that the defendants had not pressed this objection on their first appeal; that the absence of women on juries did not violate due process, since the majority admitted that states were free to provide for the exclusion of women or not as they pleased; that women had actually been called on juries in the Southern California district since 1944, so that the decision was not needed to correct an illegal situation. Justice Frankfurter was particularly exercised because the Court gave no hint of its position on the validity of {146} this prosecution under the First Amendment, which was the matter originally at issue, and pointed out that the government would no doubt begin another prosecution of the Ballards which would in turn have to be carried up to the Supreme Court for a third time before the case was finally settled.

The fire in the barn was finally put out, at least temporarily, in the 1947 case of *Fay v. New York,* which tested the constitutionality of special "blue ribbon" juries. It was alleged that from these juries women and laboring people were systematically excluded, and also that experience had shown they were more likely to convict than regular juries. The Court, in an opinion by Jackson, denied these conclusions, indicating that the *Glasser, Thiel*, and *Ballard* precedents were inapplicable here, since they concerned jury practices in federal courts. The only instances where state juries had been successfully challenged, Jackson pointed out, involved racial discrimination, and he intimated that the Court would be very unlikely to accept any claims of discrimination except those based on "race or color." Justices Murphy, Black, Douglas, and Rutledge dissented in an uncommonly mild fashion, Murphy contending that the standard of selection for blue-ribbon juries was "apparently of an economic or social nature, unjustified by the democratic principles of the jury system."[9a]

The Third Degree

The Roosevelt Court has also been extremely concerned about use of the third degree or other methods of compulsion to secure confessions. Here again the basic decision establishing the Supreme Court's power to intervene antedates 1937. It was in the preceding year that Chief Justice Hughes, for a unanimous Court, held that due process had been denied to persons convicted of murder on the sole basis of confessions extorted by means of torture at the hands of state officers.[10] Evidence in the case was conclusive that the defendants had been whipped until they agreed to sign confessions drafted by the prosecuting officers, and were threatened with renewal of the torture if they later retracted. The state's only defense was that the immunity from self-incrimination guaranteed by the Constitution in federal prosecutions {147} was not an essential element in the due process of law required of the states by the Fourteenth Amendment, a contention which the Supreme Court brushed aside with the declaration: "The rack and torture chamber may not be substituted for the witness stand."

The Roosevelt Court has extended this ban to third degree methods somewhat less brutal than those involved in the 1936 case. In *Chambers* v. *Florida,* four young Negroes charged with the murder of a white man were kept in custody and questioned, one by one, with no opportunity between grillings to obtain rest or sleep, for five days and nights until they made confessions. The Court, in a burning opinion by Justice Black, reversed the convictions. In *Ward* v. *Texas,* an ignorant Negro had admittedly been arrested without a warrant, taken from his home town, driven for three days from county to county, placed in a jail more than one hundred miles from his home, and questioned continuously. In addition, the defendant charged that he had been beaten, whipped, and burned. The Court, relying only on the admitted facts, set aside the conviction.

Third degree problems passed on by the Court have not always involved Negroes. *Ashcraft* v. *Tennessee* presented the case of a white man convicted of murder on a confession elicited by thirty-six hours of continuous questioning under powerful electric lights by relays of officers, investigators, and lawyers. Such a situation, the Supreme Court said, was "so inherently coercive that its very existence is irreconcilable with the possession of mental freedom by a lone suspect against whom the full coercive force is brought to bear." This ruling proved to be more controversial than the third degree decisions already discussed, which had been unanimous. In the *Ashcraft* case, Justices Jackson, Roberts, and Frankfurter disagreed on the ground that a confession obtained by questioning, "even if persistent and prolonged," is different from one obtained by the use of violence. "Interrogation per se is not, while violence is, an outlaw." Previously, the dissenters said, the test as to admissibility of a confession was "whether the confessor was in possession of his own will and self-control at the time of the confession." They predicted much confusion from the new doctrine of "inherent coerciveness" of situations in which the accused was placed. {148}

The state of Tennessee proceeded to retry Ashcraft, using all the evidence secured by the original inquisition and eliminating only the actual unsigned confession. The conviction secured under these circumstances was again reversed by the Supreme Court. This time Jackson was absent from the Court, Roberts had resigned, and Frankfurter now accepted the previous opinion as binding on him, so that the decision was unanimous. The Court thus appears to have firmly adopted the test of "inherent coerciveness" as ground for invalidation of confessions.

The Court has also been concerned with the circumstances under which confessions are secured in connection with federal law violations. The most noteworthy example is the 1943 case in which the hillbilly McNabb brothers were arrested in Tennessee after the shooting of a federal "revenooer" with which they were pretty clearly connected. They were taken to Chattanooga where they were held in custody by federal officers and questioned over a period of two days, without the aid of friends or benefit of counsel. They were not brought before a U.S. commissioner or judge. Finally, a confession was secured on which conviction was subsequently based. The confession was made voluntarily, and no violence was used.

The conviction was attacked on the grounds of unconstitutional self-incrimination, but the Supreme Court found it unnecessary to rule on that issue. Instead, the conviction was voided because the federal officers had not, after making the arrests, taken the prisoners immediately before the nearest judicial officer for the purpose of a hearing, commitment or taking bail, as required by statute. Their detention was consequently unlawful, and a conviction based on evidence secured during the detention, regardless of the voluntary nature of the confession, was held invalid. Justice Reed dissented, indicating that he was concerned over "broadening the possibilities of defendants escaping punishment by these more rigorous technical require-ments in the administration of justice."[11]

Federal Protection of Civil Rights

The Court's generally strict attitude on the use of the third degree, the right to counsel, the representative character of juries, and other {149} aspects of criminal trials, has given defendants in such cases a new measure of procedural protection, and has stimulated a considerable number of habeas corpus actions seeking Supreme Court review of state convictions, in some instances dating back many years. The fact that this avenue of recourse has been opened up to the highest court in the land is of tremendous import for the enforcement of stricter standards of criminal justice.

But in a sense the federal protection thus provided is negative in character, for it is the individual defendant who must take the initiative in bringing his case before the federal courts on a due process plea. Unfortunately the social and legal inequalities in the status of certain minority groups, particularly the Negroes, are so serious that this negative protection affords only slight relief. Increasingly pressure has been put on the federal government to enforce the standards of the Fourteenth Amendment upon state law enforcement officials in a more positive fashion, and perhaps even to protect individuals against interferences with their civil rights emanating from private individuals as well as from state officials.

During Frank Murphy's tenure as Attorney General, he was largely responsible for the establishment of a Civil Rights Section in the Criminal Division of the Department of Justice, which was charged with utilizing such federal legislation as was available for a positive program of protecting individual rights. The statutory basis for the work of the Section was admittedly rather sketchy, consisting principally of two sections of civil rights acts passed during the Reconstruction period after the Civil War. The Supreme Court had declared much of the civil rights legislation of that period unconstitutional, and Congress had repealed most of the remainder, but these two provisions were miraculously unscathed. One of them, Section 51 of Title 18 of the U.S. Code, deals with threats to civil rights arising from the actions of private individuals, while Section 52 covers actions of public officers. The latter section reads:

> Whoever, under color of any law, statute, ordinance, regulation, or custom, willfully subjects, or causes to be subjected, any inhabitant of any State, Territory, or District to the deprivation of any rights, privileges, or immunities secured or protected by the Constitution and {150} laws of the United States, or to different punishments, pains, or penalties, on account of such inhabitant being an alien, or by reason of his color, or race, than are prescribed for the punishment of citizens, shall be fined not more than $1,000, or imprisoned not more than one year, or both.

Section 51 had been relied on in a considerable number of controversies since its original passage as part of the Enforcement Act of 1870, but Section 52, originating in the Civil Rights Act of 1866, had been practically a dead letter until the Civil Rights Section dug it out of the dust. In 1941, these two sections taken together were declared constitutional by the Supreme Court in *United States* v. *Classic*, a prosecution brought by the Civil Rights Section against election officials in Louisiana who had tampered with the ballots in a federal election.

The first test of the broader effectiveness of Section 52 came in the 1945 decision of *Screws* v. *United States*. The facts of this case are, as the Supreme Court said, "shocking and revolting." Screws was the sheriff of a backward Georgia county. He and two other officers arrested a young Negro late at night at the latter's home for the theft of a tire. The Negro was taken handcuffed to the courthouse where as he got out of the car he was beaten with fists and a blackjack until he was unconscious, then dragged feet first through the courthouse yard into the jail and thrown on the floor gravely injured. He was removed to a hospital where he died within the hour. There was evidence that Screws held a grudge against the prisoner and had threatened to "get" him. After futilely seeking to persuade Georgia authorities to prosecute Screws, the Civil Rights Section brought this federal action. A conviction was secured in the district court, and affirmed by the circuit court of appeals.

The Supreme Court's handling of the case has been called by Cushman "a masterpiece of confusion." There can be no doubt that the majority of the Court sincerely wanted to uphold this conviction. They were confronted, however, with the contention that Section 52 lacks the basic specificity necessary for criminal statutes under our system, because as applied to the broad and rather vague rights of the Fourteenth Amendment it fails to provide an ascertainable standard of {151} guilt, and so leaves a state law enforcement officer uncertain as to what rights he must respect if he is to avoid criminal prosecution under Section 52.

Justice Douglas, writing the opinion of the Court, in which Stone, Black, and Reed joined, was able to rescue the statute from the fate of unconstitutional vagueness, but at the cost of giving Screws a new trial. Douglas reasoned that the word "willfully" made the statute sufficiently specific by requiring that anyone convicted under the section must have had a conscious "purpose to deprive a person of a specific constitutional right. . . . One who does act with such specific intent is aware that what he does is precisely that which the statute forbids." This interpretation of the statute must be given effect, however, in the trial judge's charge to the jury, and since the judge in the Screws trial had not done so, a new trial was ordered (at which, incidentally, Screws was acquitted).

To the intense mind of Justice Murphy, the Douglas opinion was technical mumbo-jumbo. The matter was very simple to him. The Fourteenth Amendment guarantees the right not to be deprived of life without due process of law; Screws had brutally killed a prisoner in his custody; Section 52 makes it a federal crime for a public officer to deprive a person of a constitutional right; ergo, Screws had committed a federal crime. Justice Rutledge likewise saw the matter in this light, but he also bore the full force of the dilemma in which the Court found itself. For the remaining three justices—Roberts, Frankfurter, and Jackson—were of the opinion that Section 52 was flatly unconstitutional. Thus if Rutledge voted his convictions, the Court would be split into three groups of four, three, and two justices respectively, and unable to dispose of the case. To avoid this outcome, Rutledge concurred in the Douglas opinion, making a five-judge majority for declaring Section 52 constitutional but requiring a new trial.

The Roberts-Frankfurter-Jackson opinion (no individual author being indicated) protested strongly this revival of a "dead letter" statute born in the "vengeful" period of Reconstruction. They argued that the statute was too vague, that a state law officer who breaks the state law by killing a prisoner cannot be considered to have acted "under color of law," and that federal prosecution of state officers {152} would lead to a breakdown in criminal justice. They feared that "this shapeless and all-embracing statute can serve as a dangerous instrument of political intimidation and coercion" in the future. The cure for such crimes as that committed by Screws "is a re-invigoration of State responsibility."

The Roosevelt Court has decided few cases which offer deeper insights into judicial motivations than were revealed in this bout with a statute that is hardly satisfactory for the purpose it was called on to serve in this proceeding. There can be no doubt that the crime committed was equally shocking to the sensibilities of all nine justices, but widely differing reactions were elicited. The Court's decision is "equivocal," as Carr says,[12] but its equivocal character resulted from competition, in the minds of the four justices who along with Rutledge made up the majority, between a desire to punish a heinous infringement of human rights and a determination that the standards of criminal justice should not be lowered even at the expense of giving a despicable culprit a new trial. The warm sensibilities and the crusading fervor of the Roosevelt Court for human rights were pitted against its equally strong insistence on giving all criminal defendants their full share of constitutional protection. It is not surprising that the conflict between these two motivations produced some unsatisfactory and overly technical quibbling about the absence of the word "willful" in a charge to the jury.

While the Civil Rights Section considered the Screws decision a victory, the legislation construed there can never be a very strong reed for a positive program of federal protection of civil rights, and the Court will never be free from difficulties in interpreting it. Congressional adoption of new legislation is desperately needed.

The Search and Seizure Mystery

In 1928 the Supreme Court decided in the well-known *Olmstead* case that wire-tapping by federal officers was not forbidden by the search and seizure clause of the Fourth Amendment, and that evidence secured in this fashion could be used in criminal prosecutions. This decision was vigorously denounced by Justices Holmes, Brandeis, {153} Stone, and Butler. Holmes called wire-tapping a. "dirty business" and said that, whether it was unconstitutional or not, "the government ought not to use evidence obtained, and only obtainable, by a criminal act."

Six years later Congress undertook to wipe out most of the effect of the *Olmstead* decision by providing, in the Communications Act of 1934, that no person not authorized by the sender "shall intercept any communication and divulge or publish" its contents. The Supreme Court promptly ruled, in a 1937 case, with only McReynolds and Sutherland dissenting, that this language rendered inadmissible in a federal criminal trial evidence secured by federal officers through wiretapping.[13] Later, in 1939, the Court held that the statute also prohibited federal prosecuting officers from making indirect or derivative use of the proscribed evidence.[14]

These decisions indicated that the Court's standards had changed considerably since the *Olmstead* case, and nothing would have seemed more certain than that the Roosevelt Court would seize the first opportunity to overrule it. But when the chance came in 1942, the Court by a 5 to 3 vote refused to take it. Government agents had installed a detectaphone, sensitive enough to hear conversations through a wall, in an office adjacent to one in which two lawyers were carrying on a conspiracy to violate the bankruptcy act. They were subsequently convicted with the aid of evidence thus obtained. The Court held that there had been no search and seizure in this case, and specifically declined to overrule the *Olmstead* decision.[15] On the same day, by the same vote, the Court ruled that the Communications Act did not prevent the use at a trial of evidence which a witness had been induced to give because of information the government had secured by wire-tapping.

In both of these cases the dissenters were Stone, Frankfurter, and Murphy (Jackson not participating). Black and Douglas, who normally are most sensitive to claims of this sort, voted with the majority. Again in 1946 a pair of search and seizure cases brought forth the same kind of division on the Court. The first case involved federal agents who, having been sold gasoline without ration coupons at a filling station which was suspected of black market operations, required {154} the owner to turn over to them all the gas coupons he had on the premises. The district court found that the owner had voluntarily consented to this search and seizure. Douglas' majority opinion for the Supreme Court stressed more the fact that the gas ration coupons were public documents, property of the O.P.A. and at all times subject to recall by it. The Court's opinion said:

> Where the officers seek to inspect *public* documents at the place of business where they are required to be kept, permissible limits of persuasion are not so narrow as where private papers are sought.

Justice Frankfurter, with Murphy and Rutledge concurring, dissented in a long and learned opinion which came to the vigorous conclusion that the decision was a dangerous breach in constitutional protection and "flows from a view of the Fourth Amendment that is unmindful of the history that begot it and of the purpose for which it was included in the Bill of Rights."[16]

On the same day in 1946 the Court split in the same fashion over F.B.I. action in securing, during the audit of a government contractor, a cancelled check which was seized and used as the basis for criminal prosecution. The majority again upheld the official action, in view of the fact that the contract entered into with the government specified that the accounts and records of the contractor would at all times be open to the government.[17]

The next term brought worse and more of it. Equipped with two warrants of arrest, F.B.I. agents had arrested one Harris for mail fraud and in connection therewith had conducted a five-hour search of the four-room apartment in which he was arrested, in the hope of finding materials used in his check forging operations. Instead they stumbled onto a number of selective service classification cards and registration certificates which were unlawfully in his possession. Harris' defense against prosecution on this score was that this evidence had been obtained by unreasonable search and seizure. Again the Court refused to allow the claim, but the vote this time was 5 to 4, Jackson now ranging himself alongside the three previous dissenters, who joined in vehement protests against the validity of what Murphy called "a general exploratory crusade."[8] The opposing view, which {155} by any standards certainly constitutes approval of a drastic invasion of personal rights, owed its adoption to the votes of Black and Douglas who, contrary to their tendencies in most other civil liberties matters, persisted in their restrictive notions of the protection afforded by the search and seizure clause.

In switching over from their normal libertarian position on this one issue, Black and Douglas passed Frankfurter and Jackson going in the other direction. The search and seizure clause thus appeared to possess the mysterious qualities of a mirror which turns left into right and right into left. This unaccustomed position on the Court's right must have caused no little soul-searching on the part of both Black and Douglas, with results that became evident when the Court decided two more search and seizure cases early in 1948. In *United States* v. *Di Re*, evidence of possession of counterfeit gasoline ration coupons had been secured by search of the defendant's person without a warrant of any kind. In *Johnson* v. *United States,* federal agents had demanded admission without a warrant into a hotel room from which the odor of burning opium was issuing, and had made the arrest after admission and search. The convictions were reversed in both cases on constitutional grounds, these decisions constituting a major change in the Court's attitude, for which Douglas, who voted with the majority in both cases, was primarily responsible. Justice Black, however, remained unreconstructed on the search and seizure issue, dissenting with Vinson in the first case and with Vinson, Reed, and Burton in the second.

Military Tribunals and Martial Law

The most striking appeals against federal criminal proceedings heard by the Roosevelt Court have been the habeas corpus actions brought by the German saboteurs in 1942 and by the Japanese generals, Yamashita and Homma, in 1946 to test the legality of their convictions by military commissions. The military proceedings in the saboteurs' case were unanimously approved by the Court (Justice Murphy not sitting), which ruled that the military commission established by the President had jurisdiction to try the charges against the defendants, that the constitutional guaranties of grand jury indictment and jury trial {156} do not apply to trials before a military tribunal for offenses against the law of war, and that the commission had followed lawful procedure in conducting the trial.[19] The significance of the Court's decision in this case has been summed up by Cushman as follows:

> The Supreme Court stopped the military authorities and required them, as it were, to show their credentials. When this had been done to the Court's satisfaction, they were allowed to proceed.[20]

The disposition of the appeals taken by the Japanese generals from their convictions by a military commission for violations of the law of war proved more troublesome, principally because of certain aspects of the procedure employed by the commission. The regulations prescribed by General MacArthur directed the commission to admit such evidence "as in its opinion would be of assistance in proving or disproving the charge, or such as in the commission's opinion would have probative value in the mind of a reasonable man." Relying upon this provision, the commission admitted depositions and hearsay and opinion evidence. Moreover, the defense counsel were given only three weeks to prepare their defense against the original charge, and three days to deal with a supplemental bill of particulars.

The Court, in *Application of Yamashita,* avoided passing judgment on these procedures by holding that "the commission's rulings on evidence and on the mode of conducting these proceedings against petitioners are not reviewable by the courts, but only by the reviewing military authorities." Justices Murphy and Rutledge, however, filed eloquent dissents objecting to the "departures from constitutional norms inherent in the idea of a fair trial." Murphy's view of the Yamashita prosecution was that "petitioner was rushed to trial under an improper charge, given insufficient time to prepare an adequate defense, deprived of the benefits of some of the most elementary rules of evidence and summarily sentenced to be hanged." The Court made the same disposition of the Homma case, with the same dissent.

Duncan v. *Kahanamoku* involved the validity of criminal convictions of civilians resident in Hawaii by military tribunals established in that area during the war. Martial law had been declared by the Governor of Hawaii on December 7, 1941, an action which the President {157} approved two days later. Civil and criminal courts were forbidden to try cases, and military tribunals were set up to replace them. In August, 1942, a Honolulu stock broker was arrested on a charge of embezzling stock. He was brought before a military court, his request for trial by jury was refused, and he was convicted and sentenced to four years' imprisonment. In February, 1944, well over two years after Pearl Harbor, a civilian shipfitter employed in the Honolulu Navy Yard engaged in a brawl with two armed Marine sentries in the Yard. By this date military control of Hawaii had been relaxed, and the courts had been authorized to conduct criminal trials. However, prosecutions for violations of military orders, which covered a wide range of day-to-day civilian activities, were still required to be conducted before military tribunals. The shipfitter was convicted before such a court and sentenced to six months' imprisonment.

Both cases came to the Supreme Court on the contention that the Hawaii Organic Act had not authorized the trial and punishment of civilians by military courts, and that if it did confer such authority the act was unconstitutional. The Court majority found it unnecessary to reach the second question, for they held that when Congress had granted the Governor of Hawaii power to declare "martial law," it had not meant to supersede constitutional guaranties of a fair trial which apply elsewhere in the United States. The division between civil and military power

> had become part of our political philosophy and institutions prior to the time Congress passed the Organic Act. The phrase "martial law" as employed in that Act, therefore, while intended to authorize the military to act vigorously for the maintenance of an orderly civil government and for the defense of the island against actual or threatened rebellion or invasion, was not intended to authorize the supplanting of courts by military tribunals.

Justice Murphy, always difficult to restrain when a civil liberties issue is present, would have preferred to go beyond this position to a clear denunciation of the military trials as in unconstitutional conflict with the Bill of Rights. Chief Justice Stone concurred in another separate opinion, his view being that the military had the right to forbid regular court trials while threat of invasion was imminent, but {158} that by the time of the first of these trials conditions in Hawaii were such that the civil courts were capable of functioning without endangering the public safety.

Justices Burton and Frankfurter were the dissenters. They felt that "the conduct of war under the Constitution is largely an executive function," in which "executive discretion to determine policy is . . . intended by the Constitution to be supreme," at least on the battlefield. The original declaration of martial law after the Pearl Harbor attack was clearly justified, and the executive authorities should be allowed a reasonable period in which "to decide when and how to restore the battle field to its peace time controls." The dissenting justices concluded that executive discretion had not been abused in this case, and they felt that the Court in condemning, from the safe vantage point of February, 1946, the military decisions made in 1941 and 1942, might be establishing a precedent "which in other emergencies may handicap the executive branch of the Government in the performance of duties allotted to it by the Constitution and by the exercise of which it successfully defended the nation against the greatest attack ever made upon it."

Law in the Making

One is tempted, in reviewing these decisions where the interpretation of constitutional standards for criminal prosecutions is at issue, to feel that here the autobiographical factor plays a larger part than in any other significant area of judicial action. The product seems so clearly to be personal rather than institutional. It is harder here for judges to cast their private judgments in the form of logical deductions from established precedents. It is harder to give the impression that they are merely finding the law, not making it up out of their heads, or hearts.

This is particularly true where state law enforcement actions are at issue. It is difficult enough to put anything other than personal meaning and content into the standards prescribed by the Bill of Rights for the federal government—unreasonable search and seizure, for example. But state action is circumscribed only by the vague "due process" {159} requirement of the Fourteenth Amendment. Confronted with the necessity of applying this standard to the facts of particular cases, the best that the pre-Roosevelt Court had been able to do was Justice Cardozo's rule that the state remains free to enforce its own notions of criminal justice unless "in so doing it offends some principle of justice so rooted in the traditions and conscience of our people as to be ranked as fundamental."[21]

But how much does this standard limit personal judgment? Take a recent case, perplexing in the extreme and entirely without precedent. Willie Francis, a Louisiana Negro under sentence of death, was placed in the state's electric chair for execution. A mechanical defect prevented him from receiving sufficient current to cause death, and he was taken from the chair unharmed. The governor refused executive clemency, and the state supreme court held there was no cause for judicial intervention to prevent the sentence from being carried out by a second trip to the chair. The United States Supreme Court approved this decision by a 5 to 4 vote.[22] Justice Reed's decision for the Court, in which Vinson, Black, and Jackson joined, sought to make due process a more specific guide in this dilemma by equating it with two of the standards found in the Bill of Rights, double jeopardy and cruel and unusual punishment; but on neither ground was the Louisiana action found to be invalid.

Justice Frankfurter concurred with these four, but he preferred Cardozo's principle, application of which, he felt, would not justify judicial intervention here. He did not believe that mitigation of a sentence of death on a convicted murderer because the first attempt to carry it out was an "innocent misadventure," was demanded by principles of justice "rooted in the traditions and conscience of our people." If he voted that way, he was convinced that "I would be enforcing my private view rather than that consensus of society's opinion which, for purposes of due process, is the standard enjoined by the Constitution." But how did Justice Frankfurter know what was the "consensus of society's opinion" on a question that had never arisen before? Was his judgment, despite this disclaimer, any the less his own "private view" than that of the four dissenters—Burton, Douglas, Murphy, and Rutledge—who came to the opposite conclusion? {160}

Justice Frankfurter apparently was not himself entirely satisfied with this explanation, for he returned to the problem in the 1948 case of *Haley* v. *State* with perhaps the most remarkably frank and courageous analysis of the personal basis of judicial decisions ever included in a Supreme Court opinion. This was a case in which a fifteen-year-old boy had been sentenced to life imprisonment on the basis of an allegedly coerced confession. Frankfurter voted with the left wing bloc to reverse the conviction, and he felt it desirable to explain why, despite "doubts and difficulties," he had come to that conclusion. His opinion deserves quotation at some length.

> The doubts and difficulties derive from the very nature of the problem before us. They arise frequently when this Court is obliged to give definiteness to "the vague contours" of Due Process or, to change the figure, to spin judgment upon State action out of that gossamer concept. Subtle and even elusive as its criteria are, we cannot escape that duty of judicial review. The nature of the duty, however, makes it especially important to be humble in exercising it. Humility in this context means an alert self-scrutiny so as to avoid infusing into the vagueness of a Constitutional command one's merely private notions. Like other mortals, judges, though unaware, may be in the grip of prepossessions. The only way to relax such a grip, the only way to avoid finding in the Constitution the personal bias one has placed in it, is to explore the influences that have shaped one's unanalyzed views in order to lay bare prepossessions.

> A lifetime's preoccupation with criminal justice, as prosecutor, defender of civil liberties and scientific student, naturally leaves one with views. Thus, I disbelieve in capital punishment. But as a judge I could not impose the views of the very few States who through bitter experience have abolished capital punishment upon all the other States, by finding that "due process" proscribes it. Again, I do not believe that even capital offenses by boys of fifteen should be dealt with according to the conventional criminal procedure. It would, however, be bald judicial usurpation to hold that States violate the Constitution in subjecting minors like Haley to such a procedure . . .

> But whether a confession of a lad of fifteen is "voluntary" and as such admissible, or "coerced" and thus wanting in due process, is not a matter of mathematical determination. Essentially it invites psychological judgment—a psychological judgment that reflects deep, even {161} if inarticulate, feelings of our society. Judges must divine that feeling as best they can from all the relevant evidence and light which they can bring to bear for a confident judgment of such an issue, and with every endeavor to detach themselves from their merely private views . . .

> While the issue thus formulated appears vague and impalpable, it cannot be too often repeated that the limitations which the Due Process Clause of the Fourteenth Amendment placed upon the methods by which the States may prosecute for crime cannot be

more narrowly conceived. This Court must give the freest possible scope to States in the choice of their methods of criminal procedure. But these procedures cannot include methods that may fairly be deemed to be in conflict with deeply rooted feelings of the community. . . . Of course this is a most difficult test to apply, but apply it we must, warily, and from case to case.

Justice Frankfurter's approach is bold and useful, and his prescription for, and practice of, public judicial psycho-analysis is sincere. Yet even after applying his own remedies he must admit that the judicial task in this field involves "an evaluation of psychological factors" of which there is no "formulated expression," and that the tests he proposes for the guidance of judges suffer from "inherent vagueness." The best he can say for his principles is that "such as they are we must apply them."

A comparison of judicial voting records in the nonunanimous decisions handed down since 1941 involving questions of constitutional standards in criminal prosecutions yields a curve which can hardly be explained on any basis other than that the "private views" of the judges were at work making the law. Table XVIII gives the lineup of votes for and against the constitutional claims of criminal defendants in 51 cases decided since the 1941 term. Justices Murphy and Rutledge are shown to have taken the most extreme view of the state's responsibilities in handling criminal prosecutions. The Black-Douglas duo was markedly more solicitous for the rights of criminal defendants than the average position of the Court, but fell far short of the intensity of the Murphy-Rutledge position. The remaining justices were all below the average of the Court, except for Stone, whose record is not exactly comparable since it is not based on the more recent cases. {162}

These figures demonstrate the close similarity between judicial positions on the rights of criminal defendants and on the civil liberties problems considered in the preceding chapter. Obviously judicial private views do not vary much from one part of the Bill of Rights to another. In both these areas the fundamental value conflict is between the claims of the individual for inviolability of his physical and intellectual freedom and the claims of society for the maintenance of order and security. Justices, like other men, attach varying weights to these values. Justice Murphy is the most extreme in his defense of the individual against society, and is constantly speaking out with passion on the subject, as when he said: "The law knows no finer hour than when it cuts through formal concepts and transitory emotions to protect unpopular citizens against discrimination and persecution." On the other side of the Court Justice Reed's comment in his *McNabb* dissent that the more rigorous technical requirements upon which the Court was insisting were going to make it easier for criminals to escape justice, demonstrates a point of view which places greater stress on the protection of society. {163}

TABLE XVIII

ALIGNMENTS OF JUSTICES IN NONUNANIMOUS CASES INVOLVING CONSTITUTIONAL
RIGHTS OF CRIMINAL DEFENDANTS IN STATE AND FEDERAL PROSECUTIONS,
1941-1946 TERMS

	No. Cases	Decisions for Defendant		Total
		State Cases	Federal Cases	
No. Cases		18	33	51
Majority	51	28%	48%	41%
Murphy	50	94	88	90
Rutledge	41	93	88	90
Black	51	83	55	65
Douglas	51	78	55	63
Stone	34	42	45	44
Frankfurter	51	11	55	39
Jackson	32	18	40	28
Reed	51	22	30	27
Roberts	26	0	47	27
Burton	25	14	17	16
Vinson	10	0	0	0

It would of course be a great over-simplification to conceive that the judicial decisions on all these criminal cases were determined in the framework of an individual-society dichotomy. The issues involved are seldom uncomplicated by additional factors. In a number of instances, for example, the dominant question in the minds of some justices has appeared to be one of state-federal conflict. Thus in the Screws dissent, Frankfurter, Jackson, and Roberts based their argument in large part on their distaste for federal intervention in a problem of law enforcement which they felt belonged to the states. It is not without significance that these three justices, as shown in Table XVIII, voted for the defendants' position in federal cases much oftener than in state cases. Justice Frankfurter has protested on numerous occasions that the Court was not showing due deference to state judicial systems. As he said in *Williams* v. *Kaiser:*

> . . . to assume disobedience instead of obedience to the Law of the Land by the highest courts of the States is to engender friction between the federal and state judicial systems, to weaken the authority of the state courts and the administration of state laws by encouraging unmeritorious resorts to this Court, and wastefully to swell the dockets of this Court.

It is, as a matter of fact, largely in these terms of federal-state relations that the more recent appeals from state convictions have been argued on the Court. The historic position, as first stated in *Barron* v. *Baltimore* in 1833, has been that the Bill of Rights applies to the federal government only, not to the states. The due process clause of the Fourteenth Amendment has been accepted as imposing certain limitations on state judicial procedure which will guarantee a fair hearing before an unbiased and uncoerced tribunal, but in such basic decisions as *Hurtado* v. *California* (1884), *Maxwell* v. *Dow* (1900), *Twining* v. *New Jersey* (1908), and *Palko* v. *Connecticut* (1937) the Court has held that indictment by grand jury, trial by jury, protection against self-incrimination and against double jeopardy were not such fundamental attributes of a fair trial as to be protected against state action by the due process clause. The result has been that practices which would be unconstitutional in federal prosecutions have not necessarily been considered as grounds for reversing state convictions. {164}

So far as the First Amendment is concerned, this double standard for federal and state action was broken down in 1925 when in the *Gitlow* case the Court held that the "liberty" protected against state action by the Fourteenth Amendment included all the liberties of the First Amendment. The left wing of the Roosevelt Court has sought valiantly to eliminate the double standard for criminal prosecutions in the same manner. Their drive to accomplish this purpose came to an unsuccessful climax in the notable Court session on June 23, 1947, when in no less than four separate challenges to state judicial action the Black-Douglas-Murphy-Rutledge bloc met defeat. These cases included the Foster, Gayes, and Fay proceedings which have already been discussed, but the best treatment of the federalism issue came in the fourth case, *Adamson* v. *California.*

This case involved a state law permitting the failure of a defendant to explain or to deny evidence against him to be commented on by the court and by counsel and to be considered by the court and the jury. Under California procedure a defendant who took the stand to explain or deny evidence against him could be subjected to cross examination. In the *Adamson* case the defendant was forced to forego testimony in person because of fear that cross-examination would disclose his previous convictions. The Supreme Court agreed that this procedure would amount to unconstitutional self-incrimination if it took place in a federal court, but held that the Fourteenth Amendment did not bar its adoption in state courts, the privilege against self-incrimination not being inherent "in the right to a fair trial."

Justice Reed wrote the *Adamson* majority opinion, but the real duel was between Frankfurter, concurring, and Black, dissenting. It was Black's contention that "one of the chief objects" of the Fourteenth Amendment "was to make the Bill of Rights applicable to the states." *Twining* v. *New Jersey,* the only previous decision holding that states were free "to extort evidence from one accused of crime," had failed to appraise the historical evidence relating to the adoption of the Amendment, Black contended. The *Twining* theory, he went on, was a mischievous one, giving the Court "boundless power under 'natural law' periodically to expand and contract constitutional standards to conform to the Court's conception of what at a particular time constitutes 'civilized decency' {165} and 'fundamental principles of liberty and justice.'" As for himself, he doubted whether the Court was "wise enough to improve on the Bill of Rights by substituting natural law concepts."

Frankfurter, on the other hand, stood squarely on the Twining decision and the judicial precedents. He scorned Black's historical evidence, pointing out that during the seventy years between the adoption of the Amendment and "the beginning of the present membership of the Court" (meaning Black's appointment in 1937), 43 judges had passed on the scope of the Amendment, of whom "only one, who may respectfully be called an eccentric exception, ever indicated the belief that the Fourteenth Amendment was a shorthand summary of the first eight Amendments. . . ." He also made good use of the case for according "an alert deference" to the judgment of state courts. But it is harder to understand his open deprecation of at least some of the protections of the Bill of Rights as "merely legal forms" which "seemed important to eighteenth century statesmen."

It was obvious that the *Adamson* case, decided on the last day of the term in 1947, was only one chapter in a continuing controversy. The next install-ment came in March, 1948, in the case of *In re Oliver*, which involved the constitutionality of a summary conviction for contempt of court by a Michigan judge sitting as a "one-man grand jury" after a secret trial and without giving the defendant a reasonable opportunity to defend himself. The Court was almost unanimous in condemning this travesty; though Frankfurter and Jackson dissented from the decision, they did so on other grounds. But Justice Rutledge took occasion to draw a moral from the *Adamson* case and the precedents on which it rested, whose chickens, he felt, were now coming home to roost.

> The [Oliver] case demonstrates how far this Court departed from our constitutional plan when, after the Fourteenth Amendment's adoption, it permitted selective departure by the states from the scheme of ordered personal liberty established by the Bill of Rights. In the guise of permitting the states to experiment with improving the administration of justice, the Court left them free to substitute, "in spite of the absolutism of continental governments," their "ideas and processes of {166} civil justice" in place of the old time-tried "principles and institutions of the common law" perpetuated for us in the Bill of Rights. Only by an exercise of this freedom has Michi-gan been enabled to adopt and apply her scheme as was done in this case. It is the immediate offspring of Hurtado v. *California . . . and later like cases.*

> So long as they stand, so long as the Bill of Rights is regarded here as a strait jacket of Eighteenth Century procedures rather than a basic charter of personal liberty, like experimentations may be expected from the states. And the only check against their effectiveness will be the agreement of a majority of this Court that the experiment violates fundamental notions of justice in civilized society.

So the argument continues, as the Bill of Rights is given scope and purpose by the translating of private meanings into public law.

CHAPTER SEVEN

Bureaucracy: No Alien Intruder

R EGULATION OF BUSINESS through federal administrative agencies dates back to 1887, when the Interstate Commerce Commission was established, and to 1914, when the Federal Trade Commission was set up. These administrative tribunals and other agencies with regulatory powers, such as the Department of Agriculture, began operations under the review and supervision of a judicial system distrustful of instruments of administrative adjudication. The courts were well aware, as James M. Landis has pointed out, that this movement toward administrative regulation was in large part the result of legislative distrust of the courts, and judges would have been less than human had their initial reaction not been to strike back at the legislatures and thwart this policy "under the guise of constitutional and statutory interpretation."[1] The early years of the Interstate Commerce Commission were made largely barren of accomplishment by paralyzing judicial interpretations of its statutory powers, and the Supreme Court kept the Federal Trade Commission on a kind of probationary status for almost twenty years.

Under the New Deal, regulatory boards and commissions multiplied to such an extent that alphabetical agencies came to be regarded as the trademark of the Roosevelt administration. Review of their decisions and enforcement of their orders has become one of the most important functions of the Supreme Court. During the five {167} terms from 1941 to 1946 the eight most important federal regulatory agencies were parties in no less than 143, or 16 per cent of all the Court cases decided by full opinion during that period. The generally favorable attitude of the Roosevelt Court toward administrative regulation is indicated by the fact that these agencies were successful in almost three-fourths of their appearances before the Court. However, there was a remarkable amount of disagreement among the judges in the decision of administrative cases, and conflicting tendencies and doctrines have been much in evidence.

The King Is Dead

Many of the basic issues concerning administrative regulation had been fought out before the first Roosevelt appointment to the Court. The scope of the federal commerce power, drastically narrowed by the N.R.A. and Guffey Coal Act decisions, had reverted to the breadth characteristic of the early Marshall conception of the commerce clause when the Court upheld the National Labor Relations Act in April, 1937. This basic decision left the Roosevelt Court little to do in interpretation of the limits of federal regulatory powers except mopping up operations and burial of such battle casualties as *Hammer* v. *Dagenhart*. Divided in so many fields, the Roosevelt Court has probably been nowhere so unanimous as in its acceptance of the constitutionality of federal regulatory statutes.

The charge of delegation of legislative powers as a basis for invalidating regulatory legislation has been sent back into the limbo from which the pre-Roosevelt Court had snatched it. In the course of American constitutional interpretation numerous statutes had been alleged to delegate legislative power to executive agencies, but no such charge had ever been upheld by the Supreme Court until the "Hot Oil" decision of 1935. The Court there held that in giving the President authority to exclude from interstate commerce oil produced in excess of state regulations, Congress had supplied no adequate standards to guide or control the President in the use of this power.[2] A ruling along this line had been so little anticipated that the government's brief of 227 pages and 200 more of appendix devoted {169} only 13 pages to the delegation point.[3] Once having discovered the possibility of using this weapon for striking down legislation, however, the Court, like Robert Frost's farmer, liked "having thought of it so much" that it quickly invalidated two other statutes on the same ground.[4]

The Roosevelt Court, however, has betrayed scant interest in charges of unconstitutional delegation, and has been willing to accept very broad legislative standards as sufficient control over administrative discretion. Justice Roberts, it is true, remained largely unreconstructed on this point. In 1939 he roundly criticized the Agricultural Marketing Agreement Act as adopting standards for the guidance of the Secretary of Agriculture which were "no standards whatever," and which actually left that official free "to form a judgment by balancing a price-raising policy against a consumer-protection policy, according to his views of feasibility and public interest. . . . The resolution of all such problems," Roberts concluded, "is of the essence of lawmaking."[5] In 1942 he returned to the attack with a contention that the wartime Price Control Act unconstitutionally delegated legislative powers to the Price Administrator, but his view won no support.[6]

In thus refusing to try to draw hard and fast lines between legislative and executive functions the Roosevelt Court is once again acting in the Holmes tradition. It was in a 1928 dissent that Holmes rebuked a majority decision which pedantically insisted upon a strict separation of executive from legislative powers, with the warning:

132

The great ordinances of the Constitution do not establish and divide fields of black and white. Even the more specific of them are found to terminate in a penumbra shading gradually from one extreme to the other. . . . It does not seem to need argument to show that however we may disguise it by veiling words we do not and cannot carry out the distinction between legislative and executive action with mathematical precision and divide the branches into watertight compartments, were it ever so desirable to do so, which I am far from believing that it is, or that the Constitution requires.[7]

In this connection it is noteworthy that the Roosevelt Court, when given an opportunity to invalidate the Lovett salary rider as an unconstitutional legislative infringement on the executive appointing power, {170} shied away from any excursion into that field and utilized instead the more specific "bill of attainder" provision as the ground for nullifying the congressional action.

The practical disappearance of serious challenges to the constitutionality of federal regulatory legislation has turned the Roosevelt Court to the task of determining the limits of administrative authority under congressional grants. Its examination has customarily resulted in support for the statutory interpretations propounded by the administrative agencies. Thus the Court found that the Federal Communication Commission's responsibility to achieve the "public interest" in its licensing of radio stations justified it in exercising control over network practices found to be inimical to the public interest, even though the Communications Act did not specifically convey authority over the network field.[8] Again, the Court in 1945 ruled that the Wage and Hour Administrator, when he found that a minimum wage order covering the embroideries industry could not be made effective because 40 per cent of the work in that industry was done at home, had authority under the Fair Labor Standards Act to prohibit industrial homework in that industry. Justice Roberts objected, alleging that "the philosophy of the Court's opinion can be nothing less than that the Administrator may, if he finds it necessary, rewrite the statute."[9]

The Court's acceptance of administrative interpretations of law has been on other occasions the subject of criticism by Justice Roberts. In a case where the Court majority had upheld the Bituminous Coal Division in its conclusion that a particular producer was within the coverage of the coal code, he commented:

This court obviously fails in performing its duty and abdicates its function as a court of review if it accepts, as the opinion seems to do, the Director's definition of "producer" and then proceeds to accommodate the meaning of related provisions to the predetermined definition. So to do is a complete reversal of the normal and usual method of construing a statute.[10]

Underlining the tendency of the Roosevelt Court to give broad scope to administrative grants of authority are two recent cases in which the administrative interpretation was overriden by the Court on {171} the ground that the agency had not construed its statutory powers boldly enough. The first instance concerned the Interstate Commerce Commission's statutory responsibility for attaching such conditions to its approval of railroad abandonments as "the public convenience and necessity may require." This standard differs from the one which the law sets up to govern railroad consolidations; in those matters the Commission is authorized to impose "just and reasonable" conditions which "will promote the public interest." Under this latter provision it was settled I.C.C. policy, approved by the Supreme Court, to require protection for displaced employees as a condition of approving consolidations. But the Commission felt that the more limited statutory language applicable to abandonment cases did not justify a similar requirement there. The Roosevelt Court in 1942 unanimously reversed the Commission on this point, admonishing that such a narrow interpretation was not consistent with the broad purpose of the Transportation Act of 1920, and holding that "there is nothing in the Act to indicate that the national interest in purely financial stability is to be determinative while the national interest in the stability of the labor supply available to the railroads is to be disregarded."[11]

Justice Roberts must have participated with mixed feelings in thus forcing upon a reluctant administrative agency powers it contended that Congress had not given it. A similar instance occurred when the Federal Power Commission insisted that it could not grant a license to build a hydroelectric dam on an Iowa stream until the applicant had secured a permit required by state law. The Supreme Court in 1946, with only Frankfurter dissenting, told the Commission that state laws did not constitute such a limitation on its powers.[12]

The most significant feature in recent judicial decisions affecting administrative regulation, however, has not been simply a tendency toward a broad interpretation of administrative powers. This development has been, in fact, merely a symptom of a different concept of the function of judicial review, and a different judicial attitude toward administrative adjudication. While these changes had been many years in the making, the fulfillment of tendency can be best seen in the Court's long struggle with the celebrated *Morgan* case.

This proceeding, arising out of the Department of Agriculture's {172} action in fixing maximum rates to be charged by marketing agencies at the Kansas City stockyards, came up to the Supreme Court in 1936, 1938, and 1939, and was finally disposed of in 1941.[13] On the first two occasions the Court held the official action invalid as lacking in fundamental elements of due process and "fair play." The two latter decisions upheld the Department, the 1941 opinion frankly confessing that the Court had been wrong in 1936. The transformation that took place in the Court's thinking and its underlying assumptions between the first and last of these decisions is so great that in reviewing the cases one almost comes to feel like an archaeologist cutting through successive strata in which the judicial artifacts reveal a pattern of rapid ideological and cultural change. Without laborious digging and sifting in these deposits, however, the fact of a fundamental shift in judicial attitude toward the administrative process may be established by one quotation from the decision in the third case, in which Justice Stone wrote:

> In construing a statute setting up an administrative agency and providing for judicial review of its action, court and agency are not to be regarded as wholly independent and unrelated instrumentalities of justice, each acting in the performance of its prescribed statutory duty without regard to the appropriate function of the other in securing the plainly indicated objects of the statute. Court and agency are the means adopted to attain the prescribed end . . . neither can rightly be regarded as an alien intruder, to be tolerated if must be, but never to be encouraged or aided by the other in the attainment of the common aim.

A controlling philosophy which sees "court and agency" as co-workers for the attainment of a common aim requires that the courts limit themselves to those functions which they are better fitted than the agencies to perform. A basic assumption of the Roosevelt Court has been that administrative agencies possess an expertness and a competence in economic and social fields which the Court does not share, and that consequently in areas where this expertness is relevant the Court will not disturb or contradict administrative conclusions. This premise is not by any means original with the Roosevelt Court. It is many years since the Supreme Court first referred to the Interstate {173} Commerce Commission, grandfather of the agency tribe, as an administrative tribunal "appointed by law and informed by experience."[14] But the Roosevelt Court has probably acted on this premise more consistently than did any of its predecessors, though its self-abnegation has certainly fallen far short of that which caused a Minnesota supreme court justice to write in an 1897 opinion concerning the *expertise* of the Minnesota Railroad and Warehouse Commission:

> How is a judge who is not supposed to have any of this special learning or experience, and could not take judicial notice of it if he had it, to review the decisions of commissioners, who should have it and should act upon it. It seems to us that such a judge is not fit to act in such a manner. It is not a case of the blind leading the blind, but of one who has always been deaf and blind insisting that he can see and hear better than one who has always had his eyesight and hearing, and has always used them to the utmost advantage in ascertaining the truth in regard to the matter in question. Before a judge can act intelligently in such a matter he must have an amount of this special knowledge and experience which it will take him years to acquire. It is not sufficient that he take his first lessons from the par-

tisan and perhaps perjured experts, or so-called experts, produced by the parties at the trial.[15]

While the Roosevelt Court has not gone this far, it has stressed the limitations of the judge, who is an expert only in matters of law. The fact-finding of administrative agencies has come to be accepted as final except under extraordinary circumstances. The doctrine developed by earlier courts that "constitutional" and "jurisdictional" facts—that is, facts which are essential in determining the constitutionality of administrative action or the jurisdiction of administrative agencies—must be finally determined by judges and not by administrative officers has quietly faded away, at least so far as business regulation is concerned.[16]

It is probably in connection with rate-fixing and utility regulation that this deference to the superior factual knowledge and understanding of administrative regulatory agencies has produced the most marked results. Justice Frankfurter during his earlier years on the Court was the most vocal in formulating the new philosophy in this field. In the *Driscoll* case, where the Court was reviewing the fixing of utility rates by a state regulatory commission, he said: {174}

> The determination of utility rates—what may fairly be exacted from the public and what is adequate to enlist enterprise—does not present questions of an essentially legal nature in the sense that legal education and lawyer's learning afford peculiar competence for their adjustment. These are matters for the application of whatever knowledge economics and finance may bring to the practicalities of business enterprise.

In another case where Justice Frankfurter spoke for the Court in refusing to upset a rate fixed by the I.C.C., he said that "the problem is enmeshed in difficult judgments of economic and transportation policy," and added:

> We certainly have neither technical competence nor legal authority to pronounce upon the wisdom of the course taken by the Commission. It is not for us to tinker with so sensitive an organism as the grain rate structure only a minor phase of which is caught in the record before us.[17]

The most notable application of this attitude toward rate proceedings came in 1942 with the case of *Federal Power Commission* v. *Natural Gas Pipeline Co.*, a decision hailed by Justice Black as starting "a new chapter in the regulation of utility rates." What made this true was a flat statement by Chief Justice Stone, speaking for the Court and turning his back upon decades of controversy over various theories of valuation, to this effect:

The Constitution does not bind rate-making bodies to the service of any single formula or combination of formulas. Agencies to whom this legislative power has been delegated are free, within the ambit of their statutory authority, to make the pragmatic adjustments which may be called for by particular circumstances. Once a fair hearing has been given, proper findings made and other statutory requirements satisfied, the courts cannot intervene in the absence of a clear showing that the limits of due process have been overstepped. If the Commission's order, as applied to the facts before it and viewed in its entirety, produces no arbitrary result, our inquiry is at an end.

Broad as this statement was in support of administrative discretion, there were certain respects in which the decision was unsatisfactory {175} to Justices Black, Douglas, and Murphy. They felt that, even though the Court had liberated the Commission from the prison of "formulas" and had completely supported the administrative action, the opinion had not disposed of the notion of due process as an "unlimited grant to courts to approve or reject policies selected by legislatures in accordance with the judges' notion of reasonableness. . . ." In fact, they suggested that the decision gave "renewed vitality" to this concept, for the Court seemed to assume that "regardless of the terms of the statute, the due process clause of the Fifth Amendment grants it power to invalidate an order as unconstitutional because it finds the charges to be unreasonable."

Nor were these three justices satisfied that the Court's opinion had stated explicitly enough "the freedom which the Commission has both under the Constitution and under this new statute." In order to make sure that the references in Stone's opinion to "constitutional requirements" and to "the limits of due process" would not be "deemed to perpetuate the fallacious 'fair-value' theory of rate making," and in order "to lay the ghost of *Smyth* v. *Ames*," the three justices pointed out that the opinion relieved the Commission from the compulsion of giving any consideration to the "reproduction cost" theory. "The Commission may now adopt, if it chooses, prudent investment as a rate base—the base long advocated by Mr. Justice Brandeis." But, they continued, it should be no concern of the Court *what* theory was used. In view of the statutory provision making the fact-finding of the Commission conclusive, if supported by substantial evidence,

> we do not think it is permissible for the courts to concern themselves with any issues as to the economic merits of a rate base. . . . Irrespective of what the return may be on "fair value," if the rate permits the company to operate successfully and to attract capital all questions as to "just and reasonable" are at an end.

Their concurring view concluded:

The problem of rate-making is for the administrative experts not the courts and . . . the *ex post facto* function previously performed by the courts should be reduced to the barest minimum which is consistent with the statutory mandate for judicial review. That review {176} should be as confined and restricted as the review, under similar statutes, of orders of other administrative agencies.

Relying upon this decision, as embellished and interpreted by the three concurring justices, the Federal Power Commission in its next big rate proceeding refused to place any reliance upon reproduction cost new, and based its computations on actual legitimate cost. When the *Hope Natural Gas Co.* case reached the Supreme Court, the decision was written by Justice Douglas, who thus had a chance to make the concurring views of the previous decision the official position of the Court. He said:

Under the statutory standard of "just and reasonable" it is the result reached not the method employed which is controlling. . . . It is not theory but the impact of the rate order which counts. If the total effect of the rate order cannot be said to be unjust and unreasonable, judicial inquiry under the Act is at an end.[18]

Three members of the Court (Frankfurter, Reed, and Jackson—Roberts not participating) considered that this *Hope* decision was carrying cooperation with administrative agencies too far, and would result in eliminating all semblance of legislative as well as judicial control over administrative action. Reed could not agree that "it makes no difference how the Commission reached the rate fixed so long as the result is fair and reasonable." In the first place, the statutory provision for just and reasonable rates was enacted "in the light of the relation of fair and reasonable to fair value and reasonable return." In the second place, he suggested that if the majority's interpretation of the statute was correct, then Congress had unconstitutionally delegated its rate-making power to the Commission, "in toto and without standards." Justice Frankfurter supported the view that the terms "just and reasonable" were meaningless save in relation to appropriate standards, and said:

It will little advance the public interest to substitute for the hodge-podge of the rule in *Smyth* v. *Ames* . . . an encouragement of conscious obscurity or confusion in reaching a result, on the assumption that so long as the result appears harmless its basis is irrelevant. {177}

If Justice McReynolds had been on the bench that day, he might again have mourned that the Constitution was gone.

Long Live the King!

But judicial supervision, phoenix-like, dies only to rise again. Belief in the rightness of administrative decisions is not the ultimate value of the composite and complex mind of the Roosevelt Court. Its general support of administrative agencies has been founded upon an acceptance of their statutory goals and a confidence that they were acting in the public interest. This confidence, however, can be shaken by events. The record indicates that a substantial bloc of the Roosevelt Court has in fact lost a measure of confidence in one particular administrative agency, the Interstate Commerce Commission, with the result that the statutory interpretations and the decisions of that commission have been subjected to close scrutiny and surprisingly severe attack.

This coolness toward the I.C.C. has been manifested principally by the more liberal members of the Court, who have been disturbed by some of the holdings of this old, conservative, and railroad-minded agency. They have objected both to the substance and to the form of I.C.C. decisions. Substantively, they have protested alleged I.C.C. discrimination against truck and waterway competition.[19] They have charged the Commission with permitting truck monopolies to be established.[20] They have complained when the I.C.C. permitted wartime rate increases over the protest of price control officials.[21] The asperity of these objections to I.C.C. legal interpretations is well illustrated by Justice Douglas' comments in a case where the Commission had excluded a trucker from the benefits of the so-called "grandfather clause" in the Motor Carrier Act of 1935:

> Great deference is owed a commission's interpretation of the law which it enforces, especially where the meaning of the statutory language, generally or in specific application, gains body and flavor from the content of the highly specialized field in which the expert body works. . . . But that is quite different from acceding to the suggestion that the non-technical word "control" may be interpreted in a {178} way which goes against all human experience and which does violence to its ordinary and accepted meaning. . . . We should not permit . . . statutory grants to be whittled away on the basis of technical and legalistic grounds which find no expression in the statute however much the administrative chore may be alleviated.[22]

From the standpoint of form, I.C.C. decisions have been questioned on the ground that findings have not been stated with sufficient clarity nor the grounds for decisions put in such a way that courts can understand the basis on which the agency acted. In a 1942 decision Justice Douglas spoke for a majority of the Court in holding that "the precise grounds for the Commission's determination . . . are not clear. . . . The defect is not merely one of the absence of a 'suitably complete statement' of the reasons for the decision; it is the 'lack of the basic or essential findings required to support the Commission's order.'"[23] In a more recent decision the Court through Justice Rutledge asked for "sufficient explication to enable the parties and ourselves to understand, with a fair degree of assurance, why the Commission acts as it does."[24] To the same effect was a four-judge dissent from the liberal wing in 1943 protesting an "obscure and vague report" of the I.C.C. and warning: "We must know what a decision means before the duty becomes ours to say whether it is right or wrong."[25]

Throughout this barrage the attacking justices denied that they were in any way seeking to limit the proper powers of administrative agencies, to expand the role of judicial review, or to lay down purely formal requirements as to findings. "We do not undertake," they said in one of these proceedings, "to tell the Commission what it should do in this case. That is not our function. We only require that, whatever result be reached, enough be put of record to enable us to perform the limited task which is ours."[26] On the other hand, the defenders of the I.C.C., coming principally from the right wing of the Court, were equally emphatic that the discretion of the Commission was being invaded on grounds that were little short of frivolous. Justices Frankfurter and Jackson said of one of these reversals:

> It overturns the exercise of a discretion which Congress has delegated to the Interstate Commerce Commission upon grounds which seem {179} to us so unsubstantial as really to be a reversal on suspicion. . . . What this amounts to is that the Court refuses to tell the Commission what it thinks about the evidence until the Commission tells what it thinks about the law. We cannot regard this as the most helpful use of the power of judicial review.[27]

If there was any doubt that I.C.C. policies, not its practices, were the real cause of these divisions, it was dispelled in 1947 by the decision in *New York* v. *United States.* This was the famous "class rates" case, in which the I.C.C. had responded to the strong pressures against alleged favoritism in freight rates to the northeastern section of the country, by an order raising class rates 10 per cent in Official (Eastern) territory and reducing them 10 per cent in Southern and Western territory. The Commission's action was upheld in a long opinion by Justice Douglas, erstwhile principal opponent of the Commission.

Only two points in Douglas' opinion need to be stressed. One was his acceptance of the Commission's finding that the conditions peculiar to the respective territories did not justify the differences in territorial class-rate structures, concerning which he said that "on a subject of transportation economics, such as this one, the Commission's judgment is entitled to great weight." Second, the order to increase rates was attacked as unjustified unless the existing rates were noncompensatory or otherwise threatened harmful effects on the revenues or transportation efficiency of the carriers in question. Douglas' interpretation of the law, on the contrary, was that rates, even though "reasonable," could be raised to remove a discrimination between territorial zones.

The only objectors to this majority view were Jackson and Frankfurter, the very justices who had defended the I.C.C. most vigorously in its earlier brushes with Douglas et al. of the left wing. In Frankfurter's view, his colleagues who had been straining at gnats in their previous I.C.C. reversals, the most recent one only six weeks earlier, were now swallowing camels. It was now his turn to protest that the Commission had failed "to be explicit and definite in its findings," which had to be sought for "as would a needle in a haystack." He was frankly suspicious of a process which revealed that "putting 10% on {180} and taking 10% off respectively will beget just the right adjustment. . . . Administrative experts no doubt have antennae not possessed by courts. . . . But courts, charged as they are with the review of the action of the Commission, ought not to be asked to sustain such a mathematical coincidence as a matter of unillumined faith in the conclusion of the experts."

Thus both wings of the Court have been willing to reverse the I.C.C. when its policies were "wrong," and have adjusted their arguments accordingly. Somewhat less grounded in purely "policy" considerations is the Roosevelt Court's tendency to disregard administrative contentions where the fundamental right of an individual or corporation to a full hearing and a fair opportunity to present his case before the administrative agency and the reviewing court appear to be limited. The Federal Communications Commission especially has tangled with the Court on this issue and come out second best. In 1943 the Court held the F.C.C. to have acted erroneously in granting a Boston radio station the right to operate on a frequency already occupied by a Denver station, without making the Denver station a party to the proceeding or permitting it to participate in the administrative hearing.[28] To a similar effect the Court ruled in 1945 that when the Commission, confronted with two mutually exclusive applications for the same broadcasting privileges, granted one application without a hearing and set the other for hearing, the second applicant was in effect denied the fair hearing which Congress had granted.[29]

The Roosevelt Court's concern for the granting of full and prompt judicial redress against F.C.C. regulations even led it into an apparent reversal of one of its long-established canons of judicial review, the so-called "final order" rule. This event occurred when the Commission's chain broadcasting regulations, announced in 1941, were subjected to judicial review in advance of their actual application. It has in the past been consistently held that administrative regulatory action does not become ripe for judicial review until it has reached the stage where actual compulsion is being exercised by the regulatory agency on the party affected. The administrative action complained of or appealed from, under this view, must not be a mere request, refusal to obey which entails no legal consequences; it must be a definite {181} order, which cannot be ignored without peril, and an order having immediate effect.

In spite of the fact that the 1941 chain broadcasting regulations merely laid down the rule which the Commission proposed to follow in the future in granting licenses, Chief Justice Stone and four of his colleagues held that conformity with the regulations was practically compulsory upon radio stations, and that this conformity would cause immediate injury to the chains which was cognizable by a court of equity.[30] The applicability of the regulations did not depend upon future administrative action, the Court contended, but operated immediately to control the acts of station owners and determined in advance the rights of all persons affected by the regulations. Stone's opinion went on:

> The ultimate test of reviewability is not to be found in an overre-fined technique, but in the need of the review to protect from the irreparable injury threatened in the exceptional case by administrative rulings which attach legal consequences to action taken in advance of other hearings and adjudications that may follow, the results of which the regulations purport to control.

Justices Frankfurter, Douglas, and Reed (Black not participating) considered this conclusion thoroughly unsound, and replied:

> To say that the courts should reject the doctrine of administrative finality and take jurisdiction whenever action of an administrative agency may seriously affect substantial business interests, regardless of how intermediate or incomplete the action may be, is, in effect, to imply that the protection of legal interests is entrusted solely to the courts.

The Roosevelt Court has in fact exhibited a considerable concern for safeguarding the status of the judiciary as the protector of legal interests, this view having led it to reject proposed limitations on the power of the federal courts to stay administrative action by writ of injunction, except upon clear and unqualified directions from Congress. The Court did, it is true, uphold the Price Control Act in its provisions denying to the Emergency Court of Appeals power to issue temporary restraining orders or interlocutory decrees staying or restraining {182} price regulations. A limitation of this kind was considered justifiable, on the ground that:

> . . . where an injunction is asked which will adversely affect a public interest for whose impairment, even temporarily, an injunction bond cannot compensate, the court may in the public interest withhold relief until a final determination of the rights of the parties, though the postponement may be burdensome to the plaintiff. . . . What the courts could do Congress can do as the guardian of the public interest of the nation in time of war. The legislative formulation of what would otherwise be a rule of judicial discretion is not a denial of due process or a usurpation of judicial functions.[31]

But when, under the same statute, it was urged upon the Court that Congress had made it *mandatory* for federal courts, upon application by the Price Administrator, to issue injunctions against violations of the act, the Court balked, saying that it preferred an interpretation of the statute which would afford "a full opportunity for equity courts to treat enforcement proceedings under this emergency legislation in accordance with their traditional practices."[32] Similarly, the Court ruled that Congress had not intended to deprive the Court of Appeals of the District of Columbia of its power to stay orders of the Federal Communications Commission pending appeal.[33]

The inner conflicts which cause the Roosevelt Court to come down now heads and now tails on these issues of judicial review are nowhere better revealed than in a pair of cases decided within a few weeks of each other during the 1943-44 term. Both concerned the constitutional right to judicial review of administrative action, and the answers given in the two cases appear contradictory. The first proceeding was *Switchmen's Union v. National Mediation Board,* decided in 1943 by a 4 to 3 vote (Black and Rutledge not participating). The question involved was whether certifications by the National Mediation Board of representatives for collective bargaining purposes were intended by Congress to be subject to judicial review. There was a general provision of the Judicial Code, giving federal district courts jurisdiction of all "suits and proceedings arising under any law regulating commerce," which might have been interpreted {183} as covering the situation. But an examination of the legislative history of the Railway Labor Act, which was the statute immediately involved, and the failure of Congress to include provisions for judicial review in that act, led the majority of the Court to conclude that Congress had intended to make the administrative decision final. The opinion stated:

> . . . if Congress had desired to implicate the federal judiciary and to place on the federal courts the burden of having the final say on any aspect of the problem, it would have made its desire plain.

The majority, composed of Justices Douglas, Frankfurter, Murphy, and Stone, appreciated that a rather extreme position was being taken here. As Frankfurter summarized the *Switchmen's Union* decision, it meant that "the courts could not even exercise the function of keeping the National Mediation Board within its statutory authority."[34] Such a denial of judicial power went too far for Justices Reed, Jackson, and Roberts, who warned the Court:

> Where duties are delegated, as here, to administrative officers, those administrative officers are authorized to act only in accordance with the statutory standards enacted for their guidance. Otherwise we should risk administrative action, beyond or contrary to the legislative will.

They believed that the general review provision of the Judicial Code covered the case, and said:

> We cannot conclude that because no statutory review exists no rem-
> edy for misinterpretation of statutory power is left. No such pre-
> sumption of obliteration of rights may be entertained.

From this drastic limitation of judicial review the Court reacted sharply only a few weeks later in *Stark v. Wickard.* Here a group of milk producers sought an injunction against certain provisions of a milk marketing order affecting handlers of milk in the Greater Boston area. The two lower courts took the view that judicial review of the order was not available to milk producers, on the ground that they had no legally protected right giving them standing to sue. The {184} Supreme Court reversed this holding, however, by a 6 to 2 vote (Black and Frankfurter dissenting, Jackson not participating).

It fell to Justice Reed, who had disagreed with the *Switchmen's Union* decision, to write the opinion here and to attempt to distinguish the rulings in the two cases. There were two steps to the process. The first was to hold that a "right" had been created for milk producers by the Agricultural Marketing Agreement Act such as had not been created for railway employees by the Railway Labor Act. The milk producers, according to the Court, were given a statutory right to protection of the minimum price fixed by the milk market-ing order. "Such a right created by statute is mandatory in character and obviously capable of judicial enforcement," provided that the complainant has "something more than a general interest in the proper execution of the laws" at stake. The Court considered that the producers had "a personal claim" which gave them standing to complain, whereas in the *Switchmen's Union* decision "no personal right of employees, enforceable in the courts, was created" by the statute there involved.

But there was a second difficulty. The statute made no provision for judi-cial review of marketing orders under these conditions. Turning his back on the *Switchmen's Union* case, Justice Reed held that even though there was "no direct judicial review granted by this statute for these proceedings," it was not to be "lightly assumed that the silence of the statute bars from the courts an otherwise justiciable issue. . . . The authority for a judicial examination of the validity of the Secretary's action is found in the existence of courts and the intent of Congress as deduced from the statutes and precedents."

Six justices participated in both these decisions. The conflicting results were due to a shift of three of them—Stone, Murphy, and Douglas—between cases. Justices Reed and Roberts were for providing judicial review in both instances, while Frankfurter was consistent in his opposition. Supported by Black, he subjected the majority decision in *Stark v. Wickard* to a vigorous attack, saying it was founded on "doctrinaire notions" as to a kind of "natural law" or "common law of judicial review," and failed to recognize that judicial review is "derived from the materials furnished by the particular statute in {185} regard to which the opportunity for judicial review" is asserted. He continued:

However useful judicial review may be, it is for Congress and not for this Court to decide when it may be used—except when the Constitution commands it. In this case there is no such command. Common-law remedies withheld by Congress and unrelated to a new scheme for enforcing new rights and duties should not be engrafted upon remedies which Congress saw fit to particularize. To do so impliedly denies to Congress the constitutional right of choice in the selection of remedies, and turns common-law remedies into constitutional necessities simply because they are old and familiar.

But Frankfurter's fight for limitation of judicial review has been a losing one. *Switchmen's Union* has been bowing to *Stark* v. *Wickard*. In a 1947 case where the action of the Board of Governors of the Federal Reserve System in removing certain directors of a national bank was attacked, the Federal Reserve Board contended that its removal orders were not subject to judicial review unless a charge of fraud was involved. But the Court majority held that the courts had the duty of keeping the Board within "the limits of its statutory grant of authority."[35] Only Frankfurter and Rutledge spoke up for restricting judicial review. Rutledge felt that because the Federal Reserve System

is a highly specialized and technical one, requiring expert and co-ordinated management in all its phases, I think their judgment should be conclusive upon any matter which, like this one, is open to reasonable difference of opinion. Their specialized experience gives them an advantage judges cannot possibly have, not only in dealing with the problems raised for their discretion by the system's working, but also in ascertaining the meaning Congress had in mind in prescribing the standards by which they should administer it.

Two weeks later the Court again spurned a plea for limiting judicial review.[36] This time it was O.P.A.-approved eviction certificates which were the subject of consideration. The Price Control Act sought to prevent judicial hamstringing of its purposes by carefully limiting court review to persons "subject to" O.P.A. regulations or orders. The O.P.A. had ruled that a person came in this category only if a {186} regulation or order "prohibits or requires action by him," and the courts had upheld the agency's interpretation. In this case the O.P.A. had granted eviction certificates to certain New York landlords, and when the tenants affected sought to protest, they were met with the contention that they were not "subject to" the orders, and so could not be heard. This the Supreme Court refused to admit, holding that "whether a person is 'subject to' the Act is dependent to some extent upon whether the order immediately, substantially and adversely affects him, as well as whether the order requires or prohibits action by him." The Court preferred to broaden judicial review rather than, by a too literal or too consistent interpretation of the Price Control Act, to withhold protection from a group which the statute was principally designed to aid.

The same insistence upon preserving broad scope for judicial review was manifested in connection with draft cases during the war. The Court's policy in this field was hammered out in a series of decisions running from 1944 to 1947. In the first important case, *Falbo v. United States*, the Court, with only Justice Murphy dissenting, affirmed the conviction of a man who had been classified by his draft board as a conscientious objector and ordered to report for "work of national importance," and who had refused to obey the order on the ground that he was an ordained minister and entitled to total exemption. The Court's position was that a draft board order was merely an intermediate step in a process which would not reach its conclusion until the selectee was actually accepted by the Army, Navy, or civilian public service camp, and it found no evidence that Congress had provided for resistance to or attack on the selection process until it had reached its conclusion. "Surely if Congress had intended to authorize interference with that process by intermediate challenges of orders to report, it would have said so." Thus the Court applied the familiar rule that administrative remedies must be exhausted before judicial review is available. Justice Murphy contended that this rule, designed to prevent "litigious interruption" of the administrative process, was not applicable under the present circumstances, where its effect was to strip a man under criminal prosecution of his only defense. {187}

It was not until two years later, in 1946, after the close of hostilities, that the Court was required in the *Estep* case to come to grips with the problem of *how much* judicial review was to be available to a selectee who had followed the *Falbo* doctrine. Two members of Jehovah's Witnesses, under prosecution for refusing to be inducted, sought in defense to challenge the classifications made by their draft boards. The statute did not provide for such review. Its language, in fact, was that decisions of the local boards "shall be final." But the silence of Congress is not decisive, said Justice Douglas for the Court. Judicial review may be required by the Constitution, and even if not so required, "the question whether judicial review will be provided where Congress is silent depends on the whole setting of the particular statute and the scheme of regulation which is adopted." The Court did not hold here that judicial review of draft board orders was a constitutional necessity, but it did conclude that since the boards operate under a statute and rules which limit and define their jurisdiction, orders issued in violation of the law or regulations were not intended by Congress to be enforced by criminal sanctions.

> We cannot readily infer that Congress departed so far from the traditional concepts of a fair trial when it made the actions of the local boards "final" as to provide that a citizen of this country should go to jail for not obeying an unlawful order of an administrative agency.

What did "final" mean then? It meant simply that Congress was limiting judicial review to less than its customary scope, that the courts were not to weigh the evidence or to determine whether the board's decisions are "erroneous." The courts were to consider only the "jurisdiction" of the board, and that question was reached "only if there is no basis in fact for the classification which it gave the registrant."

Justice Frankfurter, along with Stone and Burton, challenged this holding as "denying the evident purpose of Congress and disregarding the terms in which it expressed that purpose." Congress, they felt, had demonstrated its conviction that "it was dealing with matters which were more fittingly lodged in the exclusive discretion of the Selective Service System." Moreover, in making judicial review {188} available to test the "jurisdiction" of draft boards, the Court, Frankfurter declared,

> revives, if indeed it does not multiply, all the casuistic difficulties spawned by the doctrine of "jurisdictional fact." In view of the criticism which that doctrine, as sponsored by Crowell v. Benson . . . brought forth and of the attritions of that case through later decisions, one had supposed that the doctrine had earned a deserved repose.

In spite of this strong language, however, Frankfurter found an ambiguity in the trial court's charge which led him to concur with the majority in reversing the conviction. Burton and Stone found no such loophole, and they dissented.

Gibson v. *United States*, decided later in 1946, reaffirmed, this time unanimously, the Court's determination to keep the draft system under judicial control. The two men involved here were both Jehovah's Witnesses classified as conscientious objectors. One had refused to go to the national service camp; the other went and stayed for five days, then departed without leave. On prosecution it was contended that the first, like Falbo, had not completed the administrative process, and that the second had gone too far and so cut off his right of defense. The Court held both entitled to seek judicial review, and to offer the defense that the board orders were "arbitrary and illegal."

One year later, however, the Court reached the limits of the *Estep* principle in *Cox* v. *United States*. The case involved members of Jehovah's Witnesses who had protested draft board refusal of classification as ministers of religion. The five-judge right wing majority of the Court held that the reviewing judge was limited to the role of determining "whether there was any substantial basis for the classification order," a familiar standard in administrative law, but one whose application in this field the left wing found objectionable, Murphy contending that it would "allow the judge to do little more than give automatic approval to the draft board's action."

It may be significant that the *Estep* and *Gibson* cases were decided in 1946, after the pressure of war's necessities and alarums had abated. In the same way the most significant defense of civil liberties challenged {189} by the Civil War came out of the *Milligan* case, decided in 1866. Perhaps if the test cases on Japanese evacuation from the west coast could have been delayed for a year or two more, instead of coming up for decision in 1943 and 1944, a different result might have been reached there.

Rudder and Bowsprit

Divisions such as are evident in the Court's handling of these administrative cases make it imperative to examine more systematically the position of the individual justices in this field. For this purpose attention may be confined to the 143 cases coming up from the eight administrative agencies which were the source of the greatest amount of litigation during the six terms from 1941 through 1946. Seven of these agencies are permanent parts of the federal establishment—the Interstate Commerce Commission, the Federal Trade Commission, the Federal Power Commission, the Federal Communications Commission, the Securities and Exchange Commission, the National Labor Relations Board, and the Wage and Hour Division of the Department of Labor. The eighth was the wartime Office of Price Administration.

Table XIX indicates the number of appearances of each of these agencies before the Court during the six-year period, the measure of success each achieved in its cases, and the extent of judicial disagreement in deciding the cases. It will be noted that the N.L.R.B. was the most effective agency in securing Court approval of its actions. Almost all the F.C.C. and S.E.C. decisions were disputed ones, whereas all the F.T.C. cases were decided unanimously. There is perhaps some significance in the fact that judicial disagreement was least in the case of the three oldest regulatory agencies.

Members of the Court disagreed in deciding 90 of the 143 administrative cases, and their votes in these nonunanimous decisions are analyzed in Table XX. The first conclusion, evident from a glance at the vote for all agencies, is that a generally favorable attitude toward the bureaucracy has extended throughout most of the Roosevelt Court. The only two justices who fell substantially below the average position of 67 per cent support for all agencies were the late Chief {190} Justice Stone, whose position was 51 per cent favorable, and Justice Roberts, who voted for the agencies in only 14 per cent of the nonunanimous cases. The other justices were very close to the Court average, except for Black and Murphy, who were somewhat above it. {191} The figure for Vinson is based on only one term of service, and so is not too reliable as an index to his position.

Actually, however, the differences in the attitudes of the various justices with respect to administrative regulation are considerably more marked than this first analysis would indicate. Certain significant variations are obscured by lumping all the agencies together. Particularly the votes on Interstate Commerce Commission cases need to be separated from the others, for, as already noted, the pattern of judicial alignments in I.C.C. proceedings is quite at variance with that prevailing in decisions affecting other administrative agencies. When the I.C.C. cases are eliminated, the judicial lineup is seen to run the gamut from almost complete support to almost complete opposition.

TABLE XIX

SUPREME COURT FAVORABLE AND NONUNANIMOUS DECISIONS
IN ADMINISTRATIVE CASES, 1941-1946 TERMS

	Total Decisions	Decisions for Agency	Nonunanimous Decisions
All agencies	143*	72%	63%
NLRB	28	86	68
SEC	9	78	89
FPC	10	75	50
ICC	46	74	57
W & H	21	67	67
OPA	19	63	74
FTC	5	60	0
FCC	8	38	88

*Appearances of agencies total 146, because in three cases OPA and ICC were on different sides of the same proceeding.

TABLE XX

ALIGNMENTS OF JUSTICES IN NONUNANIMOUS ADMINISTRATIVE CASES, 1941-1946 TERMS

	No. Cases	Decisions for Administrative Agency		
		All Agencies	All Agencies Except I.C.C.	I.C.C. Only
No. Cases		90	67	26
Majority	90	67%	67%	65%
Black	83	81	97	44
Murphy	89	76	85	54
Douglas	84	66	82	27
Rutledge	70	67	74	50
Burton	27	67	67	67
Reed	88	67	66	69
Jackson	76	62	54	83
Frankfurter	90	61	52	85
Vinson	12	50	44	67
Stone	74	51	39	78
Roberts	63	14	2	42

From Justice Black, who voted favorably to the agencies 97 per cent of the time, their support drops gradually to 85 per cent from Murphy, 82 per cent from Douglas, and 74 per cent from Rutledge. Justice Burton, at 67 per cent, is at the average position for the Court, while Reed is only a point below. Then the curve falls away for the right wing of the Court, with Jackson at 54 per cent, Frankfurter at 52 per cent, Vinson at 44, Stone at 39, and finally Roberts in almost continuous opposition.

In the I.C.C. cases, on the other hand, the trend is almost exactly reversed. Justices Black, Douglas, Murphy, and Rutledge managed to cast only 43 per cent of their total votes in favor of the I.C.C., whereas the Reed-Jackson-Frankfurter-Stone combination voted for the I.C.C. 79 per cent of the time. Even Justice Roberts achieved a 42 per cent measure of support for the I.C.C., which is phenomenal considering his attitude toward government regulation generally. He voted for administrative agencies in only nine of the nonunanimous decisions from 1941 to 1945, and in eight of those cases it was the I.C.C. he was supporting.

It is clear, then, that on the administrative regulation issue there is a left wing which is generally favorable to all administrative agencies except the I.C.C., and a right wing which is very enthusiastic about the I.C.C. but somewhat less so where other agencies are concerned. However, within these wings there are significant individual differences. Justice Black is the most consistent supporter of administrative {192} agencies on the Court. Aside from I.C.C. cases, he voted against an administrative agency in a nonunanimous decision only twice during the six-year period. The first time was in a decision rebuking the Federal Power Commission for excessive timidity in concluding that it could not grant a federal hydroelectric license until a state permit had been secured; and the second was when the O.P.A. tried to prevent renters from testing an eviction order.

Justice Douglas has been more relentless in his opposition to the I.C.C. than any other member of the Court; and he has continued his fight against the alleged inadequacies of their findings, whereas the other members of the left-wing posse have shown signs of giving up the chase on this issue. An enthusiastic supporter of price control, he nevertheless voted against the O.P.A. twice in disputed decisions during the 1945 term, because he believed that states and counties were not subject to the Price Control Act; and he concurred with Black in the O.P.A. reversal mentioned above.[37]

Justice Murphy seldom votes against an administrative agency, other than the I.C.C., unless a civil liberties issue is involved. For example, he objected to giving the Wage and Hour Division the power to subpoena records of a newspaper company, on the ground that the subpoena power can be safely entrusted only to the courts. He refused to believe that Congress had meant to give the F.C.C. authority over network broadcasting. He, along with Rutledge, objected to the enforcement provisions of the Price Control Act, with their limitation on the right of defendants in criminal proceedings to challenge the validity of regulations invoked against them.

Justice Frankfurter is easily the most interesting of the right-wing justices in his reaction to administrative issues. An authority on administrative law before he came on the Court, he has been especially concerned with judicial review of administrative cases. His voting record is almost exactly the reverse of the pattern evidenced by Black and Douglas. He has been much more favorable toward the I.C.C. than the average member of the Court, but he has voted for the contentions of the seven other regulatory bodies substantially less often than the Court as a whole. {193}

Frankfurter's view of proper judicial-administrative relationships stresses two major contentions. The first is that the courts must leave the substance and policy of administrative regulation to the expert agencies, limiting the role of judicial review to insuring the "observance of those procedural safeguards in the exercise of legislative powers which are the historic foundation of due process."[38] This has, of course, been one of the major tenets of the Roosevelt Court, and there has been little occasion for Frankfurter to labor the point except in a few cases, particularly those involving the I.C.C., where he has contended that some of his colleagues were backsliding into earlier habits of detailed judicial supervision over administrative agencies.

However, the record does not indicate that Frankfurter has managed to achieve complete consistency in this respect. His refusal to credit the expertness of the I.C.C. when in the 1947 "class rates" case it handed down what he regarded as a "political" decision which pleased the Black-Douglas wing of the Court, has already been noted. He has also exhibited a curious reluctance to honor the *expertise* of the S.E.C., whose policies—it may not be irrelevant to note—stem in large part from the period when Douglas was its chairman. (Because of this Douglas almost never participates in an S.E.C. case). In the first *S.E.C.* v. *Chenery Corp.* case, decided in 1943, Frankfurter launched against the findings of that agency the kind of attack that he had considered objectionable when directed by Black and Douglas against the I.C.C. He denied, just as they had done in the I.C.C. cases, that the right-wing majority for which he was speaking in the *Chenery* case was seeking to limit the agency's discretion or confine its powers.

> In finding that the Commission's order cannot be sustained, we are not imposing any trammels on its powers. We are not enforcing formal requirements. We are not suggesting that the Commission must justify its exercise of administrative discretion in any particular manner or with artistic refinement. We are not sticking in the bark of words.

In rebuttal, Black said much the same things that Frankfurter had said when the I.C.C. was under attack on similar grounds: {194}

> The Court can require the Commission to use more words; but it seems difficult to imagine how more words or different words could further illuminate its purpose or its determination. A judicial requirement of circumstantially detailed findings as the price of court approval can bog the administrative power in a quagmire of minutiae. Hypercritical exactions as to findings can provide a handy but almost invisible glideway enabling courts to pass "from the narrow confines of law into the more spacious domain of policy."

When the *Chenery* case came back for a second decision on the last day of the term in 1947, the Court held that the agency had corrected its earlier errors, and upheld its conclusion as resting "squarely in that area where administrative judgments are entitled to the greatest amount of weight by appellate courts. It is the product of administrative experience, appreciation of the complexities of the problem, realization of the statutory policies, and responsible treatment of the uncontested facts. It is the type of judgment which administrative agencies are best equipped to make and which justifies the use of the administrative process." This was pure Frankfurter logic, but it was written by Murphy, with Frankfurter dissenting. Right and left thus appear to be able to use each other's arguments with equal facility; and on the Roosevelt Court as in the hunting of the Snark the bowsprit gets mixed with the rudder sometimes.

Second, Frankfurter generally evidences to a greater degree than any other member of the Court a predisposition to accept legislative limitation on access to the courts, and to give a comparatively narrow interpretation of the right to judicial review. In pursuit of this policy he veers to the left—even to the far left—from his normal position on the right of the Court. The best illustration of this tendency in operation is found in the *Switchmen's Union* and *Stark* v. *Wickard* decisions, which have already been analyzed. Further examples of his attitude on this point are found in the Court's recent F.C.C. decisions. In no less than 4 of the 7 nonunanimous F.C.C. cases decided since 1941, Frankfurter opposed the majority ruling on the ground that the Court was insisting upon a greater measure of judicial review over, or power to stay, administrative action than Congress had meant to provide. He believed that the majority was forgetting that "the federal {195} courts are entrusted with the correction of administrative errors or wrongdoing only to the extent of Congressional authorization," and he warned:

> Hardship there may well come through action of an administrative agency. But to slide from recognition of a hardship to assertion of jurisdiction is once more to assume that only the courts are the guardians of the rights and liberties of the people.[39]

But here again the curious capacity of the S.E.C. to make Frankfurter forget his principles should be noted. For in the 1947 case of *Penfield Co.* v. *S.E.C.,* he and Jackson were found protesting that a majority decision unduly limited judicial review, and arguing that a district judge should be entitled to use his own discretion in determining whether to enforce an S.E.C. subpoena.

Additional evidence of the strange alignments that have developed on questions of judicial review is found in the draft cases, where the strongest support for broadening review has come from the left of the Roosevelt Court, with the contractionists on the right—an exact reversal of the old established situation. It is the Court's left wing that resurrects the *Crowell* v. *Benson* doctrine of jurisdictional facts, or at least a reasonable facsimile thereof, and the right wing that wants to keep it buried. It is the left wing of the Court which in the Bridges case questions the findings of an administrative tribunal and protests the use of hearsay evidence in an administrative proceeding, while the right, in the persons of Stone, Roberts, and Frankfurter, insists on upholding the finality of administrative fact-finding and reminds the Court that "no principle of law has been better settled than that the technical rules for the exclusion of evidence, applicable in trials in courts, particularly the hearsay rule, need not be followed in deportation proceedings . . . more than in other administrative proceedings."[40] The explanation is of course left-wing concern over protection of essential liberties, which can be accomplished only through strong judicial action.

But the most extreme instance of left-wing insistence on opening up administrative determinations to court review came in the 1945 *Burley* case.[41] Here a five-judge majority, composed of Rutledge, Black, {196} Douglas, Murphy, and Reed, held, contrary to long settled practice, that after a collective bargaining representative under the Railway Labor Act had submitted employee claims to the National Railroad Adjustment Board and had received an adverse decision, the individual employees could still seek to enforce their claims through their own court action. It was the right wing of Frankfurter, Stone, Roberts, and Jackson which protested this drastic dislocation of settled habits in adjusting railroad labor relations. Complaints about the decision poured in from the Brotherhoods, the Railway Labor Executives' Association, and the organizations of industrial and craft unions. The furor was so great that the Court felt compelled to grant a rehearing of the case. But in the second decision the liberal majority stuck to the principle of its previous ruling, causing Frankfurter, along with Stone and Burton (Jackson not participating), to lament "the far-reaching mischief of unsettling nonlitigious modes of adjustment" and the maintenance of a doctrine which had "created havoc in the railroad world."[42]

* * *

Future developments with respect to judicial review of administrative regulation are rendered somewhat uncertain by congressional adoption of the Administrative Procedure Act in June, 1946. While it was the announced purpose of this act to put into statutory form the principles of judicial review already stated by the Supreme Court, the drafters appear to have sought to widen the coverage of judicial review in several important respects.[43] The new statute will unquestionably engender a harassing flood of litigation which will begin to reach the Supreme Court within the next year or so. The findings of this chapter indicate that the law will be interpreted by a Court which has shown general understanding of and sympathy for the administrative process. Moreover, the Court's administrative decisions have not shown the veering toward the right which has been characteristic of the Court for the last year or two in other fields.

In comparison with its predecessors, then, the Roosevelt Court has been responsible for a markedly different attitude toward administrative agencies, which are no longer treated as "alien intruders" in the courts. Talk of abdication, however, is hyperbole in this sphere as elsewhere. {197} The Court appears conscientiously to have attempted to follow its announced policy of serving as "co-worker" with the administration in the attainment of legislative goals. It may have swerved now to this side and now to the other side of that line. There may have been on occasions immoderate exaltation of the administrative agency and undue depreciation of judicial authority. But on other occasions the worm has turned, producing decisions which have expanded judicial authority in entirely new directions. In a recent decision the Court thought it well to give notice that it does not intend to become a mere junior partner with the bureaucracy, reminding that "Courts no less than administrative bodies are agencies of government. Both are instruments for realizing public purposes."[44] Left and right may disagree as to the public purposes in behalf of which the courts should intervene, but both agree that judicial powers must be maintained adequate to protect their respective values against administrative attack.

CHAPTER EIGHT

Labor's Day

IN 1941 Edward S. Corwin wrote: "Constitutional law has always a central interest to guard. Today it appears to be that of organized labor."[1] There are many who have put this thought in less restrained and professorial language. There was, for instance, the flurry set off by the Supreme Court's decision in 1942, holding that the New York local of the teamsters' union had not violated the Federal Anti-Racketeering Act by demanding that out-of-state trucks entering New York replace their drivers by members of the local union or pay the union the regular rate for one day's work. The Court, in an opinion by Justice Byrnes, ruled that the anti-racketeering statute had been adopted by Congress in 1934 with the intention that it should apply to economic extortion by professional gangsters, not to traditional labor activities.[2] This reasoning appealed to that noted legal authority and labor expert, Westbrook Pegler, as the equivalent of saying that "if a union has had the custom of placing lye in the soup at a cannery as a means of coercing the employer, that, too, becomes familiar union practice blessed by the Supreme Court of the United States."

In this and other labor decisions the Roosevelt Court has exhibited what Pegler and others with a less pungent gift of language have charged is a "queer attitude," exposing the people of the United States "to willful and wanton wrongdoing by a political element allied with the New Deal, with no chance of redress and without any legal protection." A somewhat more sober and factual analysis of recent labor {199} decisions would seem to be in order, however, to determine the nature and extent of labor's primacy on the Roosevelt Court.

The Wagner and Fair Labor Standards Acts

The Roosevelt Court has had the responsibility of interpreting the two most important labor statutes passed under the New Deal, the National Labor Relations Act of 1935 and the Fair Labor Standards Act of 1938. The constitutionality of the former had of course been approved before the first Roosevelt justice took his seat, but since 1937 there has been a steady stream of problems arising out of the administration of the statute. These legal questions have nearly always come before the Court in the form of review of orders issued by the National Labor Relations Board, for which judicial enforcement was sought, and the Court has been consistently favorable in its reactions. The Board has appeared before the Supreme Court in 59 cases since its establishment. In 46 of these proceedings its orders have been enforced in full, while in 9 more the order was enforced with modifications. In only 2 instances have Board orders been set aside, one case was remanded to the Board, and in the remaining case the Board's request for remand or modification of an enforced order was denied.

This is scarcely the place for an extended analysis of Supreme Court decisions interpreting the Wagner Act, but certain major tendencies should be pointed out. The first N.L.R.B. cases to go to the Court were concerned with the allowable area of coverage of the statute under the commerce clause of the Constitution. The *Jones & Laughlin* decision laid down the general rule that the statute was appropriately invoked wherever labor disputes would have an "effect" upon interstate commerce. Such effects were clearly present in a gigantic steel concern operating on an interstate scale, but the Court found the effects no less present in a plant engaged in the production of truck trailers, a fairly small men's clothing manufacturer, a fruit packing plant, a large electric company which distributed power only on an intrastate basis, and a small concern engaged in processing goods belonging to others which had been shipped across a state line.[3] By 1939 the Court's broad interpretation of the coverage of the act had {200} become sufficiently well established so that coverage cases practically ceased to appear on the Supreme Court docket. The principal exception was the 1944 decision in which, following the ruling that the insurance business constitutes interstate commerce, the Wagner Act was held to be applicable to insurance companies.[4] It is significant that the Supreme Court has never ruled against the N.L.R.B. on a question of coverage under this statute.

The Supreme Court has also been quite clear, at least since 1939, that the Board's conclusions and determinations as to the facts of labor disputes are to be accepted by the reviewing courts. In that year the Court did in two cases set aside findings by the Board that employers had refused to bargain collectively with representatives of their employees.[5] Justice Black who, along with Reed, dissented from these two decisions, contended that they tended to nullify the congressional effort to have the problems of industrial conflicts "administered by more specialized and experienced experts than courts had been able to afford." The following year saw Black's view adopted as the Court unanimously rebuked a lower court for encroaching on the exclusive jurisdiction of the Board to make findings of fact on the record, and stressed the strict necessity for judicial adherence to the congressional demarcation of power between administrative agencies and the reviewing courts.[6]

The discretion of the Board in affording remedies to effectuate the policies of the act has been held subject to judicial control, but in this process also the administrative judgment has not often been overridden. An outstanding instance where this did happen occurred when the Board ordered the reinstatement of the celebrated Fansteel sit-down strikers. The Court majority refused in 1939 to enforce this order, over the dissent of Justices Stone, Reed, and Black.[7] In line with this ruling the Board has subsequently refused to reinstate employees not taken back after a strike because of bad conduct. But in few other areas has the Court sought to restrict the Board's remedial authority. The Court has even agreed that under the Wagner Act a corporation can be required to "instate" applicants for employment never previously employed by a company, who were denied jobs because of their union activities and affiliations, and in addition to give {201} them "back pay" from the time they applied for work until they were offered jobs.[8] A strong case can of course be made for this rule, since a refusal to hire is just as effective an anti-union measure as the discharge of an employee. Logical as the Court's position appears to be, however, one may well share the doubt which C. O. Gregory has recently expressed as to whether Congress realized that in adopting the Wagner Act it was imposing on employers a contractual obligation toward persons who had never been in their employ.[9]

The Court has likewise generally supported the Board's interpretation of the collective bargaining obligations of employers. A general collective bargaining agreement, it has been held, precludes conflicting individual contracts, if it does not entirely outlaw them. Nor may an employer bargain with employees in such a manner as will be "subversive of the mode of collective bargaining which the statute has ordained." Thus an employer violates the act if on his own motion he offers employees wage increases without making the offer through the established bargaining channels, for such unilateral action is held likely to discredit the union in the eyes of the employees.[10] Similarly an employer who was approached by union members a short time before the date set for collective bargaining, with the proposition that if they could be granted a wage increase they would be glad to discard their union memberships, was held to have been guilty of an unfair labor practice in acceding to their request.[11]

The Court did not until 1947 have occasion to pass on the very troublesome question as to whether the organizational guaranties of the act extend to supervisory employees. In the absence of specific language in the statute, the Board had temporized with this issue and had actually, what with changes in the composition of the agency, decided it both ways. Finally, however, the Board held that foremen were entitled to all the benefits of the statute, though indicating that they would probably not be permitted to be represented by the same union that spoke for the production employees of a plant.

The Supreme Court upheld the Board's certification of a foremen's union in the *Packard Motor Car Co.* case by a 5 to 4 vote. Justice Jackson for the majority felt that the case was a simple one of statutory construction. The act defined "employee" as meaning "any employee." {202} While there was also a definition of "employer" as "any person acting in the interest of an employer, directly or indirectly," the Court could not accept this language as having the effect of removing supervisory employees from the employee class, contending that every employee acts "in the interest" of his employer. Whatever might be the pros and cons of wise industrial policy on the question of foreman organization, the Court felt that it had no right to upset the Board's decision if it was supported by the law.

The four dissenters were headed, surprisingly enough, by Justice Douglas, and included Vinson, Frankfurter, and Burton. Douglas suggested that if foremen could organize, so could vice presidents. He was convinced that when Congress had passed the Wagner Act it was legislating against the activities of foremen, not in their behalf, and that it had never considered the wisdom or unwisdom of a policy of foreman organization. He would therefore leave the question to Congress, rather than judicially promulgate a policy which Congress had not approved, unless perhaps "unwittingly." The congressional action for which Douglas proposed to wait came very quickly, in the form of a provision in the Taft-Hartley Act freeing employers from the obligation to bargain with "supervisors."

Perhaps the severest test to which the Court has been put by the Board in recent years came in the case of *Wallace Corp.* v. *N.L.R.B.* This proceeding involved a small West Virginia plant in which a C.I.O. and an independent union agreed to an election to determine which should represent the plant employees, with the stipulation that whichever union won would insist on a closed shop. The independent was successful, bargained for and received a closed shop contract, and then refused to admit to the independent certain leaders and members of the C.I.O. union, who were consequently discharged by the company. The Board held the employer guilty of an unfair labor practice on the ground that the independent was company-dominated and that the company had signed the closed shop contract knowing that the independent intended to exclude some of the C.I.O. members. A five-judge majority, headed by Justice Black, upheld the Board order as supported by the evidence, and on the general principle that the closed shop provision of the Wagner Act was not intended to be used {203} by a company and a plant majority "to penalize minority groups of workers."

The employer may well have been guilty of collusion with the independent union in this case, as found by the Board, though the company made a protest, at least for the record, against the discriminatory action of the independent. However, the principle of the decision appeared broad enough to impose responsibility on any employer, however innocent, for the conduct of any union to which a closed shop contract was granted. The four-judge minority in the *Wallace* case, composed of Jackson, Stone, Frankfurter, and Roberts, stressed the anomaly of this result. They could find in the Wagner Act no authority for the Board to supervise union membership or union practices, no matter how unfair they might be. And especially were they sure that *employers* had not been required or given power to police the unions in their plants. Yet the *Wallace* decision would seem to require the employer to underwrite the fairness of closed shop unions, and to do that he would have to maintain some degree of supervision over their membership practices. Such a result, they felt, "is a strange contradiction in an Act whose chief purpose was to sterilize the employers and to free workmen of the influence they exerted through control of the right to work." It would also, they hazarded, make employers extremely wary of granting closed shop contracts. The dissenting opinion by Justice Jackson concluded, with some eloquence:

> This and other cases before us give ground for belief that the labor movement in the United States is passing into a new phase. The struggle of the unions for recognition and rights to bargain, and of workmen for the right to join without interference, seems to be culminating in a victory for labor forces. We appear now to be entering the phase of struggle to reconcile the rights of individuals and minorities with the power of those who control collective bargaining groups.

Court interpretation of the second major piece of New Deal labor legislation, the Fair Labor Standards Act, began with the *Darby* decision of 1941, in which the statute was unanimously upheld as an exercise of the federal government's commerce power. The extent of the coverage of this act has proved somewhat more difficult to establish {204} than was the situation with the Wagner Act, and cases raising this issue continue to come up to the Court ten years after the legislation was adopted. One reason for this difference is that the coverage of the Wage and Hour Act was purposely limited by Congress to an area less wide than that affected by the Wagner Act. Congress made the applicability of the 1935 statute as broad as the commerce power itself, by proscribing unfair labor practices "affecting commerce." On the other hand the 1938 act, apart from certain specific exemptions such as for agricultural workers and employees in retail establishments, was made applicable only to employees "engaged in commerce or in the production of goods for commerce." Because of this more limited coverage the constitutional criteria developed in other commerce clause cases are not necessarily applicable in determining the appropriate area for application of the Wage and Hour Act.

A second reason for the Court's difficulties in interpretation of this statute is that the Wage and Hour Act is not administered by a quasi-judicial body like the N.L.R.B., which can make the initial determination as to whether the act properly applies to a specific type of employment. The Administrator of the Wage and Hour Division has no standing as an administrative tribunal for the primary adjudication of these problems, but can only bring suit in the federal courts to enjoin violations of the standards set by the act. The result is that the courts have "the independent responsibility of applying ad hoc the general terms of the statute to an infinite variety of complicated industrial situations," without "the benefit of a prior judgment, on vexing and ambiguous facts, by an expert administrative agency."[12]

Consequently the Supreme Court has been caught up, as it has itself described its task, "in the empiric process of drawing lines from case to case, and inevitably nice lines." How "nice" the line may be is well illustrated by two recent cases involving the service employees in two New York office buildings.[13] In the first building, owned by and housing the central offices of the Borden Company, admittedly an interstate concern, the Court considered the elevator operators and other building service personnel to be a necessary part of the Borden Company's interstate business, and consequently covered by the statute. The other building was owned by a New York real estate {205} company and housed a miscellaneous assortment of tenants. Because of these circumstances the Court was constrained to hold that *its* service employees were not engaged in the production of goods for commerce and so not entitled to the protection of the act. Fully aware that a distinction as fine as this one would escape many onlookers, the Court said in defense of its decision: "On the terms in which Congress drew the legislation we cannot escape the duty of drawing lines. And where lines have to be drawn they are bound to appear arbitrary when judged solely by bordering cases."

Most of the time the Court has drawn the lines in such a way as to bring the particular type of employment involved within the coverage of the act. The Court has considered as engaged in commerce or in the production of goods for commerce the service employees of a New York loft building used for light manufacturing purposes, employees of a window cleaning firm who wash windows in industrial plants, an employee of a drilling company engaged in drilling oil wells under contract, the operator of a drawbridge on a toll road, and employees of a daily newspaper regularly sending only ½ of 1 per cent of its copies outside the state.[14] But, unlike the Wagner Act cases, the Court has also demonstrated an ability to arrive at the opposite result. In addition to the office-building service employees, the act has been ruled inapplicable to a cook employed by a commissary company and assigned to the preparation of meals for a railroad maintenance-of-way crew, persons receiving training in order to become qualified for employment as railroad employees, and Western Union messengers.[15]

The Court's previous troubles with interpretation of the Fair Labor Standards Act pale into insignificance, however, in comparison with the storm aroused by its portal-to-portal pay decision in the 1946 *Mt. Clemens Pottery* case.[16] This was the third encounter of the Court with the portal pay issue, which arose out of the statutory provision that "No employer shall . . . employ any of his employees . . . for a workweek longer than forty hours," except as they are paid extra for overtime work. There was no definition of "workweek" or of what is to be considered "work" in the act. In 1944 the Supreme Court decided that the workweek of miners in underground iron ore mines included the time spent by them each day in going from the mine portal {206} to the working face and return.[17] In 1945 the Court reached the same conclusion on underground travel in bituminous coal mines.[18] The circumstances of this case, it will be recalled, supplied the occasion for Jackson's public attack on Black from Nuremberg the following year.

In the *Mt. Clemens* case the Court by a 5 to 2 vote held that employees of a pottery were entitled to be paid for the time they spent walking from the time-clock to their working place on the employer's premises, and in their activities preparatory to work such as putting on gloves, opening windows, and assembling their tools. The Court did, however, qualify this holding by noting that negligible amounts of time consumed in such operations need not be compensated for.

> When the matter in issue concerns only a few seconds or minutes of work beyond the scheduled working hours, such trifles may be disregarded. Split second absurdities are not justified by the actualities of working conditions or by the policy of the Fair Labor Standards Act.

Justices Burton and Frankfurter (Jackson not participating) dissented on the ground that Congress had not meant in this act to redefine the standard industrial conception of workweek, and that the shortness of the preparatory period at this plant would not justify the cumbersomeness of a system for adequately recording it.

The *Mt. Clemens* ruling had been rather clearly forecast by the interpretations of the Wage and Hour Administrator. But former Secretary of Labor Frances Perkins called it a "crazy decision," and the flood of suits for back and overtime pay which began to pile up, threatening to reach a total of five or six billion dollars, seemed likely to result in a huge windfall for employees, a terrific burden on industry, and a heavy tax loss to the government. On February 8, 1947, however, the trial court to which the *Mt. Clemens* case had been remanded ruled that the preparatory time spent by employees at this plant was in fact negligible, and so no compensation was due. The case did not return to the Supreme Court.

While the portal-to-portal pay issue has now been terminated by amendment of the Fair Labor Standards Act, it has left a serious division on the Court concerning interpretation of that statute. On {207} February 17, 1947, the Court unanimously rejected two employee claims which, while not raising a portal pay issue, had no doubt been encouraged by the decisions on that problem.[19] Justice Jackson made this the occasion for a blistering attack on the Court's record in interpretation of the statute. The Court, he said, had treated the act as one to regulate industrial labor relations, which he was convinced it was not. The Court had refused to follow the terms of agreements collectively bargained, or to abide by long-established industry customs. The result was that

> This Court has foreclosed every means by which any claim, however dubious, under this statute or under the Court's elastic and somewhat unpredictable interpretation of it, can safely or finally be settled, except by litigation to final judgment.

Controversy of a milder sort has been engendered in connection with several important questions concerning the statutory powers of the Administrator of the Wage and Hour Division. In this area liberal and conservative decisions have about balanced each other. In 1942 the Court by a 5 to 4 vote held the Administrator lacking in statutory authority to delegate to subordinates his power to sign and issue subpoenas.[20] But in 1946 the much broader matter of the use of the administrative subpoena and its relation to the search and seizure and self-incrimination clauses of the Constitution was decided favorably to the Administrator by a 7 to 1 vote.[21]

Another and somewhat more involved pair of cases in which differing attitudes toward administrative powers were expressed was *Addison v. Holly Hill Fruit Products* and *Gemsco, Inc. v. Walling*. In the former, decided in 1944 by a 5 to 4 vote, the Court denied the Administrator the authority to distinguish between small and large canning plants in determining the applicability of the statute. But the following year a 7 to 2 vote held the Administrator to be equipped by statute with the sweeping authority to prohibit industrial homework as a necessary means of making effective a minimum wage order for the embroideries industry.

Since the Fair Labor Standards Act was passed, and up through the 1946 term, the Administrator has been before the Supreme Court {208} in 21 cases, in 14 of which his position was upheld by the Court. Private actions brought under the statute have gone to the Court in 22 cases, with the decision favoring the employee, in whole or in part, on 14 of those occasions.

The attitude of the individual justices in Wagner and Fair Labor Standards Acts decisions, as well as in workmen's compensation cases and others where labor issues have been raised, may be summarized at this point. Table XXI covers votes in 88 nonunanimous labor decisions handed down during the six terms from 1941 through 1946. The division is largely along expected lines, with Murphy, Black, Rutledge, and Douglas strongly sympathetic to labor claims. Reed comes closest to being the center man in this field, while the remaining justices fall well below the average position of the Court. Roberts is of course isolated on the far right.

TABLE XXI

ALIGNMENTS OF JUSTICES IN NONUNANIMOUS LABOR CASES, 1941-1946 TERMS

	No. Cases	Decisions Favorable to Labor				Total
		N.L.R.B.	Wage and Hour Act	Workmen's Compensation	Other	
No. Cases		19	30	24	15	88
Majority	88	84%	63%	71%	53%	68%
Murphy	88	100	90	100	87	94
Black	88	100	100	100	60	93
Rutledge	66	86	91	100	69	88
Douglas	87	95	80	100	64	86
Reed	88	79	70	54	60	66
Jackson	73	56	52	55	40	52
Frankfurter	88	58	47	42	27	44
Stone	71	40	40	20	27	32
Burton	28	60	33	14	29	32
Vinson	15	25	0	67	25	27
Roberts	59	7	0	6	14	5

Labor and the Sherman Act

Some of the most controversial of the Roosevelt Court's labor decisions have resulted from its struggles with application of the Sherman Act {209} to the activities of organized labor. In this field the Court has been responsible for a dramatic reversal of previously established doctrines, and has exhibited a degree of facility, not to say legerdemain, in statutory interpretation which has left some members of the legal profession gasping in astonishment.

The story of the Sherman Act as applied to labor is a long and complicated one, and only a bare summary of the developments up to 1940 can be provided here. Whether Congress meant to include labor unions when it declared in 1890 that combinations or conspiracies in restraint of trade were illegal has been the subject of bitter argument. The decisive answer was given by the Supreme Court in 1908, when the *Danbury Hatters* decision held a nationwide secondary boycott, organized by the hatters' union as a method of forcing a closed shop on a Danbury company, illegal under the Sherman Act.[22] Organized labor deeply resented this decision, and was instrumental in securing the adoption of the Clayton Act in 1914, Section 6 of which sought to restate the position of labor under the Sherman Act.

Actually, however, the Clayton Act provision was weak, simply providing that labor unions were not to be considered illegal per se, and that the antitrust laws were not to be interpreted to restrain unions "from lawfully carrying out" their "legitimate objects." The Supreme Court soon exposed the hollowness of this protection by holding in 1921 that the Clayton Act was "merely declaratory" of existing rules, and had not freed intimidation by pickets or secondary boycotts from injunctive restraint by the courts.[23] Following this line, the Court declared in the 1925 *Second Coronado* decision that a local coal strike, accompanied by lawlessness and violence, had involved violation of the Sherman Act. Ordinarily, the Court admitted, "the mere reduction in the supply of an article to be shipped in interstate commerce by the illegal or tortious prevention of its manufacture or production is . . . an indirect and remote obstruction to that commerce," and so not actionable under the federal commerce power. But when, as the Court held the situation to be in this case, "the intent of those unlawfully preventing the manufacture or production is shown to be to restrain or control the supply entering and moving in interstate commerce, {210} or the price of it in interstate markets, their action is a direct violation of the Antitrust Act."[24]

Two years later in the *Bedford Cut Stone* case the Court enjoined a secondary boycott by the stone cutters' union, whose members had been refusing to handle stone cut by the leading nonunion Indiana limestone quarry. Justices Brandeis and Holmes, dissenting, urged that the rule of reason, which the Court had developed as a test to distinguish between good and bad trusts, should be applied in this case to justify the action taken by a weak union to prevent a powerful combination of corporations from breaking it up.[25]

Throughout this period it was the court injunction which was the principal instrument of labor's misfortune, and much of the legislative interest of organized labor was devoted to establishing stricter controls over the issuance of injunctions. Section 20 of the Clayton Act purported to regulate the granting of labor injunctions, but in the *Duplex* decision of 1921 the Court drew the teeth of this section by holding that Congress had merely intended to state the law as previous judicial decisions had held it to be. The next legislative effort was the Norris-LaGuardia Act of 1932, in the drafting of which Professor Felix Frankfurter took a leading part. This statute forbade the federal courts to issue injunctions in labor disputes except under carefully prescribed and limited conditions. "Labor disputes" were defined very broadly by Section 13, and by Section 4 the courts were denied power to interfere with all the normal types of union self-help. In general, an injunction may issue under the Norris-LaGuardia Act only if unlawful conduct is threatened or committed which will result in greater irreparable damage to the complainant than the union will suffer if its conduct is prohibited, and if local peace officers are unable or unwilling to furnish adequate protection. The effect of the statute is, as Gregory says, virtually to invite unions "to exert a variety of economic pressures in organizational campaigns and in collective bargaining" by making such economic pressures non-enjoinable.[26] The statute does not of course control state courts, but several states adopted similar laws.

This was the status of the law and of the Court's holdings when the Roosevelt Court encountered its first substantial anti-trust action involving labor in 1940, the famous *Apex* case.[27] A nonunion Philadelphia {211} hosiery plant had been seized by its employees in a sit-down strike, had locked up the plant, excluded all officials and non-strikers from entrance, broken windows and machinery, and deliberately refused to turn over to the company for interstate shipment some 134,000 dozens of manufactured hosiery standing ready in the plant. The company sued the union for triple damages under the Sherman Act, but a majority of the Supreme Court concluded that, however illegal these acts might have been under state law, they did not constitute the kind of interference with interstate commerce Congress had been thinking about when it passed the Sherman Act.

The Court, wrote Justice Stone for the majority, had never applied that act to laborers or others as a method of policing interstate transportation. Nor had the Court, he continued, ever applied the act in any case, whether or not involving labor organizations, unless it had found the existence of some form of restraint upon commercial competition in the marketing of goods or services. The Court had consistently refused, he contended, to apply the act in cases, like the present, where local strikes conducted by illegal means prevented substantial interstate shipments, but in which it was not shown that the restrictions on shipment had operated to restrain commercial competition in some substantial way. The purpose of the Sherman Act was to afford "a remedy, public and private, for the public wrongs which flow from restraints of trade in the common law sense of restriction or suppression of commercial competition." The *Apex* case did not present such a situation, for the object of the workers had been to promote unionization, not to restrain competition in the market for the company's product.

None of the Court's earlier labor decisions, Stone argued, conflicted with this view of the law. In the *Danbury, Duplex,* and *Bedford* cases the labor activities had been directed at control of the market, and were so widespread as substantially to affect it. The situation most like the present one was that found in the *Coronado* case, but the reason why the Court applied the act in the *Second Coronado* decision was its finding of a definite purpose and intent to injure interstate commerce. Unless, Stone concluded, a conspiracy to prevent or obstruct transportation in commerce is *intended* to have, or in fact {212} has, the effects on the market which the Court relied on to establish violation in the *Second Coronado* decision, it is not within the reach of the Sherman Act.

The Stone opinion, which spoke for Reed, Frankfurter, Murphy, Black, and Douglas, and from which Chief Justice Hughes, Roberts, and McReynolds dissented, was a strong one. It offered a compellingly reasonable interpretation of the congressional intent embodied in the Sherman Act, and it substituted for the ill-defined test of intent to obstruct or prevent interstate commerce the more logical and clearly defined test of intent to monopolize supply, to control prices, or to discriminate between buyers, in a manner which suppresses commercial competition. The weakest part of Stone's opinion derived from his unconvincing effort to prove that it was not inconsistent with the earlier Sherman Act labor decisions. A direct overruling of the *Danbury, Duplex, Bedford,* and *Second Coronado* decisions would have seemed preferable as a basis for the proposition which the *Apex* case seemed to support; namely, that elimination of competition between union and nonunion made goods was a normal and lawful objective of nationally organized labor unions, and not subject to the prohibitions of the Sherman Act.

This extraordinary tenderness for outmoded precedents was to get the Court into more serious complications in its next important Sherman Act proceeding, *United States* v. *Hutcheson,* decided in 1941. The case arose out of a jurisdictional dispute between the carpenters' union and the machinists' union as to which should get certain work in a St. Louis brewery. When the company decided in favor of the latter, the carpenters' union went on strike, picketed the plant, and organized among workers a boycott of the company's beer. The Anti-Trust Division of the Department of Justice, which, under Thurman Arnold's direction, had recently organized a drive against what it conceived to be illegal restrictive practices of labor unions, began a criminal prosecution against the president of the carpenters' union for violation of the Sherman Act.

This time Justice Frankfurter, speaking for the same six-judge majority, held that, as in the *Apex* case, no violation of the act had been shown. He reached this conclusion despite the fact that a similar {213} secondary boycott had been held a violation of the Sherman Act in the *Danbury Hatters* decision in 1908. The Clayton Act of 1914 had in Section 20 appeared to legalize secondary boycotts, but the Supreme Court had ruled otherwise in its 1921 *Duplex* decision. Thus the precedents which Stone had refused to disturb in the *Apex* case seemed to condemn Hutcheson and his carpenters.

Justice Frankfurter's ingenuity proved equal to the occasion, however. His argument was that the protection of Section 20 of the Clayton Act, almost fatally limited when in the *Duplex* decision the Court confined its application to the immediate employer-employee relation, had been restored to its original breadth when Congress passed the Norris-LaGuardia Act in 1932. That statute, he reasoned,

> explicitly formulated the "public policy of the United States" in regard to the industrial conflict, and by its light established that the allowable area of union activity was not to be restricted, as it had been in the Duplex case, to an immediate employer-employee relation. Therefore, whether trade union conduct constitutes a violation of the Sherman Law is to be determined only by reading the Sherman Law and section 20 of the Clayton Act and the Norris-LaGuardia Act as a harmonizing text of outlawry of labor conduct.

Thus the *Duplex* case, which Stone had been so careful to distinguish in his *Apex* decision, was now held by Frankfurter to have been dead at the hands of Congress since 1932. Freed from its pall, Section 20 of the Clayton Act stood forth again as a broad charter granting immunity to unions for their self-help activities. Only two limitations were recognized by Frankfurter on the immunizing qualities of Section 20—the union must be acting "in its self-interest" and must not "combine with non-labor groups." The jurisdictional strike and the secondary boycott organized by Hutcheson met these two tests, and so the Sherman Act did not apply.

Now Justice Frankfurter was undoubtedly correct in arguing that the Norris-LaGuardia Act was passed because of congressional dissatisfaction with judicial interpretations of the Sherman and Clayton Acts as applied to labor, and that the three statutes were consequently "interlacing." The difficulty with the use which he made of this view was that the Norris-LaGuardia Act was solely concerned with establishing {214} limitations on the granting of injunctions in labor disputes. It had nothing whatever to do with revising the standards of criminal responsibility under the Sherman Act. Frankfurter was of course well aware of this fact, since he is credited with having drafted the Norris-LaGuardia Act. But his position was that if the protection of that statute was available only against the injunctive process, the result would be that officials of a labor union could be held criminally responsible under the Sherman Act for actions which were non-enjoinable under the Norris-LaGuardia Act. As he put it:

> . . . to argue, as it was argued before us, that the *Duplex* case still governs for purposes of a criminal prosecution is to say that that which on the equity side of the court is allowable conduct may in a criminal proceeding become the road to prison.

Such a result, the justice felt, would be "strange indeed," and he went on:

> That is not the way to read the will of Congress, particularly when expressed by a statute which . . . is practically and historically one of a series of enactments touching one of the most sensitive national problems. Such legislation must not be read in a spirit of mutilating narrowness.

But neither, of course, must such legislation be given unintended meanings by an overly helpful Court desirous of achieving consistency where perhaps the legislature had had no desire or intention of being consistent. Chief Justice Hughes had fallen into this same fallacy in the *Apex* case, where his dissent had stressed the anomaly that would result because *employers* were being subjected to the Wagner Act on the theory that their unfair labor practices might lead to conduct which would prevent shipment of their goods in commerce, while *employees* under Stone's interpretation of the Sherman Act were being left free directly and intentionally to obstruct or prevent such shipments in commerce. An anomaly this may be, but it is not the task of the Supreme Court to rewrite congressional legislation to eliminate all anomalies or inequalities in treatment, unless basic constitutional guaranties are contravened. Clearly Justice Frankfurter's concern to achieve a consistency between the Norris-LaGuardia Act and the Sherman {215} Act in the *Hutcheson* decision led him, in a fashion contrary to all his professed principles, rather far into the field of judicial legislation.

It is true that the Sherman Act set up such vague standards that, if it was to be enforced at all, judicial legislation was compelled. Justice Holmes was even inclined at first to hold the statute unconstitutional on this ground of uncertainty. An act formulating such broad concepts especially demands that the Supreme Court achieve *rightness* and balance in its interpretation. Certainly the pre-Roosevelt Court had failed to achieve such balance in its application of the Sherman Act to labor. The Roosevelt Court could have gone to the opposite extreme and held the act completely inapplicable to labor. While there is fairly strong evidence that this may have been the original congressional intent, it would have been an abrupt break with thirty years of constitutional interpretation, and Stone rightly rejected this suggestion in his *Apex* argument.

The Court's strategic problem then became one of mapping out an allowable and socially justifiable area for the self-help activities of labor, with such assistance as the more recent statutes and judicial decisions could give. The rule which Stone worked out in the *Apex* decision—namely, that a labor organization employing its power for self-help does not violate the Sherman Act unless it purposely affects competition in the marketing of goods and services—was not bad, even though it was less consistent with the precedents than he attempted to make it appear. But Justice Frankfurter was not satisfied with this rule and, in an excess of cleverness, produced a doctrine in the *Hutcheson* case which justifies all self-interest actions of unions subject to the sole limitation that labor "does not combine with non-labor groups" to achieve its ends. It was not necessary to go this far to exempt Hutcheson's boycott from the Sherman Act. Justice Stone concurred in the result in that case without accepting Frankfurter's devious reasoning, simply by distinguishing the methods of the Hutcheson boycott from those declared invalid in the *Danbury* case, and by justifying an "unfair" announcement by a union as "an exercise of the right of free speech guaranteed by the First Amendment which cannot be made unlawful by act of Congress."

The chickens hatched by the Frankfurter interpretations came {216} home to roost in 1945, to the considerable embarrassment of Frankfurter himself. *Allen Bradley Co.* v. *Local Union No. 3* presented the situation of an electrical workers' union which had entered into closed shop agreements with the makers and sellers of electrical equipment in metropolitan New York, rendering it completely impossible for competitors to break into this market. Such a combination of labor and employers and manufacturers of goods was of course in defiance of the one restriction named in the *Hutcheson* decision, and the Court, with only Justice Murphy dissenting, said: "We think Congress never intended that unions could, consistent with the Sherman Act, aid non-labor groups to create business monopolies and to control the marketing of goods and services." But Justice Roberts, concurring, pointed out the hollowness of this holding, for nothing in the opinion would condemn the re-establishment of these same barriers to marketing of outside electrical equipment in the New York area, if the union simply relied on its own resources and avoided any connivance with employers. The result is that Frankfurter's *Hutcheson* doctrine can easily be manipulated to permit the type of market controls which Stone's *Apex* decision had declared illegal.

Additional loopholes in the *Allen Bradley* ruling were soon discovered when *United Brotherhood of Carpenters and Joiners* v. *United States* was decided in March, 1947. This was a criminal prosecution of various employers and unions for conspiring to monopolize interstate commerce in millwork and patterned lumber in the San Francisco Bay area by methods quite similar to those employed in the New York electrical workers case. The *Allen Bradley* decision made it clear that the Sherman Act covered such a conspiracy. But Section 6 of the Norris-LaGuardia Act was offered in defense. It provides:

> No officer or member of any association or organization, and no association or organization participating or interested in a labor dispute, shall be held responsible or liable in any court of the United States for the unlawful acts of individual officers, members, or agents, except upon clear proof of actual participation in, or actual authorization of, such acts, or of ratification of such acts after actual knowledge thereof

This section was widely understood to have been adopted because of {217} such judicial rulings as the *Danbury Hatters* decision awarding damages against union members for their union's acts in an unlawful conspiracy, and another case where both the unions and their members had been held liable for all overt acts of their co-conspirators. In the present case the Court majority, through Justice Reed, ruled that the effect of the section was to restrict responsibility or liability in labor disputes to "those associations, organizations or their officers or members who actually participate in the unlawful acts," except as it could be proved that the particular act or acts generally of that type and quality had been expressly authorized or ratified after actual knowledge of their occurrence. Since the jury had not in this case received a charge setting forth this limited liability of organizations for the acts of their agents, the judgments were reversed as to all defendants, both union and employer.

Justice Frankfurter wrote a scathing minority opinion, in which Vinson and Burton concurred (Jackson not participating). He considered that the congressional purpose behind Section 6 of the Norris-LaGuardia Act had been wholly misconstrued by the Court. According to his interpretation, Congress had been intending merely to remedy a judicial misapplication of the law of agency under which "labor unions were held responsible for the conduct of individuals in whom was lodged no authority to wield the power of the union." But the Court majority had gone far beyond this, and had imposed conditions for the establishment of union liability which would be "practically unrealizable." Under the Court's doctrine, no union or business organization could be proved guilty unless it specifically authorized its officers to violate the Sherman Act or gave carte blanche approval in advance to anything they might do. His conclusion was:

> Practically speaking, the interpretation given by the Court to section 6 serves to immunize unions, especially the more alert and powerful, as well as corporations involved in labor disputes, from Sherman Law liability. . . . For those entrusted with the enforcement of the Sherman Law there may be found in the opinion words of promise to the ear, but the decision breaks the promise to the hope.

One final example of the Court's great reluctance to apply the Sherman Act against labor is found in the 1945 case of *Hunt* v. *Crumboch*, {218} handed down the same day the *Allen Bradley* case was decided. The facts were that in a 1937 organizing strike a member of the teamsters' union was killed, and a partner in a trucking firm was tried for the homicide and acquitted. The strike was successful in imposing the closed shop, and the trucking firm sought membership for its employees in the union. The union refused to deal with this employer because of their antagonism resulting from the murder, and since his employees were refused admission into the union, his firm lost its interstate trucking contracts and was driven out of business. By a 5 to 4 vote the Court held the union's action not to be a violation of the Sherman Act, on the ground that nothing more was involved than the action of laborers in combination refusing to sell their services.

Dissents from this euphemistic interpretation were written by Roberts and Jackson. Frankfurter and Stone concurred in them, but did not express their own views. Thus it is impossible to know why Frankfurter drew back from a result rather clearly required by his *Hutcheson* decision. He could not of course fail to note that Jackson's dissent was able to use Stone's *Apex* decision in arguing against the result arrived at here, while it significantly refrained from mentioning the *Hutcheson* case. It is perhaps safe to assume that Frankfurter would be equally willing to forget it.

Picketing as Free Speech

It is not so long since picketing of all kinds was held by the courts to be tortious conduct, and peaceful picketing was regarded as a contradiction in terms. Gradually the view developed that peaceful picketing by strikers who had a direct economic interest to serve might be permitted by the state, but "stranger picketing" remained outside the law. In 1921 the Supreme Court cautiously admitted that "strikers and their sympathizers" might maintain one picket "for each point of ingress and egress" at a plant or place of business. Unless severely limited in this way, the Court concluded, picketing "indicated a militant purpose, inconsistent with peaceable persuasion."[28]

It is a long jump from 1921 to 1940, when in the case of *Thornhill* v. *Alabama* Justice Murphy, speaking for a majority of the Roosevelt {219} Court, put peaceful picketing of all kinds under the protection of the free speech clause of the Constitution. In this case two of the Court's major concerns—protection of civil liberties and protection of the rights of labor—merged to yield an unprecedented principle of constitutional law. Foundations for this development, as for so many of the other doctrines of the Roosevelt Court, had been laid by Justice Brandeis. The 1937 case of *Senn* v. *Tile Layers' Protective Union* arose under a Wisconsin statute authorizing the giving of publicity to labor disputes and making peaceful picketing lawful and non-enjoinable. Justice Brandeis' opinion held that a statute thus protecting stranger picketing was not unconstitutional, and noted:

> Clearly the means which the statute authorizes—picketing and publicity—are not prohibited by the Fourteenth Amendment. Members of a union might, without special statutory authorization by a State, make known the facts of a labor dispute, for freedom of speech is guaranteed by the Federal Constitution. The State may, in the exercise of its police power, regulate the methods and means of publicity as well as the use of public streets. If the end sought by the unions is not forbidden by the Federal Constitution, the State may authorize working men to seek to attain it by combining as pickets, just as it permits capitalists and employers to combine in other ways to attain their desired economic ends.

The *Thornhill* case, decided three years later, involved the reverse situation of a state law making peaceful picketing a misdemeanor, which as applied in this instance rendered punishable a mere conversation between a picket on company property and a nonunion worker. The Supreme Court, with only Justice McReynolds dissenting, took the position that the coverage of this statute was so broad as on its face to preclude all practicable and effective, methods of enlightening the public as to the facts of a labor dispute. Since "in the circumstances of our times the dissemination of information concerning the facts of a labor dispute must be regarded as within that area of free discussion that is guaranteed by the Constitution," the Court concluded that a statute blocking such dissemination so completely must be adjudged unconstitutional.

That picketing was a type of speech and a method of disseminating information Murphy regarded as requiring no proof. He did recognize {220} that it was a type of speech often accompanied by violence and breach of the peace, but these abuses were not considered as necessarily inherent in every act of picketing. He intimated that the state retained its right by "narrowly drawn" statutes to deal with "picketing en masse" or other methods which threatened "imminent and aggravated danger" to lawful interests.

Now there are other ways of looking at picketing than as a type of speech entitled to constitutional protection. Four justices of the Supreme Court in the *Senn* decision only three years earlier had held that peaceful stranger picketing was "so inherently illegal that, like libel, it could not constitutionally be made lawful even by legislation." Even Brandeis in the majority opinion in that case had not held that picketing was speech, but merely that it was not forbidden by the Fourteenth Amendment. As competent and generally fair-minded an observer as C. O. Gregory concludes:

> What even peaceful picketing usually boils down to is a simple process of proscription. The picketed person is bad because he is either not doing what we, the picketers, want him to do, or because he is doing something which we don't want him to do, and such information is thrust at passers-by, whether they want it or not. Such a procedure is, indeed, a dubious venture into the world of ideas and opinions, and hardly seems to be the sort of thing contemplated by the constitutional guaranty of free speech. Rather, it suggests a sort of psychological embargo around the picketed premises, depending for its persuasiveness on the associations most people have in mind when they think about picketing. Hence it is likely that people hesitate to cross picket lines more because they wish to avoid trouble and to escape any possible scorn that might be directed toward them for being antiunion, than because they are persuaded intellectually by the worth of the picketing union's cause.[29]

Justice Murphy's opinion, however, raised no such problems as these in accepting, without analysis, peaceful picketing as on a par with other types of expression of opinion and entitled to the full constitutional protection guaranteed to speech. Subsequent decisions have furnished occasion for the Court to consider this doctrine somewhat more carefully. In 1941 it was applied, in an opinion by Justice Frankfurter, and over the dissent of Hughes and Roberts, to protect peaceful {221} stranger picketing in the case of *A. F. of L. v. Swing.* But on the same day Frankfurter wrote another opinion holding that the *Thornhill* rule did not prevent the Illinois supreme court from enjoining *all* picketing in a labor dispute which had been so marred by past violence that the state court believed it was impossible for future picketing to be maintained on a peaceful basis.[30] Justices Black, Douglas, and Reed attacked this conclusion, the latter contending that the right maintained by *Thornhill v. Alabama* had collapsed on the first attack. Reed's opinion emphatically endorsed the conception of picketing as speech, though there may have been an unconscious recognition of the coercive quality of picketing in his statement that "the right to picket peacefully in industrial disputes is a recognized means for the marshaling of public opinion on the side of the worker." Justice Black's dissenting opinion sought not so much to give added weight to the speech concept of picketing as to show that the court injunction issued in this case was in such broad terms as actually to prohibit not merely picketing, but all other practicable methods of communicating the facts of this labor dispute to the public. Surprisingly enough, Murphy, author of the *Thornhill* decision, went along with the Frankfurter opinion.

Coming two by two like the animals entering the Ark, another pair of picketing decisions was announced on March 30, 1942. In *Bakery and Pastry Drivers Local v. Wohl,* the Court unanimously struck down a New York court injunction against picketing, but the language of Justice Jackson's opinion was not entirely satisfactory to Douglas, Black, and Murphy, who interpreted it to mean that "a State can prohibit picketing when it is effective but may not prohibit it when it is ineffective." More important, their opinion contained the first clear admission since the *Thornhill* decision that

> Picketing by an organized group is more than free speech, since it involves patrol of a particular locality and since the very presence of a picket line may induce action of one kind or another, quite irrespective of the nature of the ideas which are being disseminated.

It is these aspects of picketing, Douglas concluded, that "make it the subject of restrictive regulation." {222}

In the second case decided that day, *Carpenters and Joiners Union v. Ritter's Cafe,* the dissension was more acute. The facts here were that a Texas restaurant owner was having a home built by a nonunion contractor over a mile away from the business section of town where his cafe was located. The carpenters' union proceeded to picket Ritter where it would hurt him most, at his cafe. The state court enjoined picketing of the restaurant, but did not attempt to prevent publicizing the situation in any other way. Justice Frankfurter and four of his colleagues upheld this action on the ground that Texas had the right to restrict picketing "to the area of the industry within which a labor dispute arises." Any other view, he continued, "would compel the states to allow the disputants in a particular industrial episode to conscript neutrals having no relation to either the dispute or the industry in which it arose."

Underlying Frankfurter's opinion was a definite departure from the view of picketing set forth in the *Thornhill* decision. Picketing was here spoken of inferentially as a method of "industrial warfare," and more specifically its status as a form of speech was qualified by this language:

> It is true that by peaceful picketing workingmen communicate their grievances. As a means of communicating the facts of a labor dispute peaceful picketing may be a phase of the constitutional right of free utterance. But recognition of peaceful picketing as an exercise of free speech does not imply that the states must be without power to confine the sphere of communication to that directly related to the dispute.

Thus only two years after *Thornhill* the Court majority was willing to concede only that picketing may *be* free speech, and even if so regarded was entitled to constitutional protection only within certain "spheres" directly related to industrial disputes. The sphere theory is hard to reconcile with past thought on free speech problems. It is true that freedom of speech has never been regarded as absolute, and that considerations of time and place have always been held pertinent in determining whether constitutional protection is to be extended, as demonstrated by Justice Holmes' famous statement that no one has the right to cry fire in a crowded theater. But the type of restriction {223} held valid by the Court in the Ritter case has no counterpart in previous free speech decisions, and the language about "conscription of neutrals" is sufficient indication that the Court did not believe it was dealing simply with a technique of disseminating ideas.

Four justices—Black, Douglas, Murphy, and Reed—protested that the *Ritter* decision fatally undermined the protection accorded picketing by the *Thornhill* doctrine. "Until today," Justice Reed said (meaning since 1940), "orderly, regulated picketing has been within the protection of the Fourteenth Amendment." That this view was somewhat over-pessimistic became evident when in 1943 the Court unanimously upheld the peaceful picketing of a cafetera by a union whose grievance was that the cafeteria was operated by its owners and so hired no employees for the union to organize.[31]

The Court has by no means deserted the *Thornhill* rule. It certainly has not subscribed to the view of picketing which Gregory suggests as the true one, namely, "that it is simply a species of coercion traveling under the guise of speech for the purpose of enjoying constitutional immunity from state regulation."[32] The attitude it has adopted is accurately summarized by E. M. Dodd when he says:

> Picketing is thus recognized as being at once a means of communicating grievances and a method of exerting economic pressure. Because of the former aspect, it cannot be wholly forbidden; because of

173

the latter, it may be limited in ways which are more likely to seem appropriate if one thinks of limiting the scope of economic warfare than if one conceives of a picket's placard as the equivalent of a political pamphlet.[33]

The Court, then, still regards picketing as communication, but a type of communication less likely than other forms to convince by persuasion and more likely to lead to violence, and so subject to an unusual amount of permissible regulation. As Justice Reed, one of the justices most concerned over protecting the right to picket, said in his *Ritter* dissent:

> We do not doubt the right of the state to impose not only some but many restrictions upon peaceful picketing. Reasonable numbers, quietness, truthful placards, open ingress and egress, suitable hours or other proper limitations, not destructive of the right to tell of labor difficulties, may be required. {224}

Determining the allowable limits of such regulation is a difficult new burden which the Court has assumed, but its course is clearly preferable to the two alternatives of giving picketing either absolute protection or no protection whatever under the Bill of Rights.

The States and Labor Regulation

The pro-labor tide which put the Norris-LaGuardia Act, the Wagner Act, and the Fair Labor Standards Act on the federal statute books has long since ebbed. Anti-labor feeling in Congress has, however, only recently developed enough strength to adopt restrictive legislation such as the anti-Petrillo act, the Hobbs anti-racketeering act, and in 1947 the Taft-Hartley Act.

At the state level, however, the change in the tide began to produce results much sooner. As early as 1939 Wisconsin modified its "Little Wagner Act" in a manner unfavorable to labor, and adopted a fairly stringent Employment Peace Act. The state legislative sessions of 1943 produced laws or constitutional amendments regulating various aspects of labor activities in Colorado, Kansas, Alabama, Florida, Texas, Arkansas and several other states. That the tide is still running strong (if any such proof is needed) is indicated by the fact that three states in the November, 1946, elections adopted constitutional amendments banning the closed shop, and the legislative sessions of 1947 produced a new crop of restrictive labor laws. Already the constitutional issues raised by such legislation have begun to come before the Court, and on the basis of the decisions handed down and the general principles which the Court has enunciated in this field it is easy to predict trouble ahead for the Court as it encounters prevailing anti-labor sentiment.

The state regulations so far considered by the Court have been questioned on the ground either of the due process clause or of alleged incompatibility with the provisions of the National Labor Relations Act. The due process cases include, of course, the picketing decisions just discussed. Only one additional picketing case need be considered. The Wisconsin Employment Peace Act of 1939 had forbidden as an "unfair labor practice" picketing except in connection with {225} a strike called by majority vote. Another section of the statute stated that nothing in the act was to be construed "to invade unlawfully the right to freedom of speech." Under this authority the Wisconsin Employment Relations Board issued an order totally forbidding a union to engage "in promoting or inducing picketing," but the state supreme court, by what E. M. Dodd calls "an extraordinary feat of legerdemain," construed the order as permitting peaceful picketing and forbidding nothing except violence. So construed, the Supreme Court unanimously held the order not to violate the Fourteenth Amendment.[34]

Aside from picketing problems, the most important challenge to state labor legislation on due process grounds was *Thomas* v. *Collins*, decided in 1945. A 1943 Texas statute required all labor union organizers operating in the state to secure organizers' cards from the secretary of state before soliciting members for their organizations. Registration involved supplying the name, union affiliations, and credentials of the organizer, and the secretary of state had no discretion to refuse registration if the application was properly made. R. J. Thomas, then president of the United Automobile Workers, went to Texas in September, 1943, to test the statute. Without applying for registration Thomas addressed a union meeting, inviting all nonunion men present to join the union and, to make perfectly sure that he was violating the law, he specifically solicited the membership of a particular individual present at the close of the meeting.

By a 5 to 4 vote the Supreme Court reversed Thomas' conviction and invalidated the Texas statute as an interference with freedom of speech and assembly. Two main arguments had been relied on by the state. The first was that the registration requirement resembled the vocational or business practice regulations which states commonly adopt; according to this view, it was to be construed as affecting only the right to engage in the business of a paid organizer, and not limiting the expression of views on union membership. Justice Rutledge, for the majority, ruled that it was impossible to make this distinction; he felt it would be an "incredible feat" for a union leader to make a speech praising unionism without impliedly suggesting membership to his audience. In the absence of some grave and imminent {226} threat to the public interest, "a restriction so destructive of the right of public discussion" could not be upheld.

The second argument for the statute was that, since the secretary of state had no discretion to refuse the license, registration was only a "previous identification" requirement. But the Court was quick to point out that if previous identification could be required for speeches on labor unionism, it could be required for any social, business, religious, or political cause, and speech or assembly which could not be punished directly could be made a crime by establishment of a previous identification requirement and penalizing failure to conform with it. Justice Roberts' dissent, which spoke for Stone, Reed and Frankfurter as well, took the view that registration was a reasonable police regulation which did not interfere with freedom of speech, but merely required a paid labor organizer to identify himself as such.

The extent to which the National Labor Relations Act precludes restrictive state labor legislation has been examined in two recent decisions. The Wisconsin Employment Peace Act was tested in this respect in 1942 by *Allen-Bradley Local No. 1111* v. *Wisconsin Employment Relations Board.* This statute authorizes the state board to forbid employees to commit certain unfair labor practices, and in this instance the Board had used its authority to forbid mass picketing, obstructing entrance to or egress from a factory, threatening employees desiring to work with physical injury or property damage, and so on. The Court unanimously held that the Wagner Act had not intended to prevent states from regulating such employee and union conduct, and that employees had not by this state order been denied rights protected by the federal statute. Disorder and abuse of the picketing right were thus left clearly subject to state regulation.

In the 1945 decision of *Hill* v. *Florida,* however, a Florida statute providing for the compulsory licensing of labor union business agents was held to thwart the purposes of the Wagner Act. Issuance of licenses, in the charge of a special state board created for the purpose, was discretionary and an applicant was required to prove that he had been a citizen of the United States for more than ten years, had never been convicted of a felony, and was a person of good moral character. A 7 to 2 majority held that this type of regulation invaded the full {227} freedom granted by the Wagner Act to workers in the selection of bargaining representatives, and substituted Florida's judgment for the workers' judgment.

That these requirements actually did interfere with the collective bargaining process was demonstrated, Justice Black contended, by the fact that in this very case an employer before the N.L.R.B. had defended his refusal to bargain with a duly elected representative of workers on the ground that the representative had not secured a Florida license as a business agent. Likewise the requirement of the statute that unions file certain reports with the state was held invalid, because failure to file these reports could result in the union being enjoined from further functioning as a labor union. Justices Frankfurter and Roberts dissented on the ground that the Wagner Act did not deal with qualifications of union business agents, and consequently Florida was able to adopt its own regulations on the subject.

The cases which have thus far come up to the Supreme Court present only a few of the state labor controls already adopted or likely to be adopted in the near future. The Court has succeeded in postponing some of these issues. In two 1945 decisions the Alabama Federation of Labor and the C.I.O. sought to secure review of the Alabama Bradford Act, a comprehensive labor control law adopted in 1943. The statute required all unions to file with the state department of labor detailed reports as to the organization and finances of the union, including a showing of all receipts and disbursements with the names of recipients and the purpose thereof. The act also forbade unions of non-supervisory employees to have supervisory employees as members. Labor brought declaratory judgment proceedings, seeking a ruling that these two provisions infringed freedom of speech and assembly and were in conflict with the Wagner Act, on the theory that the report provisions were equivalent to the requirement of a license without which labor unions could not function within the state.

Another provision of the act—aimed at the selling of work permits, but broad enough to forbid unions to receive any money except initiation fees and dues—was attacked as so arbitrary and unreasonable as to infringe due process. The Supreme Court refused a ruling on {228} these issues on the ground, first, that the statute had not yet been applied and construed by the state courts, and second, that in matters of this sort the Court needed a precise set of facts, a specific controversy, on which to base its judgment, which was not supplied by the declaratory judgment type of proceeding.[35]

One year later the Court used much the same technique in avoiding a ruling on the anti-closed shop constitutional amendment adopted by Florida in 1944, which provided:

> The right of persons to work shall not be denied or abridged on ac-count of membership or non-membership in any labor union, or labor organization; provided, that this clause shall not be construed to deny or abridge the right of employees by and through a labor organization or labor union to bargain collectively with their employer.

The A.F. of L. sought a federal court injunction against enforcement of this provision on the ground that it violated the First and Fourteenth Amendments and the contract clause of the Constitution, and conflicted with the Wagner Act and the Norris-LaGuardia Act.

The Court concluded, Chief Justice Stone dissenting, that the plaintiffs had a cause which justified them in seeking relief at equity, in view of their contention that the amendment was an imminent threat to the entire system of collective bargaining capable of causing irreparable damage in the relationships between capital and labor. But the Court also held that a ruling on the merits of the question should be deferred until the Florida courts had announced the construction which they proposed to place on the amendment. It might, for instance, be regarded as not self-executing, in which case legislation would be needed before it had any effect. The federal district court was consequently directed to retain the case pending state adjudication of the issues raised. Justice Murphy dissented from such a disposition of the case, contending that it left the plaintiff's rights unprotected against the very threat which the Court had said was "real and imminent" enough to justify the equity action.[36]

Within the near future the issues which have thus been temporarily postponed will find their way back into the Court docket. It seems reasonable to anticipate that the more extreme state labor legislation will be declared unconstitutional. {229}

Labor versus Civil Liberties

The Roosevelt Court's concern for the protection of labor and for the maintenance of civil liberties generally tend to re-enforce each other, as when labor's right to picket is assimilated into the larger problem of freedom of speech. But as labor, by use of its economic powers and under the auspices of favorable government policy, has developed in power and authority it has become a force capable of threatening economic and civil liberties if they stand in the way of the fulfillment of labor's objectives. When a conflict of this kind is presented to the Supreme Court in the form of a legal controversy, its justices face the necessity of deciding between two sets of values, both of which they hold in high regard.

Only a comparatively few cases have put this dilemma before the Court in clear-cut form. Particularly noteworthy are the problems which the N.L.R.B. faced, prior to the adoption of the Taft-Hartley Act, in determining the limits within which employers may use their rights of free speech to influence collective bargaining elections held in their plants. The Board took the position that speeches to employees or plant notices or statements in pay envelopes were not entitled to constitutional protection when they sought to influence employee opinion against unionism in general or unions in particular.

The principal Supreme Court expression of opinion on this question came in 1941, in a case where the Board had held that a bulletin issued by a power company and speeches made by its officials had "interfered with, restrained and coerced" the company's employees in the exercise of their organizing rights guaranteed by the statute.[37] In an opinion for a unanimous Court, Justice Murphy held that such a ruling was not necessarily contrary to the rights of free speech, for

> conduct, though evidenced in part by speech, may amount in con-
> nection with other circumstances to coercion within the meaning of
> the Act. If the total activities of an employer restrain or coerce his
> employees in their free choice, then those employees are entitled to
> the protection of the Act. And in determining whether a course of
> conduct amounts to restraint or coercion, pressure exerted vocally
> by {230} the employer may no more be disregarded than pressure
> exerted in other ways.

The Court was, however, in doubt as to whether, standing alone, the speeches and bulletins involved in this case really had a coercive character, and held that it would be necessary for the Board to base its findings of coercion upon the whole course of company conduct revealed by the record and to put these utterances into the background and setting of the entire situation. The case was consequently remanded to the Board, which made more elaborate findings, and when the matter came up for review the second time the Court had no difficulty in granting enforcement of the Board's order.[38]

Although the Supreme Court has subsequently given indirect indication of its position on this issue by refusing to review lower court decisions limiting employers' rights to attempt to influence employee voting, the only occasion on which the Court has directly amplified its views came in some verbal by-play in the *Thomas* v. *Collins* decision. Justice Jackson concurred in the ruling of that case to the effect that Thomas' rights to free speech had been denied by the Texas statute, but he regarded this holding as "applying to Thomas a rule the benefit of which in all its breadth and vigor this Court denies to employers in National Labor Relations Board cases. . . . However," he concluded, "the remedy is not to allow Texas improperly to deny the right of free speech but to apply the same rule and spirit to free speech cases whoever the speaker."

This allegation that the Court had one rule for labor and a second rule for employers was rebutted by Justice Douglas in another concurring opinion in the same case. He denied that there was any inconsistency in the Court's opinions, contending that both employer and employee had been equally protected in their unfettered right to "speak." The apparent differences in treatment had arisen when employers used their economic power "over other men and their jobs to influence their action." Such use of economic power, Douglas averred, is coercion, and whether utilized by employer or labor union, it is not entitled to the protection of the free speech clause. Here the Court would seem again to have grounded itself on a principle thoroughly sound but, like the picketing cases, requiring rather detailed {231} inquiry into factual situations and resulting in a further complication of the task of judicial review.

No such difficult problems have bothered the Court when confronted with labor unions guilty of racial discrimination. Two 1944 cases brought before the Court actions taken by the Brotherhood of Locomotive Firemen and Enginemen discriminating against Negro firemen.[39] This brotherhood, which excludes Negroes from membership, represents the majority of railroad employees in these classifications and thus, under the Railway Labor Act, has the status of exclusive bargaining agent with the railroads. A 1941 agreement between the railroads and the brotherhood, adopted without notice or opportunity to be heard to the Negro firemen, substantially restricted the employment of Negro firemen on the roads. The Supreme Court unanimously struck down this agreement, taking the position that the Railway Labor Act in conferring the power of representation on a union imposed an obligation to represent the entire membership of the craft. While the statute did not deny to unions the right to determine eligibility to membership, and thus opened the way to racial exclusion, it did require the union "in collective bargaining and in making contracts with the carrier, to represent non-union or minority union members of the craft without hostile discrimination, fairly impartially, and in good faith."

Later in the same term a related issue arose in the *Corsi* case, as the Railway Mail Association (an A. F. of L.-affiliated organization of railway mail postal clerks) sought to secure immunity from the section of the New York Civil Rights Law which forbids any labor organization in the state to deny any person membership or equal privileges because of race, color, or creed. This organization limited its membership to eligible postal clerks who were of the Caucasian race or native American Indians. The contentions it presented before the Supreme Court were that the statute denied due process and equal protection, and was repugnant to the constitutional grant of authority to Congress over postal matters. The Court was obviously somewhat startled by the audacity of a claim that the Fourteenth Amendment, "adopted to prevent state legislation designed to perpetuate discrimination on the basis of race or color," must be regarded as protecting {232} such discrimination, and it ruled unanimously and emphatically against the union on all of its claims.[40]

John L. Lewis and the Law of the Pendulum

The decision in *United States* v. *United Mine Workers of America,* which the Court handed down on March 6, 1947, was about as bitter a pill as a Court, generally sympathetic to labor and ardently believing in strict adherence to constitutional procedure in criminal cases, could have been called on to swallow. The government had taken possession of the nation's bituminous coal mines on May 21, 1946, to end a crippling coal strike. On May 29 an agreement was entered into between Secretary of the Interior Krug and John L. Lewis on wages and working conditions. The terms of the contract were to cover the period of government possession. In October, however, Lewis asserted that the contract was subject to termination under a provision of the National Bituminous Coal Wage Agreement of April 11, 1945, which he contended had been carried over into the government contract. In accordance with this interpretation Lewis informed Krug on November 15 that the contract would be terminated five days later, and circulated copies of his letter to union members. The letter was equivalent to a strike notice, since the U.M.W. traditionally does not work without a contract.

Krug, acting on an opinion of the Attorney General, notified Lewis that he had no power to terminate the contract by unilateral action. On November 18 the government brought suit in the district court of the District of Columbia under the declaratory judgment act, seeking a judgment that Lewis had no power to terminate the agreement, and requesting a temporary restraining order and preliminary injunctive relief against Lewis' strike call. A temporary order to that effect was issued the same day, but a full-fledged strike was on by the 20th. On November 27 trial of Lewis and the union for contempt of court was begun. The case was heard without a jury, and on December 4 the court entered judgment, fining Lewis $10,000 and the union $3,500,000, and issuing a temporary injunction in terms similar to the restraining order. On December 7 Lewis announced that the strike {233} would be called off so that the

Supreme Court could review the decision free from the atmosphere of hysteria engendered by the strike. The Court's decision was announced almost three months later.

In deciding against the union and Lewis, the Court majority found it necessary to accept the following doctrines. First, the Court was required to hold that the Norris-LaGuardia Act with its limitation on the issuance of labor injunctions was not binding upon the government as an employer. Only five justices would adopt this view—Vinson, Reed, Burton, Black, and Douglas. They grounded their argument on the language of the statute, its legislative history, and the general rule that statutes which in general terms divest pre-existing rights or privileges will not be applied to the sovereign without express words to that effect. Justice Frankfurter, who reputedly wrote the Norris-LaGuardia Act, was convinced, on the other hand, that Congress was not even thinking of such a situation as temporary government seizure of a private industry when it adopted the act, and he charged that the Court was now legislating by "interpolating" an exemption for the government from the statutory terms.

Second, the same five-judge majority affirmed that the government by "seizing" the coal mines had become the actual proprietor of them, and that the miners had become government employees. To support this position they pointed out that the government had actually substituted itself for the private owners in negotiating the Lewis-Krug agreement on wages and working conditions, matters which normally constitute the subject matter of collective bargaining between employer and employees, and that the union had recognized this status by entering into the agreement. They had, however, to overlook the fact that the government did not share in either the earnings or the liabilities of the seized mines, and that the private owners continued to be liable for all taxes and subject to suit. Justice Murphy said: "In my opinion, the miners remained private employees despite the temporary gloss of Government possession and operation of the mines."

Third, the Court majority had to find a way around certain difficulties raised by the legislative history of the War Labor Disputes Act of 1943, better known as the Smith-Connally Act, under authority {234} of which the mines were seized. In the course of adopting that statute the Senate considered what remedies the government should be given against interference with its operation of seized plants. Remedy by injunction was specifically considered, but was finally omitted from the bill. The House adopted the Senate version of the legislation on this point. Frankfurter summarized: "The whole course of legislation indicates that Congress withheld the remedy of injunction. This Court now holds that Congress authorized the injunction." Jackson apparently joined the majority on this issue, making the vote here 6 to 3.

Fourth, the Court majority had to hold that Lewis and his union were rightly convicted of criminal contempt for ignoring the temporary restraining order of November 18, even if the Court had no authority to issue an injunction under the law. The restraining order was issued two days before the strike call was to go into effect. By its issuance the district court was attempting to preserve existing conditions while it was determining its own authority to grant injunctive relief. The defendants, in making their private determination of the law, acted at their peril. Their disobedience is punishable as criminal contempt.

There was more unanimity on this ruling than on any other aspect of the case, seven justices supporting it. Frankfurter, who thought the district court had no power to issue an injunction, nevertheless voted to sustain the conviction for criminal contempt

> upon the broad ground of vindicating the process of law. . . . Only where a court is so obviously traveling outside its orbit as to be merely usurping judicial forms and facilities, may an order issued by a court be disobeyed and treated as though it were a letter to a newspaper. . . . The greater the power that defies law the less tolerant can this Court be of defiance.

Black and Douglas likewise agreed, though they felt there were some extenuating circumstances. The defendants, they said, "appear to have believed in good faith, though erroneously, that they were acting within their legal rights. Many lawyers would have so advised them." But they quickly added: "This does not excuse their conduct." {235}

Justices Rutledge and Murphy were the dissenters on this point. Rutledge contended that if a court can, in any proceeding not obviously frivolous, enter restraining orders pending determination of its jurisdiction to act, and can punish violations of those orders as criminal contempt even if it turns out that the court was acting outside its jurisdiction, then a device has been discovered for enormously expanding the powers of the courts. In this case, Lewis ran the risk of being found guilty of contempt if the order was valid, but Rutledge did not think he should have been required to assume that risk even if the order was void.

Fifth, the Court was faced with the fact that the district court had violated one of the Rules of Criminal Procedure by failing, in the notice issuing to the defendants, to describe the alleged contempt as "criminal." The Court by a 7 to 2 vote held this failure was not prejudicial error, since the defendants were in fact aware that a criminal contempt was charged, and enjoyed during the trial all the enhanced protections accorded defendants in criminal contempt proceedings. Rutledge and Murphy, on the other hand, contended that this failure to give proper notice violated the Sixth Amendment.

Sixth, the Court had to overlook the maladroitness of the district judge who had tried Lewis and the union for both civil and criminal contempt in the same proceeding. The Court admitted that it would be better practice to try criminal contempts alone, so as to "avoid obscuring the defendant's privileges in any manner," but declared that the mingling of the two was not reversible error unless "substantial prejudice" was shown. Here, all the defendants' rights and privileges were held to have been fully, protected. Only Rutledge and Murphy objected to this ruling, but they did so vehemently. Rutledge said:

> In any other context than one of contempt, the idea that a criminal prosecution and a civil suit for damages or equitable relief could be hashed together in a single criminal-civil hodgepodge would be shocking to every American lawyer and to most citizens.

He was convinced that even in contempt cases such an "admixture of civil and criminal proceedings" was not constitutional.

Seventh, the Court had to consider the fines of $10,000 on Lewis {236} and $3,500,000 on the union imposed by the district judge. Not only was the latter fine an extraordinarily large one, but both fines were assessed in lump sums, with no indication as to how much was levied for damages, how much for punishment, and how much for civil coercion. The majority of the Court decided to treat Lewis' fine solely as a criminal penalty, which they held not excessive when consideration was taken "of the willful and deliberate defiance of the court's order, the seriousness of the consequences of the contumacious behavior, the necessity of effectively terminating the defendant's defiance as required by the public interest, and the importance of deterring such acts in the future."

The union's composite fine of $3,500,000 was adjudged excessive by the Court, and it was replaced by a flat criminal fine of $700,000, plus a contingent penalty of $2,800,000 for coercion, with any award for civil damages apparently eliminated.

These decisions as to the fines were approved by only a 5 to 4 vote, with Black, Douglas, Murphy, and Rutledge dissenting. As for Lewis' fine, they pointed out that if he had been criminally prosecuted for interfering with operation of a government-seized plant under the Smith-Connally Act, the maximum fine permitted would have been $5,000. (He could also have been imprisoned for one year.) They argued that courts should observe congressional standards in assessing fines for contempt. Black and Douglas proposed that Lewis' fine not be treated as criminal punishment, but that it be made a coercive civil sanction, payable only if he continued to disobey the court order. They favored the same treatment for the union fine, the entire $3,500,000 of which they would treat as contingent. Only on this basis would they consider the two fines as not excessive. Rutledge and Murphy were somewhat more forceful, holding the $700,000 criminal fine "constitutionally excessive, far beyond any heretofore sustained for violation of any statute or order of court, [and] an unlawful commingling of civil coercive and criminal penalties. . . ."

Two swallows do not make a summer, but a second important anti-labor decision only three months after the Lewis judgment was handed down certainly supplies material for "trend spotters" (to use Sam Grafton's phrase). This latter case, *U.S.* v. *Petrillo,* involved the {237} so-called "anti-Petrillo" act passed by Congress in 1946, making it unlawful to compel a radio broadcasting station to employ in its business "any person or persons in excess of the number of employees needed . . . to perforin actual services. . . ." The statute was of course aimed at certain notorious make-work practices of the musicians' union.

The district judge before whom the Petrillo prosecution was brought obviously felt that he was getting in step with the Supreme Court's recent civil liberties decisions by dismissing the case on the ground that the statute was unconstitutional. It was, he said, too vague and indefinite to meet the standards required of a criminal statute, it denied equal protection of the laws by singling out radio stations for regulation, it abridged freedom of speech, and it constituted the establishment of involuntary servitude contrary to the Thirteenth Amendment.

The Supreme Court, however, by a 5 to 3 vote (Douglas not participating), with none other than Justice Black writing the opinion, reversed the district court and sent the case back for trial. The Court held that the statute was not too vague, and did not deny equal protection. As for the free speech and involuntary servitude points, the Court ruled the statute to be unobjectionable on its face, but pointed out that trial of the case might disclose that the statute had been employed in such a way as to bring about an unconstitutional result. The dissenters—Reed, Murphy, and Rutledge—objected to the vagueness with which this statute defined criminal acts.

* * *

While the standard equipment for the symbol of Justice is a blindfold and a pair of scales, it might not be inappropriate to add a pendulum, for the law of its swing is apparent in judicial decisions as in other human affairs. When power changes hands, it is difficult for the new holders merely to redress the balance. Usually the remedial action goes so far as to set up an imbalance in the other direction. Thus the Roosevelt Court, in its concern for wiping out the old inequities under which labor suffered, developed in some areas doctrines which threatened to vest labor unions "with the worst curse {238} of modern times—too much economic power over others." Justice Jackson was making such a charge in his dissent to *Hunt* v. *Crumboch,* and his words may stand as an arresting epitaph over the Court's struggles to evolve a rightful rule for labor:

> With this decision, the labor movement has come full circle. The working man has struggled long, the fight has been filled with hatred, and conflict has been dangerous, but now workers may not be deprived of their livelihood merely because their employers oppose and they favor unions. Labor has won other rights as well, unemployment compensation, old-age benefits and, what is most important and the basis of all its gains, the recognition that the opportunity to earn his support is not alone the concern of the individual but is the problem which all organized societies must contend with and conquer if they are to survive. This Court now sustains the claim

of a union to the right to deny participation in the economic world to an employer simply because the union dislikes him. This Court permits to employees the same arbitrary dominance over the economic sphere which they control that labor so long, so bitterly and so rightly asserted should belong to no man.

Now the pendulum is swinging back again, and the Roosevelt Court must reconsider its policy. It may decelerate the backward swing by declaring unconstitutional some of the more extreme provisions of the Taft-Hartley Act and other anti-labor legislation, but that it will be pulled along in the direction of the election returns has already been demonstrated by the *Lewis* and *Petrillo* cases.

CHAPTER NINE

Alignments and Issues

IN No. 78 of the Federalist papers, Alexander Hamilton wrote:

> "To avoid an arbitrary discretion in the courts, it is indispensable that they should be bound down by strict rules and precedents, which serve to define and point out their duty in every particular case that comes before them."

If this view of the judge as automaton and of the judicial process as a ministerial function involving nothing more than the applying of agreed-upon rules and precedents to individual situations were accurate, there would be no need to examine into the question of judicial alignments and motivation. It is true that for subordinate tribunals, in stable times, and in settled fields of law, the Hamiltonian statement is not too far wide of the mark. But for a supreme court, operating in times of crisis, whose grist is almost entirely the hard cases, the difficult problems, the fields where new legislation needs interpretation, the areas of the law where precedents conflict or are nonexistent—on such a court decisions must inevitably reflect the values of the justices who make them. To paraphrase Justice Frankfurter, judges of necessity read the laws of Congress through the distorting lenses ground by their own experience.

For the discovery of the personal factors affecting judicial decisions there are available, aside from autobiographical data and clues from {240} the public life of the justices prior to their judicial appointment, only the materials furnished by the published opinions of the Court. Many of these opinions are valueless as guides to an understanding of judicial motivation. As a rule unanimous decisions fall in this category. The fact that all the members of the Court agree in the disposition of the case may mean that the issue involved is one on which the law is so clear and peremptory that any exercise of judicial discretion, guided by an individual set of values, is completely foreclosed. On the other hand, the area may be one where reasonable men could have come to divergent conclusions, but the judges did not do so in the particular case because their respective values were so similar as to lead them all to the same answer.

It is, consequently, only where the Court's decision is not unanimous that there is genuine assurance that the result was influenced by judicial preferences as to public policy. For here we see judges, working with an identical set of facts, and with roughly comparable training in the law, coming to different conclusions. These divisions furnish data which are more tangible than ordinary judicial verbalizations, and afford opportunities for analysis that goes beyond the characteristic lawyers' processes of interpretation, comparison, search for inconsistencies, and general legal exegesis. They supply the concrete data of a series of yes and no votes on a variety of issues. The sharp increase in the number of dissenting opinions since 1941 has given an unparalleled opportunity for this approach to a study of the motivations of Supreme Court justices.

The Alignments

In this book two relatively novel approaches have been developed for utilizing the data of these nonunanimous decisions. The first was the method employed in Chapter II for charting alignments revealed in the dissenting opinions filed by the Court's members. That series of charts showed the number of times the various justices dissented in company with each of their colleagues during the recent terms of the Court. On the basis of those charts certain conclusions were drawn as to the existence of blocs of judicial opinion and changes {241} of affiliation over a period of time by the individual justices. The existence of well-defined groups, referred to as left wing and right wing, was clearly evident during the earlier part of the period, but after 1941 a marked decline was apparent in the cohesiveness of the judicial bloc on the right, and later in that on the left.

Another way of developing term-by-term information on the affiliations of the justices is by reducing the data on agreements and disagreements among the justices to a percentage basis for tabular presentation. In Chapter II only the agreements in dissenting opinions were shown. In the series of tables presented in this chapter, account is taken of the agreements of every pair of justices, whether on the majority or minority side, in every nonunanimous opinion in which both participated. For example, during the 1944 term Justices Douglas and Frankfurter were both participants in 90 of the 98 divisions of opinion in Court decisions. In 47 of these they were on the same side, while in the other 43 they were in disagreement. Thus the rate of agreement between them was 52 per cent. The same data are given for every other pair of justices in every term covered.

Examination of these tables reveals a situation of shifting alignments and progressive deterioration of judicial blocs similar to the one demonstrated in Chapter II, but it is here shown somewhat more precisely and comprehensively. The combined data for the five terms from 1931 through 1935 in Table XXII indicate a pattern of division which is characterized by clearly defined blocs on both the left and the right of the Court. In this five-year period Justices

Stone, Cardozo, and Brandeis had rates of agreement with one another ranging from 79 to 89 per cent in the nonunanimous decisions, while the four-judge group on the right had internal agreement ratios of from 75 to 93 per cent. The span separating left from right is evident from the fact that Stone agreed with Butler in only 20 per cent of the nonunanimous decisions.

During this five-year period the center of the Court was composed of Hughes and Roberts. They had their highest rates of agreement with each other and with the more moderate left- and right-wing justices, their curves dropping off noticeably toward the two extremes of the Court. It is character-istic of center justices that they have neither very {248} high nor very low rates of agreement with their colleagues on either side of the Court. Hughes' range was from 54 to 77 per cent, while Roberts, who was skewed a little more to the right, had a low of 42 per cent and a high of 78 per cent. These figures compare with Stone's range from 20 to 89 per cent.

TABLE XXII

AGREEMENTS AMONG SUPREME COURT JUSTICES IN NONUNANIMOUS OPINIONS, 1931-1946 TERMS (In Percentages)

1931-1935 Terms*

	Stone	Cardozo	Brandeis	Hughes	Roberts	Van Devanter	Sutherland	Butler	McReynolds	Range
Stone	—	89	83	54	43	33	29	20	22	69
Cardozo	89	—	79	59	42	36	31	21	26	68
Brandeis	83	79	—	60	55	41	39	31	30	53
Hughes	54	59	60	—	77	77	71	60	62	23
Roberts	43	42	55	77	—	74	78	71	67	36
VanDevanter	33	36	41	77	74	—	93	82	79	60
Sutherland	29	31	39	71	78	93	—	87	78	64
Butler	20	21	31	60	71	82	87	—	75	67
McReynolds	22	26	30	62	67	79	78	75	—	57

* Justice Holmes, who served part of the 1931 term, is excluded from the table.

1936 Term

	Cardozo	Stone	Brandeis	Hughes	Roberts	Van Devanter	Sutherland	Butler	McReynolds	Range
Cardozo	—	100	90	84	71	40	32	26	13	87
Stone	100	—	91	91	78	39	35	26	17	83
Brandeis	90	91	—	83	83	45	37	30	17	74
Hughes	84	91	83	—	81	57	48	42	29	62
Roberts	71	78	83	81	—	50	42	35	23	60
VanDevanter	40	39	45	57	50	—	93	87	73	54
Sutherland	32	35	37	48	42	93	—	87	74	61
Butler	26	26	30	42	35	87	87	—	87	61
McReynolds	13	17	17	29	23	73	74	87	—	74

1937 Term*

	Black	Cardozo	Stone	Brandeis	Hughes	Roberts	Butler	Sutherland	McReyn-olds	Range
Black	—	88	68	70	67	64	17	20	9	79
Cardozo	88	—	100	81	75	60	13	8	6	94
Stone	68	100	—	91	89	83	41	15	27	85
Brandeis	70	81	91	—	98	93	50	33	37	65
Hughes	67	75	89	98	—	95	52	40	39	59
Roberts	64	60	83	93	95	—	57	57	43	52
Butler	17	13	41	50	52	57	—	80	83	70
Sutherland	20	8	15	33	40	57	80	—	100	92
McReynolds	9	6	27	37	39	43	83	100	—	94

* Justice Reed, appointed during the term after Sutherland's resignation, is excluded from the table.

1938 Term*

	Black	Douglas	Frankfurter	Reed	Stone	Hughes	Roberts	Butler	McReyn-olds	Range
Black	—	100	100	77	67	56	45	6	0	100
Douglas	100	—	100	82	73	42	50	9	0	100
Frankfurter	100	100	—	85	79	62	57	5	0	100
Reed	77	82	85	—	83	77	64	26	21	65
Stone	67	73	79	83	—	90	62	35	30	65
Hughes	56	42	62	77	90	—	73	45	41	59
Roberts	45	50	57	64	62	73	—	56	53	28
Butler	6	9	5	26	35	45	56	—	94	88
McReynolds	0	0	0	21	30	41	53	94	—	94

* Justice Brandeis, who resigned during the term, is excluded from the table.

1939 Term*

	Black	Douglas	Murphy	Frankfurter	Reed	Stone	Hughes	Roberts	McReyn-olds	Range
Black	—	100	100	95	87	81	56	36	8	92
Douglas	100	—	100	95	87	80	58	37	8	92
Murphy	100	100	—	95	90	75	55	45	11	89
Frankfurter	95	95	95	—	92	86	61	40	13	82
Reed	87	87	90	92	—	87	66	44	17	73
Stone	81	80	75	86	87	—	71	50	21	66
Hughes	56	58	55	61	66	71	—	80	50	30
Roberts	36	37	45	40	44	50	80	—	64	44
McReynolds	8	8	11	13	17	21	50	64	—	56

1940 Term

	Black	Douglas	Murphy	Frankfurter	Reed	Stone	McReynolds	Hughes	Roberts	Range
Black	—	100	84	72	67	56	32	20	11	89
Douglas	100	—	84	72	67	55	32	18	12	88
Murphy	84	84	—	86	70	76	47	36	20	66
Frankfurter	72	72	86	—	82	80	42	42	25	61
Reed	67	67	70	82	—	70	53	41	26	56
Stone	56	55	76	80	70	—	58	65	29	51
McReynolds	32	32	47	42	53	58	—	94	56	62
Hughes	20	18	36	42	41	65	94	—	67	76
Roberts	11	12	20	25	26	29	56	67	—	56

1941 Term*

	Douglas	Black	Murphy	Reed	Byrnes	Jackson	Frankfurter	Stone	Roberts	Range
Douglas	—	95	72	54	53	42	34	23	23	72
Black	95	—	78	56	61	45	36	25	14	71
Murphy	72	78	—	58	59	48	53	48	34	44
Reed	54	56	58	—	57	65	61	54	54	11
Byrnes	53	62	59	57	—	68	69	61	57	16
Jackson	42	45	48	65	68	—	64	53	60	26
Frankfurter	34	36	53	61	69	64	—	70	53	36
Stone	23	25	48	54	61	53	70	—	70	47
Roberts	23	24	34	54	57	60	53	70	—	47

1942 Term

	Black	Douglas	Murphy	Rutledge	Stone	Reed	Jackson	Frankfurter	Roberts	Range
Black	—	93	73	84	50	50	46	41	27	66
Douglas	93	—	77	87	51	50	47	46	29	64
Murphy	73	77	—	76	48	42	47	42	29	48
Rutledge	84	87	76	—	55	55	63	55	33	54
Stone	50	51	48	55	—	68	67	68	62	20
Reed	50	50	42	55	68	—	70	76	62	34
Jackson	46	47	47	63	67	70	—	64	57	24
Frankfurter	41	46	42	55	68	76	64	—	65	35
Roberts	27	29	29	33	62	62	57	65	—	38

1943 Term*

	Douglas	Black	Murphy	Rutledge	Jackson	Reed	Stone	Frankfurter	Roberts	Range
Douglas	—	86	79	72	56	56	55	47	24	62
Black	86	—	76	74	57	58	58	50	27	59
Murphy	79	76	—	81	49	53	58	49	34	47
Rutledge	72	74	81	—	59	63	62	52	40	41
Jackson	56	57	49	59	—	64	55	71	46	25
Reed	56	58	53	63	64	—	78	73	50	28
Stone	55	58	58	62	55	78	—	70	49	29
Frankfurter	47	50	49	52	71	73	70	—	62	26
Roberts	24	27	34	40	46	50	49	62	—	38

1944 Term

	Black	Douglas	Rutledge	Murphy	Reed	Jackson	Frankfurter	Stone	Roberts	Range
Black	—	79	78	74	62	53	47	41	9	70
Douglas	79	—	78	74	70	57	52	52	20	59
Rutledge	78	78	—	79	63	62	56	47	20	58
Murphy	74	74	79	—	64	57	54	46	25	54
Reed	62	70	63	64	—	64	67	72	41	31
Jackson	53	57	62	57	64	—	75	67	45	30
Frankfurter	47	52	56	54	67	75	—	74	61	28
Stone	41	52	47	46	72	67	74	—	61	33
Roberts	9	20	20	25	41	45	61	61	—	52

1945 Term

	Douglas	Black	Murphy	Rutledge	Reed	Burton	Stone	Frankfurter	Range
Douglas	—	71	62	56.	54	49	42	45	29
Black	71	—	67	59	61	57	47	43	28
Murphy	62	67	—	73	63	56	60	52	21
Rutledge	56	59	73	—	54	45	49	61	28
Reed	54	61	63	54	—	68	80	57	26
Burton	49	57	56	45	68	—	78	57	33
Stone	42	47	60	49	80	78	—	65	38
Frankfurter	45	43	52	61	57	57	65	—	22

1946 Term

	Rutledge	Murphy	Black	Douglas	Reed	Burton	Vinson	Jackson	Frankfurter	Range
Rutledge	—	77	72	55	48	46	42	34	34	43
Murphy	77	—	81	71	45	42	49	37	35	46
Black	72	81	—	68	54	53	56	40	35	46
Douglas	55	71	68	—	56	55	57	39	40	32
Reed	48	45	54	56	—	75	69	65	59	30
Burton	46	42	53	55	75	—	75	62	62	33
Vinson	42	49	56	57	69	75	—	68	68	33
Jackson	34	37	40	39	65	62	68	—	71	37
Frankfurter	34	35	35	40	59	62	68	71	—	37

These data suggest the possibility of using the range between high and low agreement rates as an index to moderation or extremism in judicial attitudes. The limits within which the range may vary for individual justices are 100 to zero. The former figure would evidence extreme opposing attitudes on the Court, for a justice with such a range would agree in every one of the nonunanimous opinions with one or more of his colleagues, and disagree in every instance with others of his colleagues. A range of zero, on the other hand, could be attained only by a justice who was a kind of common denominator for his brethren, agreeing and disagreeing with all of them an equal number of times. Broad ranges are characteristic of the justices on the two extremes of the Court, and narrow ranges mark the center justices. During the 1931-35 period, Stone on the left had a range of 69, Hughes' range in the center was 23, while Butler's on the right was 67.

The data for the 1931-35 terms can be presented somewhat more graphically by putting them on a chart, as is done in Chart A. Three types of curves are evident on the chart, demonstrating the three general divisions on the Court. For the three justices on the left the curve approximates a straight line, descending sharply from left to right. For the four right-wing justices the profile is reversed, with a tendency for the curves to flatten out as they approach the right of the chart. For the two center justices the curve is a parabola, ascending from the left to the center and then dropping off again to the right. Within each of these three categories the curves of the individual justices indicate relative degrees of location to the left or right of center.

For a single mathematical expression of the extent of the differences on the Court during a particular period, the *average of the range* of each justice's agreement relationships with his colleagues furnishes an acceptable measure. If the members of the Court were divided into {249} two perfect blocs in their nonunanimous decisions, each judge agreeing with colleagues in his own bloc all the time and never agreeing with those in the other bloc, then every justice would have a range of 100, and the average range would of course be 100. At the other extreme, if every judge agreed with every other judge in half of the nonunanimous decisions, all agreement rates would be 50 per cent and the average range would be zero. For any particular period, then, the average range could be taken as a measure of the presence or absence of separate well-defined blocs of opinion on the Court. For the 1931-35 period, the average range was 55, indicating only a moderately well-developed system of alignments. The figure is held down by the two center justices, who managed to maintain fairly close relations with each wing.

It is not necessary to comment in similar detail on the record of alignments revealed in the terms from 1936 through 1946, but at least the highlights should be noted. In the 1936 term, when the Court's conversion to the New Deal was accomplished, Hughes and to a lesser extent Roberts became practically full-fledged adherents of the Court's left wing, thus giving it control of the situation. The four right-wing justices maintained a high degree of solidarity, their internal rates of agreement ranging from 73 to 93 per cent. This tightening of the battle lines resulted in increasing the average range from 55 (for the 1931-35 period) to 68.

When Black joined the Court for the 1937 term, he was too far to the left for any of the other justices except Cardozo, and the more moderate left-wing members merged with the center to form a compact five-judge group (Reed, Stone, Brandeis, Hughes, and Roberts) in which the agreement relationships were quite high, from 82 to 98 per cent. The average range continued to climb, reaching 75 for this term.

The 1938 term saw Frankfurter and Douglas coming onto the Court and coalescing with Black into a new left-wing alignment marked by complete and unprecedented unanimity during the entire term. The center was now composed of Reed, Stone, Brandeis, and Hughes, whose inter-agreements ranged from 77 to 100 per cent. Roberts was on the right fringe of this center group, and the right {251} wing was reduced to Butler and McReynolds, who clung together faithfully in 94 per cent agreement. With this lineup, the Court developed its clearest alignment into opposing groups, with an average range of 76.

In 1939 Murphy was added to the Court's very solid left, as Reed and Stone also fell back toward the left and away from Hughes, who was deviating rightward along with Roberts. But 1940 saw considerable disintegration on the left. Black and Douglas remained in perfect harmony, but Murphy was with them only 84 per cent of the time, and Frankfurter was definitely drifting over to the center with Reed and Stone. The average range for 1939 dropped to 69, and for 1940 to 67.

CHART A

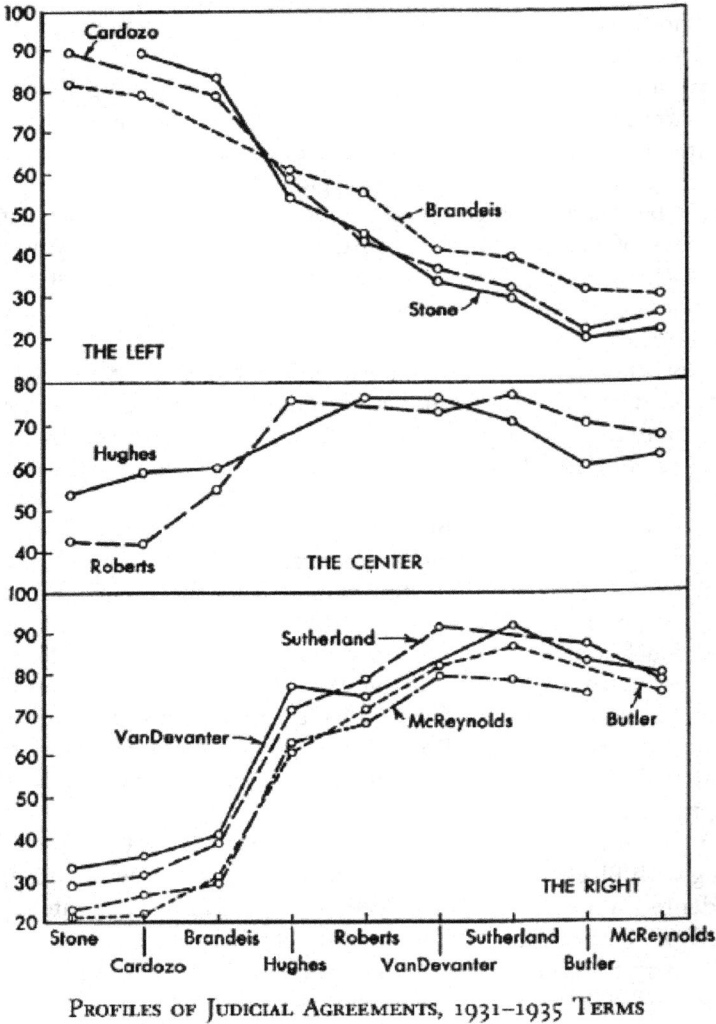

PROFILES OF JUDICIAL AGREEMENTS, 1931–1935 TERMS

In 1941 divisive forces of some kind hit the Court in full force. Black and Douglas split for the first time, and Murphy departed from their bloc in about one-fourth of the nonunanimous cases. No other pair on the Court could muster more than a 70 per cent rate of agreement, and there was no particular cohesiveness to be found either in the center or the right of the Court. The average range for 1941 suffered a drastic slump to 41, evidencing the progressive breakdown of bloc alignments. Much the same condition prevailed during the 1942 term, though Rutledge did associate himself closely with Black and Douglas in his first Court term, and the average range increased slightly to 43.

In the sessions since 1942 there have been two principal developments. One is the continued disintegration of the left wing, though it still remains as the only substantially well-defined bloc of opinion on the Court. The agreement relationships between Black and Douglas have steadily declined—from 100 per cent in the 1938-40 terms to 95 in 1941, 93 in 1942, 86 in 1943, 79 in 1944, 71 in 1945, and 68 in 1946. The two other members of the left, Rutledge and Murphy, have certain very marked affinities, but their rate of agreement for 1946 was no higher than 77 per cent. The inter-agreements for the four left-wing justices in 1946 varied from 55 to 81 per cent, as compared with 1942, when the same four justices agreed 73 to 93 per cent of the time.

The second marked trend has been the progressive disappearance of {252} extremes of agreement and disagreement among the justices. With the comparative dissolution of well-defined left- and right-wing groups, all the justices have more in common with colleagues on the other side of the Court, and less in common with members of their own wing, than was previously the case. In the 1939 term, Black's agreements varied from 100 per cent with Douglas to 8 per cent with McReynolds, a range of 92. But by the 1945 term Black's range had dropped to 28, his agreements varying from 71 per cent with Douglas to 43 per cent with Frankfurter. It is worthwhile to chart the inter-relationships for the 1945 term in the same fashion as was done for the 1931-35 terms, to demonstrate how the profiles of judicial agreement have flattened out and lost much of their certainty of direction. This is done in Chart B. {253}

CHART B

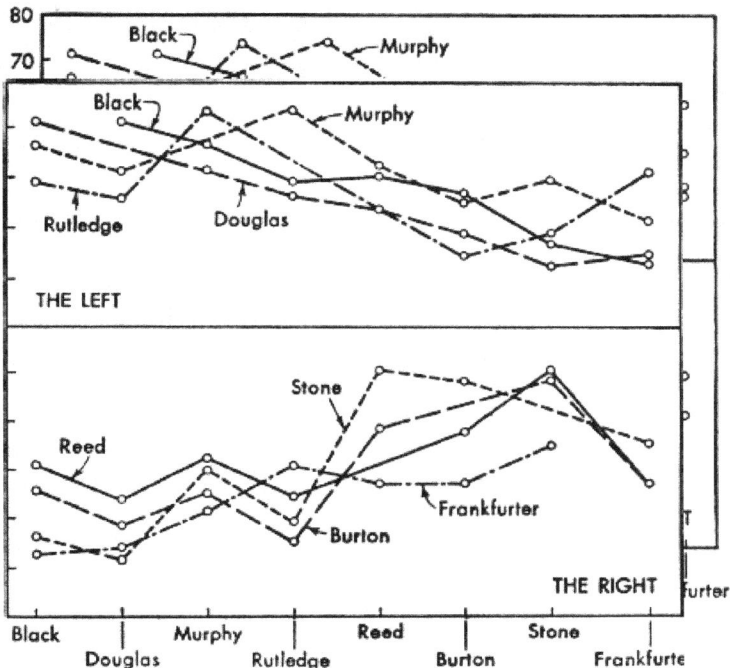

The Issues

These tables and charts reveal judicial alignments, blocs, protagonists and antagonists, and in general the structure of agreement and disagreement on the Court. They ignore, however, the ideational content of the Court's work, the issues out of which judicial conflicts are engendered. They do not throw any light upon the values in terms of which the justices have been making their decisions, nor do they afford any explanation of judicial motivation.

Chapters IV through VIII have supplied some material of the sort needed for this fuller understanding of the Court. In those chapters the decisions rendered, particularly since the 1941 term, in five general subject matter areas have been discussed, and judicial alignments noted. A large amount of the disagreement on the Court during this period was registered in cases falling in those categories. During the six terms from 1941 through 1946, 477 nonunanimous decisions were handed down, and of this number 273 (57 per cent) involved issues relating to civil liberties, rights of criminal defendants, state economic regulation and taxation, federal economic regulation, or labor. The first two of these categories are related, in that both deal with fundamental problems of personal liberty; the latter three all have a common economic matrix.

In every nonunanimous decision involving one of these problems it is possible to divide the participating justices into two groups—those more favorable and those less favorable toward the policy, interest, or value which was the subject of controversy. By this process the attitudes of the justices can be determined only relatively—that is, in relation to other members of the Court sitting in the same case, not absolutely in terms of position on an opinion scale. Two justices may both be "liberals" on a particular issue, and the difference between them may simply be that one is prepared to go a little farther than the other in promoting his views. However, if this difference is sufficient to cause the two justices to vote differently in a judicial decision, then a divergence in judicial attitudes has been demonstrated which is a significant clue as to their attachments to the particular value involved. {254}

Table XXIII uses this approach in analyzing the voting record of the justices in personal liberty decisions for the six terms since 1941. The resulting pattern of division is clear. The four justices in the left wing, whose votes favorable to personal liberty claims range from Murphy's 94 per cent to Douglas' 63 per cent, are all well above the position taken by the Court majority in these 82 cases, which was only 49 per cent favorable. The votes of the seven justices on the right all fall below the majority position, ranging from Stone's 43 per cent to Vinson's zero. As pointed out in an earlier chapter, the generally close correspondence between the positions of individual justices on the two types of personal liberty issues (columns 1 and 2) indicates that the two categories of cases have been decided within the framework of the same set of values. In the case of only two justices, Rutledge and Frankfurter, is there a substantial variation in degree of support for the two types of liberties.

TABLE XXIII

ALIGNMENTS OF JUSTICES IN NONUNANIMOUS PERSONAL LIBERTY DECISIONS,
1941-1946 TERMS

	Pro Civil Libs. (1)	Pro Crim. Defs. (2)	Fed. Civil Libs. (3)	State Civil Libs. (4)	Fed. Crim. Defs. (5)	State Crim. Defs. (6)	Total Personal Liberties (7)
No. CASES	31	51	15	16	33	18	82
Majority	61%	41%	53%	69%	48%	28%	49%
Murphy	100	90	100	100	88	94	94
Rutledge	71	90	64	79	88	93	83
Black	68	65	47	87	55	83	66
Douglas	65	63	33	94	55	78	63
Stone	42	44	25	58	45	42	43
Frankfurter	26	39	20	31	55	11	34
Jackson	33	28	50	25	40	18	30
Roberts	32	27	67	0	47	0	29
Reed	29	27	27	31	30	22	28
Burton	17	16	17	17	17	14	16
Vinson	0	0	0	0	0	0	0

It may be objected that merely because justices disagree in disposing of a case presenting a personal liberty issue is no proof that their disagreement is actually grounded in a difference of attitudes on that {255} issue. It is a rare controversy in which two or more issues are not imbedded. As McCune says:

> Each case is a wheel within other wheels. The Court accepts for decision mostly those cases that are not clear cut; it seldom gets a crack at a simple one. One principle seldom disposes of a case; others cut across it sharply, touch it at angles or impinge on it with a broad sweep.[1]

Take, for example, the *Girouard* decision where the majority of the Court overruled several previous rulings and approved naturalization of a conscientious objector. In this case Chief Justice Stone dissented from the very position he had subscribed to fifteen years earlier. His explanation was, not that his zeal for civil liberties had diminished or was less than that of the current Court majority, but that in his opinion Congress had, by failing to amend the naturalization act, ratified the earlier Court view of which he had disapproved. It thus appeared that it was Stone's greater deference to congressional action (or inaction) that led him to a conclusion opposed to the strong civil liberties view of the Court majority.

Nevertheless, it does not follow that the *Girouard* case tells us nothing about the strength of Stone's attachment to civil liberties. For the members of the *Girouard* majority were also aware of the same claims for legislative deference to which Stone yielded, but their concern for civil liberty was strong

197

enough to override them. The percentage ratings in Table XXIII can thus be taken as a reliable index of judicial attitudes, in the sense that they measure the tenacity with which the justices have upheld the libertarian position against the claims of competing values.

One method of bringing out the presence of these competing values in personal liberty cases is to divide the controversies according to whether they involve state or federal action. When this is done for the civil liberties cases (columns 3 and 4), it becomes apparent that Douglas and Black were much more positive libertarians in state than in federal cases. Their lower vote in federal cases was due partly to their refusal to believe that application of the Sherman Act and the Fair Labor Standards Act to the press was a threat to freedom. Also in the {256} seven wartime liberty cases (involving treason prosecution, Japanese evacuation, and denaturalization or other penalties for Nazi sympathizers), Douglas supported the government in every instance, while Black did so in five. Stone likewise was markedly more positive toward civil liberties in state cases, largely because of his support for the claims of Jehovah's Witnesses. Roberts had a curious record, the only liberties he considered worthy of protection being those of evacuated Japanese, indicted Nazis and Nazi sympathizers, and the Associated Press.

A similar division between state and federal cases involving procedural rights in criminal prosecutions is made in columns 5 and 6 of Table XXIII. Here the most interesting disclosure is Frankfurter's and (to a lesser degree) Jackson's higher standards for federal than for state prosecutions, while the reverse tendency appears to operate in the case of Black and Douglas. Obviously, the desirability of states retaining control of their own standards of criminal prosecution is a value which Frankfurter rates considerably higher than do Black and Douglas. When federal cases only are considered, it is noteworthy that all three of these justices have the same percentage records, and in some instances Frankfurter exhibits more concern over protection of procedural rights than Black and Douglas, as in the recent search and seizure cases.

Alignments in 191 nonunanimous decisions concerned with economic issues decided since 1941 are analyzed in Table XXIV. In addition to the cases discussed in Chapters IV, VII and VIII, nonunanimous decisions in anti-monopoly cases, involving the Sherman Act and related federal legislation or the patent laws, have been included in this table because of their obvious relevance. The importance of these economic cases to an understanding of the Court's divisions is evident from the fact that they constitute 40 per cent of all the nonunanimous decisions handed down since 1941.

It is a striking fact that on all these economic issues the four left-wing justices take a position more positive than the majority view of the Court, while with few exceptions the other seven justices fall below the Court average. The division is clearest in the labor and antimonopoly cases, operates with only one exception in attitudes against the I.C.C. (Roberts), and with only two exceptions (for the Court's {257} two newcomers) in the other federal regulatory cases. The lineup on state regulatory and tax cases is a little more jumbled, because they present not only economic issues but also the broad constitutional question of federal judicial control over state legislative policies. The {258} fact that Frankfurter and Stone depart from the right-wing position they maintain on other economic issues can be attributed to their adherence to the Holmesian doctrine that the Fourteenth Amendment should not be used to hobble state legislative decisions.

TABLE XXIV

ALIGNMENTS OF JUSTICES IN NONUNANIMOUS ECONOMIC DECISIONS,
1941-1946 TERMS

	Pro Fed. Reg.*	Anti I.C.C.	Pro Labor	Anti Monopoly	Pro State Reg.	Total Economic Cases
No. Cases	34	26	88	21	22	191
Majority	59%	35%	68%	43%	55%	58%
Black	93	56	93	100	86	88
Douglas	75	73	86	95	77	82
Murphy	76	46	94	88	81	82
Rutledge	66	50	88	93	55	75
Reed	56	31	66	19	45	52
Burton	75	33	32	43	30	41
Frankfurter	47	15	44	5	64	39
Jackson	46	17	52	8	19	38
Stone	33	22	32	33	62	34
Vinson	100	33	27	40	22	34
Roberts	0	58	5	0	10	12

* Excluding N.L.R.B. and Wage and Hour Administration cases, which are included in the Labor classification.

TABLE XXV

DEVIATION OF JUSTICES FROM POSITION OF COURT MAJORITY IN PERSONAL LIBERTY
AND ECONOMIC CASES, 1941-1946 TERMS

	Personal Liberty Cases	Economic Cases	Total Cases
No. Cases	82	191	273
Murphy	+45	+24	+31
Black	+17	+30	+26
Douglas	+14	+24	+22
Rutledge	+34	+17	+22
Reed	−21	−6	−10
Frankfurter	−15	−19	−18
Jackson	−19	−20	−19
Stone	−6	−24	−19
Burton	−33	−17	−23
Vinson	−49	−24	−31
Roberts	−20	−46	−38

The general correspondence between judicial attitudes on the economic and personal liberty cases is evident from Table XXV, which translates the percentage figures of Tables XXIII and XXIV into terms of positive and negative deviations from the position of the Court majority. While the deviations of each justice from the majority view are invariably in the same direction for both categories of issues, there are some interesting variations in the relationships between the deviations of individual justices which call for a somewhat more detailed summary of their voting records.

Justice Black's reputation for decisiveness, forthright thinking, strong attitudes, and impatience with legalism is thoroughly substantiated by the record. His deviation from the Court's average position on these 273 cases was +26, making him second only to Murphy in leftward tendencies. It is apparent that government's right to intervene in a private enterprise economy and labor's right to maintain itself through self-help and favorable government legislation stand very high in Black's scheme of values. His votes on I.C.C. cases, however, indicate that he is not motivated by a favorable attitude toward government regulation as such, but by a conviction that normally government regulation is in the public interest. If it appears that regulatory powers are being administered in a discriminatory fashion, or to protect vested interests, then his broader concern for the public welfare leads him into opposition to official action. In the two fields where individual rights are at stake, Black is only moderately above the average position of the Court.

Judging by the similarity of voting reactions, Justice Douglas' values are close to those of Black, though there have been increasing signs of divergence during recent terms. In the area of individual liberties they are not far apart, and this is also true in state regulation, labor, and anti-monopoly cases. On federal administrative regulation, Douglas favors the government substantially less often than Black, and he is the most extreme member of the court in opposition to the I.C.C. {259} With a deviation of +22 from the Court's average position, Douglas' general location is a little closer to the center of the Court than Black's.

Justice Murphy offers perhaps the clearest evidence as to the nature of the hierarchy of values in terms of which he makes his decisions. His preferences take him in the same general direction as Black and Douglas, but his deviation of +31 makes him the most extreme member of the Court's left wing. Murphy reverses the Black-Douglas pattern in that he stresses individual rights more than economic issues. He has a 100 per cent record in upholding civil liberties since 1941, and he favored the claims of criminal defendants in 90 per cent of the nonunanimous decisions. His general leftward deviation is the same as Douglas' on economic matters, though his pro-labor position is the most extreme on the Court.

The outstanding fact about Murphy, then, is the precedence which he grants to claims for individual rights and freedom from governmental infringement on personal liberties. He votes to strike down all limitations on free speech, press, assembly, or religion, being willing to go considerably farther than any other member of the Court in this direction. He insists upon a meticulous observance of the rights of defendants in criminal cases, even when they are Japanese generals. He denies that the federal government has the right to take naturalization status away from naturalized citizens under any provocation. Though he believes strongly in government regulation, he questions the constitutionality of permitting administrative agencies to issue subpoenas, contending that only the courts should have this power of compulsion. He likewise departs from his colleagues of the left in urging that application of the Sherman Act to the Associated Press threatens freedom of the press. When the A. F. of L. challenged the Florida constitutional provision outlawing the closed shop, Murphy was the only justice unwilling to delay consideration of the constitutional questions raised by the amendment until after the state courts had interpreted it. He sums up his hypersensitivity on issues of individual rights by frankly confessing that "as a judge" he has "no loftier duty or responsibility than to uphold spiritual freedom to its furtherest reaches."[2]

Justice Rutledge is closer to Murphy on these individual liberty issues than any other member of the Court, particularly as to the rights {260} of criminal defendants. These two stood together in challenging the validity of the Yamashita and Homma military trials, the power of the federal government to denaturalize naturalized citizens, and the judicial review provisions of the Price Control Act. Rutledge, however, is a little less intense in his convictions than Murphy, and his attitude is consequently somewhat more "reasonable." In the Screws decision, for example, he was really in agreement with Murphy's position, but in view of the hopeless division on the Court he was willing to compromise his own views in order to obtain half a loaf. His deviation of +22 is the same as that of Douglas, though this figure averages out their differing emphases on personal liberty and economic values.

The Court's continental divide runs between Rutledge and Reed. Beginning with Reed, the characteristic deviation on these economic and individual rights issues is toward a less favorable attitude than the majority position of the Court. Reed is below the average on every one of the individual categories, his overall deviation being –10. While he runs only slightly below the line on the economic issues, his deviation on individual rights problems is very marked. On balance he stands as the most moderate member of the right wing.

The various paradoxes of Justice Frankfurter have already been examined at several points. In his refusal to approve claims for civil liberties he has been almost the most extreme member of the Court, but he has been considerably closer to the Court's average position in cases involving procedural protection for criminal defendants. In spite of his expertness in administrative law and his militant support for the administrative process on some issues that have arisen, such as limiting the scope of judicial review, he has been considerably less favorable in this field than the Court as a whole. On the other hand, he has been able to find in the Interstate Commerce Commission almost no wrong whatever. His views on labor cases, in spite of his early tendencies as revealed in his authorship of the immoderately favorable *Hutcheson* decision, have more recently become decidedly unfavorable as compared with the Court's average attitude. Only in connection with state regulation and taxation does Frankfurter rank himself with the justices of the left.

Justice Jackson is remarkably close to Frankfurter in his general {261} reaction pattern. The figures, however, average out a certain unpredictability in Jackson's votes. He has been considerably below the average of the Court on civil liberties issues, yet he wrote the powerful opinion of the Court in the second flag salute case, and in the first *Ballard* case he was the only justice who considered that this mail fraud case against cultists infringed principles of religious freedom. This atypical reaction got Jackson into serious difficulties when the *Ballard* case came up a second time for review, for then he found himself running with the hare and chasing with the hounds, as he agreed with the majority in its dismissal of the case but joined with the minority in attacking the majority for its reasons. Jackson's opinions have a pungency, and often a sharpness of language, which make them interesting to read, whatever may be the exacerbating effect on his colleagues.

The late Chief Justice Stone ended his judicial career well to the right of the Court on which he had once been noted for dissents from the left. His record on civil liberties is something of a surprise, considering his lone stand for religious freedom in the first flag salute case. But his favorable votes in this field were largely confined to the Jehovah's Witnesses cases, and finally the Court majority went too far for him even in that field. He was also markedly out of sympathy with the Court's decisions in labor and federal regulation cases.

The positions of Justice Burton and Chief Justice Vinson are not yet too definitely defined because of their short periods of service. On the record thus far both must be considered extremely negative toward personal liberty claims. In economic matters, however, their deviation is much less marked.

Finally, Justice Roberts stood in his last years of service at the far outer reaches of the Court, as a reminder of how far it had moved from the days when as middle man he kept the Court suspended in uncertain balance. With respect to the issues of individual liberty he was not much at variance with his colleagues of the right. His conservatism was primarily of an economic sort. On all the economic issues except the I.C.C. he took by far the most negative position on the Court. On the I.C.C. the two ends of the Court seemed to meet, Roberts' record being almost identical with that of Black, but their opposition was largely expressed in different cases and for different reasons. {262}

As already pointed out, it was in cases involving these economic and individual rights issues that over half of the dissents were registered during the six terms from 1941 through 1946. A survey of the remaining nonunanimous opinions discloses no issue present in any substantial number of cases which yielded anything like the clear divisions into left and right found in the economic and individual liberties categories. There was, for example, a comparatively large number of nonunanimous decisions (44) where federal tax levies were being protested. The Court ruled for the government in 70 per cent of these cases. There may appear to be some significance in the fact that Black voted for the government 82 per cent of the time, while Roberts favored the taxpayer in all except 33 per cent of the cases. The justices in between these two extremes, however, do not fall into any pattern and do not, in fact, vary much one way or the other from the majority position of the Court. In the same way, when 34 cases are collected where a federal-state issue of some sort was raised, the judicial divisions do not conform to the established bloc patterns.

An analysis of the sort attempted in this chapter can only hope to offer some clues as to the more obvious motivations for judicial behavior. A statistical summary is bound to be a relatively crude tool. It needs to be supplemented by the more orthodox types of inquiry and deduction, which when employed by as keen an observer as Thomas Reed Powell can discover refinements in judicial motivation of the following order:

> Mr. Chief Justice White was loath to condemn fiscal exactions but somewhat hostile toward regulatory measures. . . . Mr. Justice Pitney had a feeling both for local government and for *laissez faire* and when the two preferences came into conflict, he would follow now one and now the other. . . . Mr. Justice Sanford had both a deference toward government and a deference toward Mr. Chief Justice Taft, and these two inclinations were not always harmonious.[3]

Nevertheless, it is scarcely without significance to have demonstrated such a remarkably close correlation between judicial attitudes on economic issues and individual rights problems, and to have shown that current alignments on the Court tend to be organized around variations {263} in the intensity with which these two values are held by its members. The fundamental division on the Roosevelt Court, though expressing itself in new kinds of issues, and badly complicated by the presence of competing values, appears still to be between conflicting systems of preferences on matters of social and economic policy.

CHAPTER TEN

The Plight of a Liberal Court

{264}

"IT IS well recognized among the lawyers," wrote Max Lerner in 1941, "that the new doctrinal directions of the present Supreme Court spell a return to Holmes. Five years ago those who followed the New Deal constitutional crisis were overcome by a sense of sadness at what seemed the decisive defeat of the Holmes tradition. But today when the Court assembles for conference the true Chief Justice is the image of Holmes that all but one or two of its members carry in their thinking. Rarely has a more certain defeat been followed by a more complete triumph."[1]

The early years of the Roosevelt Court were indeed largely devoted to establishing as the majority view of the court the liberal positions for which Holmes had argued so eloquently in his dissents. All the Roosevelt appointees participated in this process. Such disagreements as there were during the first three or four years of the Roosevelt Court found the newly appointed liberal members standing almost as a unit. Well might it seem at that time that the Court's only task was the simple one of turning Holmes' dissents into majority holdings.

Why, then, did the liberals on the Roosevelt Court fall apart after a few brief terms of unanimity? What turned a judicial honeymoon into a domestic wrangle? Apart from any questions of personal incompatibility, three reasons may be suggested for the failure of liberalism, {265} or what Lerner called the Holmes tradition, to supply clear guidance for the thinking of a liberal court.

First, there are the shortcomings of American liberalism as a social and economic philosophy. "For the last 35 years," John Fischer wrote recently, "the American progressive movement has been living on a collection of ideas which was put together at about the turn of the century . . . by a group of first-rate political thinkers, including such men as Brandeis, Wilson, Holmes, Veblen, Norris, Steffens, Pinchot, the elder La Follette, and Theodore Roosevelt."[2] The New Deal completed the task which the New Freedom had begun, of writing these progressive ideas into laws that are now so generally accepted that a Republican Congress does not think seriously of attacking more than a very few of them.

205

This was the New Deal's success. Its failure was in producing any consistent social and economic philosophy to give meaning and purpose to its various action programs. Priding itself on its experimental approach, guided by a man who thought of himself as a quarterback trying first one play and then another, and judging their success by immediate pragmatic tests—the New Deal, along with all its great positive contributions to American life, may well be charged with contributing to the delinquency of American liberalism.

This failure to develop the philosophic foundations of a liberal way of life had some important implications for the success of a liberal Supreme Court. One was that the force of the New Deal was expended in pursuit of a variety of oddly assorted policies, some of them mutually contradictory. The New Deal lived in a tent wide enough to cover both N.R.A. and T.V.A., and operated through an army in which both Jesse Jones and Henry Wallace could be generals. Breadth is a good thing in a political movement, but the appearance of stability it gives is false if the attachments are to a personality rather than to a set of principles, and if a substantial part of the following is composed of opportunists attracted simply by the success of the movement.

Another result of the New Deal's failure to produce a liberal philosophy was that its ability to grow was limited. Lerner spoke of a "return to Holmes." But the problem was scarcely one of "returning" to an earlier liberalism. It was necessary to go forward. The New Deal knew {266} the old liberal answers, but for the new questions it had to resort to trial and error. It failed to produce political philosophers of the stature, fertility, and generalizing ability needed to understand the facts of life in an atomic era, out of whose thinking a liberal action program for the next decade could germinate. Given these conditions, it is scarcely surprising that the Court created by the New Deal should be similarly self-contradictory and confused as to the directions in which a liberal policy should develop.

A second factor in the Roosevelt Court's difficulties was that the liberal judicial tradition it inherited was a divided one. Lerner, in accepting Holmes as the spiritual father of the new Court, was overlooking the great judge's long-time partner in dissent, Justice Brandeis. His image was likewise present in the thinking of the Roosevelt Court, and his version of liberalism was not identical with that of Holmes, in spite of the fact that they were nearly always found on the same side of decisions. This similarity in voting records concealed fundamental divergences of temper and attitude. For Holmes, liberalism was above all a rule for guidance of his actions as a judge. It was a philosophy which taught that courts must not set themselves up as censors of legislative policy, or thwart the popular will on any grounds except to save the freedoms which are necessary to democratic policy-formation. Holmes believed, as Schlesinger has put it, that "if the American people wanted to go to hell, he could not see anything in the Constitution to stop them." As a judge, it was his duty to ensure that "the people could embody their desires in law, whatever the nature of the desires."[3]

On the other hand, liberalism for Justice Brandeis was not merely a rule for deciding cases on the bench. It supplied motivation for him over the entire range of public policy. It was not as easy for him as for Holmes to develop a separate judicial personality divorced from his personality as a citizen and a voter. Brandeis could never "relieve himself of a sense of responsibility for the results of judicial decision." He could never quite believe that it was wrong for him as a judge to further the liberal goals of public policy in which he believed as a man. The Roosevelt Court has thus had not one but two preceptors from whom to take its liberal line. {267}

Finally, the Roosevelt Court has had to effectuate its liberalism under conditions that Holmes and Brandeis never had to face—the condition of being in power. There are many advantages to a minority position. It permits one to be completely logical, to adhere strictly to principle, to shun compromise. Out of power, it is easy to criticize the use of power by those who have it. But history is full of illustrations of what happens to the sharp ideology of minority political movements which suffer the fate of winning a majority. It is no less true of courts than of legislatures that liberalism out of power will seldom behave the same as liberalism which has inherited the perquisites and the responsibilities that go with success. These are some of the factors that have hampered the Roosevelt Court in its efforts to develop policies of economic, social, and judicial liberalism.

Liberalism and Judicial Pragmatism

One of the fundamental contributions of Holmes to the judicial process was his pragmatism. Historically judges have proceeded to their conclusions on the basis of concepts, fictions, absolutes which cram the disparate data of a disordered world into neat categories. This method yields clear blacks and whites, divisions based on difference of kind. It makes life easy for a judge, and lets him sleep untroubled.

Justice Holmes knew that the differences in the important cases are differences in degree. He knew that "the great ordinances of the Constitution do not establish and divide fields of black and white. Even the more specific of them are found to terminate in a penumbra shading gradually from one extreme to the other."[4] He rejected the fictions and the formulas. The great Marshall had said in 1819 that the power to tax is the power to destroy. On that abstraction, which was almost completely untrue as a generalization from experience in the field of taxation, was built up a whole elaborate structure of intergovernmental tax immunity. Holmes exposed the hollowness of this century-old judicial precept in a single sentence: "The power to tax is not the power to destroy while this Court sits." For a flat prohibition on intergovernmental taxation, Holmes proposed to substitute a flexible rule of reason. A policy of permission within limits would throw a heavier burden {268} on the Court in applying the rule to individual cases than Marshall's policy of automatic rejection, but it loosened the grip of the Court on the political process and increased the area of free legislative choice.

Holmes' battle against conceptualism was not successful while he was on the Court. In 1935 the attitude against which he had fought won one of its greatest victories as the Court majority made its invalidation of the N.R.A. turn on a distinction between "direct" and "indirect" effects upon interstate commerce, contending that this distinction must be preserved and the federal government limited to the area where direct effects were evident. "Otherwise . . . there would be virtually no limit to the federal power and for all practical purposes we should have a completely contralized government."

The next year saw Justice Sutherland in the *Carter Coal Co.* case engaged in an even more desperate attempt to demonstrate the wisdom of defining the power of the federal government to regulate commerce in conceptual rather than pragmatic terms.

> The distinction between a direct and an indirect effect turns, not upon the magnitude of either the cause or the effect, but entirely upon the manner in which the effect has been brought about. If the production by one man of a single ton of coal intended for interstate sale and shipment . . . affects interstate commerce indirectly, the effect does not become direct by multiplying the tonnage, or increasing the number of men employed, or adding to the expense or complexities of the business, or by all combined. It is quite true that rules of law are sometimes qualified by considerations of degree, as the government argues. But the matter of degree has no bearing upon the question here, since that question is not—What is the *extent* of the local activity or condition, or the *extent* of the effect produced upon interstate commerce? but—What is the *relation* between the activity or condition and the effect?

Sutherland's argument was too successful. It illuminated as by a flash of lightning a judicial dream world of logical abstractions. When the same Court came to decide the Wagner Act cases in 1937, Chief Justice Hughes gave these two embarrassing precedents as brief a nod as was possible, and then hurried on in the next paragraph to talk about facts, not concepts. Those who argued that the effect on interstate commerce of industrial strife in the Jones & Laughlin steel plant {269} did not matter were, Hughes said, asking us "to shut our eyes to the plainest facts of our national life and to deal with the question of direct and indirect effects in an intellectual vacuum." His paragraph came to a fitting pragmatic conclusion: "We have often said that interstate commerce itself is a practical conception. It is equally true that interferences with that commerce must be appraised by a judgment that does not ignore actual experience."

This was shocking to the conservative minority of the 1937 Court, so recently its majority. They were, as Charles P. Curtis, Jr., has so well said, "afraid for the future, because this new concept was one of degree, which had no logical stopping place. . . . It was a ramp, with no convenient landings for a logical mind, slightly out of breath, perhaps, to rest on. . . . To them it was 'subversive doctrine.' True enough for Justices who perform their duties under the sole compulsion and domination of logic. Not true for those who know how to handle matters of fact and matters of degree in fact."[5]

But even for those who know how and are not afraid to handle matters of degree in fact, the task is difficult. Consensus is harder to achieve, a fact amply demonstrated by the sharply increased rate of dissent in recent Court terms. The old sense of certainty is gone, and judicial decisions take on the experiential quality of life itself. Too much freedom is as difficult to endure as too little, and it is hard for anyone who is strongly attached to certain values to admit that their claims are only relative. For judges, absolutism is an occupational disease which it is almost impossible to escape.

The Roosevelt Court, true enough, has rejected the absolutes of its predecessor, but has been unable to escape developing some of its own. They mostly concern such matters as civil liberties and the rights of defendants in criminal prosecutions. On such questions the new Court has tended to be as dogmatic as the old, though now it is the Bill of Rights rather than the due process clause that is the foundation for their certainties. Murphy and McReynolds are brothers under the skin in their insistence on fixed barriers to governmental powers. Justice Jackson, disturbed by what he feels to be the dogmatism of the new liberalism in imposing procedural limitations on state law enforcement officials, suggests that his brethren reread Holmes' classic dissent in {270} *Baldwin* v. *Missouri* where he said: "I have not yet adequately expressed the more than anxiety that I feel at the ever increasing scope given to the Fourteenth Amendment in cutting down what I believe to be the constitutional rights of the States," and ponder whether his warning has not now some relevance for them.[6]

Economic Liberalism

Liberalism as an economic philosophy has gone through an interesting and complicated evolutionary process. The historic role of Adam Smith's eighteenth century sort of economic liberalism was to remove the dead hand of the state from the processes of production and exchange, to clear the channels of trade and to facilitate rapid industrialization. But by the latter part of the nineteenth century it had become evident that laissez faire and free competition sometimes worked too well and sometimes were prevented from working well enough, so that liberals began to believe in the need for reintroducing the state into the economy to regulate the excesses both of competition and of monopoly. Thus in little more than a century the program of economic liberalism was transformed from freedom for capitalism into legislative regulation of capitalism.

There has been some question as to whether Justice Holmes, whose long and active intellectual life spanned the period from the Granger legislation to the N.R.A., was an economic liberal. Certainly he lacked the knowledge of economic processes, the painstaking thoroughness of study, the burning fire for eliminating economic abuses, that motivated his colleague Justice Brandeis. His first important vote on the Supreme Court was to uphold the monopoly which the titans Morgan and Hill had set up through the Northern Securities Company. It was a legalistic rather than an economically informed point of view which saw the question in this case as no different from "whether two small exporting grocers shall go to jail."[7]

But whether or not Holmes' economic views were basically those of an economic liberal, he usually as a judge arrived at a result which favored the goals that economic liberals were seeking. He held that the great liberal doctrine of freedom of contract could not operate unless {271} there was equality of bargaining position, and so he spoke vigorously for the right of labor to organize. It may have been a conviction of the constitutional right of the majority to experiment and make fools of themselves rather than a belief in state intervention which motivated him, but the net result was his approval of workmen's compensation laws, laws against labor injunctions, minimum wage and hour laws, regulation of chain stores, guarantee of bank deposits, adequate tax programs and powers, and an interpretation of the federal commerce clause broad enough to justify federal regulation of child labor.

There is no better way to gauge the development of American constitutional thinking than to note how these positions, in support of which Holmes was often in the Court minority, have become the unquestioned assumptions of the Roosevelt Court. When Holmes' dissenting view on the 1918 child labor case was vindicated in 1941, it was by a unanimous court. The economic questions with which Holmes mainly dealt—basic constitutional authority to regulate or protect—have, in fact, simply ceased to be issues. Now the matters coming up for adjudication concern the methods of instrumenting these general legislative goals, the interpretation of statutory language, the development of proper administrative standards and procedures. On these problems Holmes has less to say to the Court, partly because they interested him less, partly because regulatory processes were still relatively immature when he left the bench. Brandeis rather than Holmes did the pioneer work on the newer administrative dilemmas—as in his views on utility valuation theory in the Southwestern *Bell Telephone* case, and on the finality of administrative fact-finding in his *Crowell* v. *Benson* dissent and his *St. Joseph Stockyards* concurrence.

Similarly in the labor field, it was Holmes' role to state the fundamental theory of the right to organize, as he did while still on the Massachusetts supreme court in his famous dissent to the decision of *Vegelahn* v. *Guntner*. There he said:

> One of the eternal conflicts out of which life is made up is that between the effort of every man to get the most he can for his services, and that of society, disguised under the name of capital, to get his services for the least possible return. Combination on the one side is {272} patent and powerful. Combination on the other is the neces-

sary and desirable counterpart, if the battle is to be carried on in a fair and equal way.

But it was Brandeis who devoted himself to the more intricate problem of determining the effect of anti-trust legislation on the allowable area of economic conflict in the *Duplex* and *Bedford Cut Stone* cases, and who analyzed and described in the former, "for about the first time in the Anglo-American law reports, the real nature of union economic needs, as the unions saw them."[8] The Roosevelt Court in its decisions involving the Clayton Act, the Norris-LaGuardia Act, and the right to picket has been basing itself on Brandeis' principles, although it may well have carried them at times beyond the limits he himself would have approved.

But the legacy of neither Holmes nor Brandeis provides solutions for many of the economic issues with which the present Court has been confronted. Their guidance is good as far as it goes, but increasingly it has been found not to go far enough. The principles they laid down provide a sure guide when the issue is between economic liberals and economic conservatives, which was the battle ground in their time. But on a Court almost entirely composed of economic liberals who believe in the principle of legislative regulation of capitalism, the old issues do not arise, or if they do manage to get in, they are disposed of unanimously.

Instead, there are new issues which are harder to decide. When Holmes set down his dissent in *Vegelahn* v. *Guntner*, there could be no doubt that labor organizations were unable to carry on the battle against capital "in a fair and equal way." Today the balance of power, in some areas at least, is much more nearly in equilibrium, and the judicial task of "pricking out a line" that will divide permissible from forbidden labor action has become correspondingly difficult. Similarly, when Brandeis dissented in the *Bedford* case, no economic liberal could have seen much threat to economic freedom in the boycott established by these few stonecutters and setters in an attempt to prevent a powerful combination of twenty-four corporations from breaking up their union. But today, when a local of the International Brotherhood of Electrical Workers, comprising practically all the production {273} and installation electricians of the New York area, operating under a closed shop, with a very restrictive policy on admission to the union, refuses to permit its members to handle any equipment not produced by members of its own local, and thus eliminates competition from outside producers for the New York market, with consequent increases in price for electrical equipment there, then economic liberals may well ponder whether the values of a competitive system have not been seriously infringed.

"The liberals," says John Fischer, "have come to the edge of the dependable old battle map which they inherited from earlier campaigns. They desperately need a brand new set of directions." It is perhaps in the field of labor that this need is currently most obvious. The old liberalism was familiar only with a weak labor movement, which needed judicial protection if it was to survive. It had no need for any theory as to the relationship between a strong labor movement and society. And so the John L. Lewis case catches a liberal Court completely unprepared, and splits it into splinter groups. Rutledge and Murphy stick to the doctrines of the old liberalism and deny the government's right of coercion. Frankfurter and Jackson refuse to take a stand on the major policy question, passing it back to Congress, but they do succeed in finding a purely judicial hook—maintenance of respect for the courts—on which Lewis can be snagged. Black and Douglas are willing to assist in judicial formulation of a new public policy for dealing with crucial conflicts between strong unions and the public interest, but insist that judicial enforcement of that policy should avoid any taint of retaliatory action. Thus liberalism in search of a labor policy mounts its horse and rides off in all directions.

Liberalism and Individual Rights

There is a seeming paradox in the liberal's attitude toward the state, for he welcomes its intervention in economic affairs, but seeks to limit very severely its restrictions on individual expression of intellectual and physical freedom. In the former area, liberalism is typically pro-state; in the latter, its fundamental bias is anti-statist. If the liberal's mental set is favorable toward the legislative regulation of capitalism, it is still {274} laissez faire when the legislative regulation of fundamental civil liberties is at issue.

This same ambivalence of attitude is found in conservatism, operating in reverse. An excellent illustration of this fact is the Supreme Court decision in the 1931 case of *Near* v. *Minnesota*. Here the liberal majority view of the Court struck down a state statute which authorized the enjoining, as a nuisance, of "malicious, scandalous and defamatory" newspapers or magazines, on the ground that such action unconstitutionally infringed the freedom of the press. But Justices Butler, VanDevanter, McReynolds, and Sutherland, inveterate opponents of state efforts toward economic regulation, found such regulation of the press unobjectionable and, fresh from a series of decisions holding the state powerless to regulate prices or business charges, complained that the majority view left the state "powerless" to cope with the evil of defamatory newspapers.

In some areas, of course, the case for social control is so strong that serious infringements on the precincts of individual freedom are approved by the most confirmed liberal. In 1905 Justice Holmes was part of a unanimous Court upholding the validity of compulsory vaccination,[9] and in 1927 he spoke for the Court in approving state sterilization of a feeble-minded woman, whose mother was feeble-minded, and who had an illegitimate feeble-minded child. "Three generations of imbeciles are enough," he concluded.[10]

In general, legislative efforts to avert threats to the health, to the physical well-being, even to the morals of the community, are not so likely to arouse liberal-conservative division. It is when society undertakes to deal with what a legislature regards as threats from ideas that the most clear-cut alignments develop. Perhaps the greatest contribution Justice Holmes made on the Court

212

was to put in a classic judicial form the liberal position on the need for free trade in ideas—"not free thought for those who agree with us but freedom for the thought that we hate."[11] "The best test of truth," he was convinced, "is the power of the thought to get itself accepted in the competition of the market."[12]

But he knew that pure laissez faire was not practicable even here. He recognized that speech and thought can be dangerous to organized {275} society under certain conditions, and he sought to supply a rule that would assist in determining when those conditions were present. "The question in every case," he wrote for a unanimous Court in upholding a conviction for violation of the Espionage Act in the *Schenck* case, "is whether the words used are used in such circumstances and are of such a nature as to create a clear and present danger that they will bring about the substantive evils that Congress has a right to prevent. It is a question of proximity and degree."

By this test he felt that Schenck, who had sought to obstruct the draft by distributing pamphlets, had been rightfully convicted. In the *Debs* Sedition Act case he also found clear and present danger, writing an opinion which he later regretted. But a few months afterwards in the *Abrams* case he refused, in one of his most impassioned dissents, to find clear and present danger in the scattering, during wartime, of antiwar leaflets from a New York City roof by five foreign-born pacifists. The conservative Court majority, which had been willing to let Holmes apply his clear and present danger test so long as it gave results favorable to the government, now ignored it and set up its own competing test of "remote and indirect tendency," under which almost any criticism of the government could be brought within the prohibitions of the Sedition Act.

But "clear and present danger" would not stay buried, so the Court tried a different tactic. In the 1925 *Gitlow* case involving a conviction under the New York criminal anarchy law, the majority felt compelled to make some reference to the doctrine, which had been pressed strongly by counsel in the case, and so proceeded practically to distinguish it out of existence, holding that it had no applicability in a situation where, as in the New York statute, the legislature had determined for itself the likelihood that certain kinds of language would tend to bring about the prohibited results. The test would have been relevant, the Court majority said, if Gitlow had been prosecuted for publishing dangerous words, but since his conviction was for publishing *forbidden* words, it had no applicability. Thus the protection of the clear and present danger doctrine was whittled down to a narrow coverage, and legislatures were left comparatively free to punish thought and speech which they adjudged dangerous. {276}

The Roosevelt Court lost little time in rescuing the Holmes doctrine from the discard. They proceeded, in fact, to refurbish it into something considerably stronger than Holmes himself had made of it, namely, a test of the constitutionality of statutes. In none of his decisions in this field had Holmes attempted to question the validity of the statute itself. He had used clear and present danger as a rule of reason to guide law enforcement officers and judges in interpreting statutory restrictions on certain kinds of speech or conduct. But in the 1940 picketing cases the Court adopted clear and present danger as an appropriate guide in determining the constitutionality of legislative restrictions on expression where the substantive evil sought to be prevented by the restriction is "destruction of life or property, or invasion of the right of privacy," and on this basis declared the two statutes involved unconstitutional. Again in the second flag salute case, and in the Texas labor case of *Thomas* v. *Collins,* the Court used the clear and present danger doctrine to justify the invalidation of state statutes.

The test has also been employed in another field where Holmes did not have occasion to use it, as a defense against contempt of court citations resulting from published comments about judicial proceedings. Again, the test was employed during World War II to reverse a conviction under the Espionage Act of 1917, where the facts were about equally incriminating with those which had led Holmes to approve a conviction in the 1919 *Schenck* case.

The Roosevelt Court has thus made of Holmes' clear and present danger doctrine a somewhat stronger protector of the right to circulate ideas and to assemble for purposes of discussion than Holmes himself had any occasion for doing.[13] But the Court has not unanimously approved this tendency. Justice Frankfurter has protested that clear and present danger is only a "felicitous phrase" which should not be taken "out of the context of the particular situation where it arose and for which it was adopted."[14] The limits that Frankfurter would impose upon the use of the constitutional test in judicial protection of civil liberties were foreshadowed before he went on the Supreme Court when he wrote:

> The tendency of focusing attention on constitutionality is to make constitutionality synonymous with propriety, to regard a law as all right {277} so long as it is "constitutional." Such an attitude is a great enemy of liberalism. Particularly in legislation affecting freedom of thought and freedom of speech, much that is highly illiberal would be clearly constitutional. . . . Here is ample warning to the liberal forces that the real battles of liberalism are not won in the Supreme Court.[15]

Perhaps the best elaboration of this view is found in Henry Steele Commager's little book, *Majority Rule and Minority Rights,* which argues that judicial review is undemocratic, ineffective, and dangerous when used to protect civil liberties no less than when used to protect property. Undemocratic—because if the courts must be called in to protect these liberties, "we concede that the majority is not to be trusted in what is perhaps the most important field of its legislative activity." Ineffective—because judicial decisions can often be easily circumvented by a new legislative formula. Dangerous—because the assumption of responsibility by the courts minimizes legislative responsibility and discourages "the people's active and intelligent interest in these matters."[16]

In the long run, Commager concludes, civil liberties will be safe only in "an educated and enlightened democracy." Judicial fiat will not create these conditions, and for the courts to take over "the peculiar guardianship of civil liberties" tends to deprive "democracy of its most effective training school— experience." But here the civil liberties argument merges into the broader question of the proper role of courts in the process of democratic policy formulation.

Activism versus Self-Restraint

Most perplexing of all the dilemmas that have harassed the Roosevelt Court is determination of the degree of deference owed by a liberal bench to the legislative will. Again and again Holmes pounded away on the theme, sometimes in opinions for the Court, more often in dissents, that the courts were not the sole, or even the primary, protectors of the public. "It must be remembered," he wrote in 1904, "that legislatures are ultimate guardians of the liberty and welfare of the people in quite as great a degree as the courts." And the legislatures had the great advantage that they were directly responsible to the {278} people and were subject to check and change in direction by them, whereas with a life-term judiciary, as Stone said, "the only check upon our own exercise of power is our own sense of self-restraint."[17]

This doctrine of judicial self-restraint operated in Holmes' day to protect liberal state and federal programs of economic legislation from invalidation by reactionary courts. But what happens when the courts become liberal, and are confronted with the product of reactionary legislatures? Can liberal justices, however firmly they may be convinced that judges are not God, be expected to sit back and permit the enforcement of a legislative program offensive to their most firmly held values, on the ground that reasonable men might have adopted that program? Or must it be admitted that liberalism in talking about judicial self-restraint was merely adopting a debating tactic by which as a minority it might seek to limit the interference of a conservative majority with liberal legislative goals? Is judicial self-restraint a means rather than an end?

An argument can be made for liberal abandonment of the self-restraint doctrine. Schlesinger ably puts the case as liberal judicial activists might state it:

> The Court cannot escape politics: therefore, let it use its political power for wholesome social purposes. Conservative majorities in past Courts have always legislated in the interests of the business community; why should a liberal majority tie its hands by a policy of self-denial that conservatism will never follow when it is in power? ... If any decision of the Court can reduce persecution, redress injustice, or promote the general welfare, it would surely be contrary to the spirit of the Bill of Rights to renounce these results for the sake of abstractions.[18]

215

In some respects this statement may seem an accurate description of the views on which the Black-Douglas-Murphy-Rutledge wing of the Court has acted. But while these justices may be properly characterized as activists in the Brandeis tradition, it does not follow that they have cynically abandoned the Holmes doctrine of judicial self-restraint. For it has never been the liberal position that legislatures are always right. It has always been recognized, by both liberals and conservatives, that there are fundamental guaranties in the Constitution which the {279} Supreme Court is charged with protecting against legislative invasion. The difference has been that the conservative has tended to feel that it was rights of property which it was the divine duty of the Constitution to protect, whereas the liberal has insisted that judicial intervention be principally employed for the protection of individual liberties.

Justice Holmes certainly did not believe that self-restraint should be carried to the extreme of judicial quietism, even though his deep-lying skepticism made it easier for him than for most justices to say that perhaps the legislature was right and he was wrong. There were paradoxes in his nature which emerged in such admissions as that "in the abstract, I have no very enthusiastic belief [in free speech], though I hope I would die for it."[19]

The best evidence that Holmes was willing to apply his doctrine of judicial self-restraint even in areas where the result was to uphold legislation that must have offended his own convictions is supplied by the 1923 case of *Meyer v. Nebraska*. That state, under the stimulus of wartime feeling, had prohibited the teaching of modern foreign languages to children until after the eighth grade. The Court majority, in an opinion by Justice McReynolds, invalidated the statute on the good conservative grounds that it deprived language teachers of their livelihood and interfered with the control of parents over their children. To Holmes, however, the important question was whether the legislature could reasonably have adopted such a statute, and on that point he said:

> I cannot bring my mind to believe that in some circumstances . . . the statute might not be regarded as a reasonable or even necessary method of reaching the desired result. . . . If it is reasonable it is not an undue restriction of the liberty either of teacher or scholar. No one would doubt that a teacher might be forbidden to teach many things, and the only criterion of his liberty under the Constitution that I can think of is "whether, considering the end in view, the statute passes the bounds of reason and assumes the character of a merely arbitrary fiat."

It should be noted that this was one Holmes dissent in which Brandeis did not join.

But even Holmes' toleration for legislative judgments had its limits, {280} and statutory infringements on personal liberties did not always meet his test of reasonableness. He was part of a unanimous Court which in 1925 condemned an Oregon statute requiring children to attend only public schools.[20]

In the 1927 *Whitney* case he gave a strong indication that he would have declared the California syndicalism act unconstitutional if the claim had been properly made in the trial court. And in two 1931 cases, involving a California "red flag" law and the Minnesota statute on "nuisance" publications already referred to, Holmes voted to declare legislative action unreasonable.[21]

Thus Holmes can be cited in support both of the activists and of the apostles of self-restraint on the present Court. The justices of the left, developing the emphasis which liberals have always placed on civil liberties, have put the First Amendment on a pedestal, out of the reach of normal principles of constitutional construction. The First Amendment, declares Justice Black, "must be taken as a command of the broadest scope that explicit language, read in the context of a liberty-loving society, will allow."[22] Legislation which runs counter to that command is unconstitutional on its face, unless it can be rescued by the test of clear and present danger.

On the other hand, Justice Frankfurter, most articulate of the present Court in defense of self-restraint, is likewise convinced that he is honoring the Holmes tradition. His views were elaborated most clearly in the two flag salute decisions. When he spoke for the Court majority in the *Gobitis* case, he quoted the famous sentence, "We live by symbols," from Holmes' speech on John Marshall in 1901, and he was undoubtedly deeply affected by what Holmes had said on the symbolism of the flag in that same address: "The flag is but a bit of bunting to one who insists on prose. Yet . . . its red is our life blood, its stars our world, its blue our heaven. It owns our land. At will it throws away our lives."[23]

Over and over again in the *Gobitis* case Frankfurter stressed that the legislative judgment must be respected. The rule of the local school board was to be treated as though it were the decision of the state legislature. The law-making body had decided that the flag salute was an appropriate means "to evoke that unifying sentiment without which there can ultimately be no liberties, civil or religious." For the Court {281} to invalidate the requirement "would amount to no less than the pronouncement of a pedagogical and psychological dogma in a field where courts possess no marked and certainly no controlling competence." For the Court to conclude that exemption from the flag salute ceremony must be granted to dissidents would be "to maintain that there is no basis for a legislative judgment that such an exemption might introduce elements of difficulty into the school discipline, might cast doubts in the minds of the other children which would themselves weaken the effect of the exercise."

At only one point in the opinion did Frankfurter evidence any doubt that Holmes would have approved of his stand, and that came when he had to refer to the Oregon public school decision, where Holmes had joined in condemning a legislative judgment making education in public schools mandatory. However, Frankfurter found that only a slight detour was necessary to avoid this obstacle. Recognizing that legislatures cannot compel all children to attend public schools, Frankfurter went on: "But it is a very different thing for this Court to exercise censorship over the conviction of legislatures that a

217

particular program or exercise will best promote in the minds of children who attend the common schools an attachment to the institutions of their country." To which Robert E. Cushman's acid rejoinder was: "The opinion does not explain why it is different."[24]

When the Court majority deserted Frankfurter in the second flag salute case, his dissent sought to make it even clearer that it was his judicial principles, not his human sympathies, which separated him from his colleagues. Schlesinger finds in this dissent "a depth and an urgency that make it a great democratic document," based on "the old Jeffersonian confidence in the people." "Were my purely personal attitude relevant," Frankfurter said, "I should wholeheartedly associate myself with the general libertarian views in the Court's opinion. . . . [But] as a member of this Court I am not justified in writing my private notions of policy into the Constitution, no matter how deeply I cherish them or how mischievous I may deem their disregard."

Is Frankfurter or Black then the better disciple of Holmes on civil liberties problems? Each has based himself on a fundamental tenet of Holmes' liberalism. Frankfurter's insistence on upholding legislatures {282} has been a more literal application of the precedents. He has said to Holmes: "Lord, behold, here is thy pound, which I have kept laid up in a napkin." The Black bloc has been more inventive, whether for good or ill. They have developed out of Holmes' passionate conviction that "the ultimate good desired is better reached by free trade in ideas," a rule which justifies judges in negating legislative action hampering such freedom.

There has been a tendency recently, as in Schlesinger's *Fortune* essay, to explain all the divisions on the present Court as resulting from this battle between the activists (Black and Douglas) who want to use the Court to promote public policies in which they believe, and the practitioners of self-restraint (Frankfurter and Jackson) who attempt to achieve judicial objectivity, remaining above the battle and leaving the task of legislating to legislatures. This difference in approach to the judicial function, Schlesinger suggests, accounts for the strained personal relations that have developed on the Court, for

> the advocates of self-denial, with their belief in the autonomy of the judicial process, cannot in their hearts resist the feeling that the activists are unprincipled; while the activists, with their skepticism about judicial objectivity, cannot in their hearts resist the feeling that self-denial is a cover for conservatism.[25]

Thomas Reed Powell takes a similar view, which is apparently the official Harvard position. "A leaning for getting the result in the particular case as if it were a legislative choice," characteristic of Black, contrasts "with a leaning to respect the outlines and many of the details of an established legal system" in Frankfurter.[26]

But Yale, which sent Douglas to the Court, produces a somewhat different interpretation. Fred Rodell, writing in 1944, professed to find that it was Black, not Frankfurter, who wanted to limit the Court's power. He spoke of

> Black's tremendous respect for legislatures, his belief that appointed judges should interfere only in rare and extreme instances with the decisions of those elected by the people. This respect is partly due to the fact that he, alone on the present Court, was once a legislator himself. His constant battle cry is—Let Congress decide this; it's none {283} of our judicial business. The respect is also due in part to his unflinching faith in democracy with a small "d." Thus Black, mild and amiable as he remains in person, has no intellectual patience with his brethren when they mistake their role for that of God-in-government. This is the core of his chief quarrel with Justice Frankfurter, a quarrel which has recently flared into their formal opinions.[27]

Surely the facts must be somewhat confusing if two such astute observers as Powell and Rodell can come to diametrically opposite conclusions. As is usual in such cases, the truth seems to lie somewhere between. Black is respectful of the legislative judgment—more so than Frankfurter—where economic matters are involved. In the Richmond tax case and the Arizona train limit case, for example, Black voted to uphold legislative actions which Frankfurter helped to overturn. Schlesinger's explanation is that Black "will invoke deference to the legislature when it does something he supports." Perhaps. But in the Jim Crow bus case from Virginia, Black recognized that his views in the Richmond and Arizona cases, if they had been adopted by the Court, would logically require him to uphold the Jim Crow law, much as he disapproved of it.

Frankfurter's views on legislative supremacy, on the other hand, have been elicited mostly in civil liberties cases. It is true that he joined in the *McCarroll* dissent with Black and Douglas, but as already pointed out his enthusiasm for congressional rather than judicial solutions of the problems of federalism has abated since that time. Again Schlesinger has an explanation. Frankfurter, he says, "will strike down laws when such action is within the well-established limitations of the Court." But on such a basis of adherence to precedents Holmes' and Brandeis' dissents could never have been made the rule of the Court. And of course no disciple of Frankfurter has ever been able to explain away his *Hutcheson* decision, perhaps the most flagrant example of judicial legislating during the past ten years.

In the civil liberties field, there can be no question as to Frankfurter's self-restraint. While he has recently receded somewhat from his original position and bowed to the majority of the Court, for a time at least he carried self-restraint perilously close to the point of judicial {284} abdication. It still remains a mystery why he should have thought that a local school board's decision to make the flag salute compulsory for public school children was entitled to greater respect than the Arizona legislature's decision that freight trains should not be more than seventy cars long.

Frankfurter's essential philosophy, Schlesinger suggests, is that "the larger interests of democracy in the United States require that the Court contract rather than expand its power." Such a rule, while certainly aiming in the right direction, is not entirely acceptable as a guide for judicial action. A more satisfactory restatement would run something like this: The Supreme Court must always remember that democratic control over public policy is more likely to be in danger from those who propose to expand judicial power than from those who propose to contract it, and that any overriding of legislative or popular decisions must consequently have overwhelmingly strong justification.

But what constitutes sufficient justification for such overriding? The Frankfurter-Commager-Schlesinger answer is "that basic decisions on all questions save the fundamental rights of political agitation [must] be entrusted as completely as possible to institutions directly responsive to popular control."[28] This was the position which not only Black, Douglas, Murphy, and Rutledge, but also Stone and Jackson decisively *rejected* in the second flag salute case. They were convinced that it was not enough for the Supreme Court simply to make sure that the channels of political agitation remained open so that people who did not believe in compelling children to salute the flag would be free to try to win a majority to their side. They held that persons under the protection of the American Constitution were entitled to have the Supreme Court act directly to safeguard them from a majority-enforced violation of their religious convictions. "The very purpose of a Bill of Rights," Jackson said for the Court in that case, "was to withdraw certain subjects from the vicissitudes of political controversy, to place them beyond the reach of majorities and officials and to establish them as legal principles to be applied by the courts." It is somewhat ironic to hear Frankfurter's refusal to accept this claim for the primacy of the Bill of Rights, the most truly Jeffersonian {285} part of the Constitution, defended as demonstrating "the old Jeffersonian confidence in the people."

The Roosevelt Court has, then, expanded its power in the only direction where such expansion is compatible with a democratic constitutionalism—in the direction of safeguarding the right to believe, to speak, to assemble, to practice one's religion, to have a fair trial. But expansion of judicial control even for these purposes is not without its limits and its dangers. No section of the Bill of Rights grants unqualified freedoms. The protections of the first ten amendments must be interpreted with sanity, with judgment, with extraordinary pains to understand the rationale of the legislative or administrative or judicial action which it is proposed to invalidate.

There is no doubt that the Roosevelt Court has sometimes failed to achieve the balance required for this task. The philosophy of human freedom is a heady brew, which tends to dissolve judicial inhibitions and turns judges into crusaders, unable to apply the standards that should guide them as "reasonable men." The dignity of the Bill of Rights is scarcely furthered by decisions protecting the right to ring doorbells or safeguarding cult leaders from prosecution for mail fraud. A concern for civil liberties and a concern for redressing the balance for labor, when mixed together in the same case, yield an explosive mixture which may get out of the control of the Court, as in the picketing cases. If further evidence were needed, Justice Murphy's example demonstrates that a hyperactive concern for individual rights can lead a judge into ventures little short of quixotic. The Court may rightly have rejected the Frankfurter notion that the battles of liberalism cannot be won on the Supreme Court, but in doing so it has admittedly added very heavy responsibilities to its load, and has created new opportunities for failure, some of which it has all too eagerly embraced.

* * *

Marx professed to believe that under communism the state would gradually wither away. Similarly there were some who conceived that under liberal domination the Supreme Court would fade out by degrees, like the Cheshire Cat. As it has turned out, both the Russian {286} state and the Court have flourished under their new regimes. Like Winston Churchill, the Roosevelt Court has not regarded its mandate as one of liquidation of an empire. It has maintained judicial powers, though using them for different purposes than its conservative predecessors. It has adhered to the notion that the American Constitution sets bounds to the legislative range of choice, and has continued to police these boundaries wherever they protect the sacred precincts of human freedom. Because it is asked political questions, it has continued to give political answers. Brooks Adams thought that experience had amply demonstrated that courts must be removed from politics, and there is much to support his view. But the American tradition did not develop in that direction. The eggs have been too thoroughly scrambled to think seriously of restoring them to their separate shells.

A liberal court, we now can see after some years of experience with one, faces much the same hazards as a conservative court. It has to learn that its goals must be the development of sound principles, not the protection of particular interests. Labor, as such, is no more entitled to judicial support than capital, as such. In either category the claims of the interest must be considered in their relationship to the goals of a democratic community.

A liberal court, wielding the great powers of the American judiciary, must bear constantly in mind the necessity of judicial self-restraint. A policy of judicial activism sponsored by a liberal court is no more consistent with the democratic process than a like conservative policy, unless the negation of legislative decisions is limited to countering assaults on authentic principles of liberty and dignity which must be maintained as essential conditions of a free society.

Liberal justices, no less than conservative, may come to think in terms of absolutes or of legal fictions and may forget that courts are part of the living process of growth and adjustment and adaptation which is the great hope of American life in a fantastically scrambled world.

Standards of this sort are not easily attained. Certainly the Roosevelt Court, the first liberal court of the twentieth century, has not attained them. But only if they are reasonably approximated—and {287} this the Roosevelt Court may fairly claim to have done—can we conclude, with Bacon, that

> it is an happy thing in a state when kings and states do often consult with judges; and again, when judges do often consult with the king and state: the one when there is matter of law intervenient in business of state; the other, when there is some consideration of state intervenient in matter of law. . . . And let no man weakly conceive that just laws and true policy have any antipathy: for they are like the spirits and sinews, that one moves with the other.

NOTES

CHAPTER I (PAGES 1-22)

1. *The Theory of Social Revolutions* (Macmillan, 1913), p. 216.

2. *Ibid.*, pp. 33, 34.

3. *The Struggle for Judicial Supremacy* (Knopf, 1941), p. 187.

4. *Hammer* v. *Dagenhart.* Citations for this and all subsequent decisions will be found in the Table of Cases.

5. *Adkins* v. *Children's Hospital.*

6. *Ribnik* v. *McBride.*

7. Quoted by Justice Frankfurter in *N.L.R.B.* v. *Donnelly Garment Co.* (1947).

8. *Lions Under the Throne* (Houghton Mifflin, 1947), p. 98.

9. Jackson, *op. cit.*, pp. 77-8.

10. *Home Building & Loan Association* v. *Blaisdell.*

11. *Nebbia* v. *New York.*

12. *Panama Refining Co.* v. *Ryan*—the "hot oil" case.

13. *Norman* v. *Baltimore & Ohio R. Co.;* see Carl B. Swisher, *American Constitutional Development* (Houghton Mifflin, 1943), p. 928.

14. *Railroad Retirement Board* v. *Alton R. Co.*

15. *Louisville Joint Stock Land Bank* v. *Radford.*

16. *Humphrey's Executor* v. *United States.*

17. *Ashwander* v. *Tennessee Valley Authority.*

18. *Ashton* v. *Cameron County District.*

19. *Morehead* v. *New York ex rel. Tipaldo.*

20. Dissenting in *Adkins* v. *Children's Hospital.*

21. Jackson, *op. cit.*, p. 139.

22. For a convenient summary of various proposals for limiting the Court's powers, see Robert K. Carr, *The Supreme Court and Judicial Review* (Farrar and Rinehart, 1942), Ch. XI.

23. *West Coast Hotel Co.* v. *Parrish.*

24. *Steward Machine Co.* v. *Davis; Helvering* v. *Davis.*

25. *Ex parte Levitt* (1937).

26. More extended biographical sketches of the justices are found in Wesley McCune, *The Nine Young Men* (Harper, 1947).

27. These and subsequent data on judicial appointments prior to 1937 are from Cortez A. M. Ewing, *The Judges of the Supreme Court, 1789-1937* (University of Minnesota Press, 1938).

28. Swisher, *op. cit.*, p. 960.

29. *Op. cit.*, p. 63.

30. *Law and Politics* (Harcourt, Brace, 1939), p. 108.

31. *American Commonwealth* (1888 ed.), Vol. I, pp. 247-8; see Benjamin F. Wright, *The Growth of American Constitutional Law* (Houghton Mifflin, 1942), p. 249.

32. *United States* v. *Butler.*

33. "The Supreme Court and American Capitalism," 42 *Yale Law Journal* 668 at 669 (1933).

34. In *Norman v. Baltimore if Ohio R. Co.*, the holder of a railroad bond bearing an interest coupon payable in gold of face value of $22.50 demanded $38.10 in payment.

35. Quoted in Felix Frankfurter, *Mr. Justice Holmes and the Supreme Court* (Harvard University Press, 1938), pp. 21-2.

36. Henry F. Pringle, *The Life and Times of William Howard Taft* (Farrar and Rinehart, 1939), Vol. II, p. 854.

37. Quoted in Felix Frankfurter, *Law and Politics*, p. 37.

38. Pringle, *op. cit.*, Vol. II, p. 955.

39. *Ibid.*, p. 967.

40. Swisher, *op. cit.*, pp. 446-7.

41. Quoted in Jackson, *op. cit.*, p. 131.

42. *Ideas for the Ice Age* (Viking, 1941), p. 259.

43. *Op. cit.*, pp. 82, 53.

44. Jackson, *op. cit.*, p. ix.

45. *The Federalist*, No. 10.

46. C. H. McIlwain, *Constitutionalism, Ancient and Modern* (Cornell University Press, 1940), p. 24.

CHAPTER II (PAGES 23-45)

1. "Battle of the Bench," *Collier's*, August 17, 1946, pp. 12-13.

2. In connection with these figures it should be explained that throughout this book opinions counted in computing statistics of dissent are all full opinions plus per curiam decisions reported with opinion in the same manner as full opinions. This practice conforms with that used by the Department of Justice in the preparation of Supreme Court statistics. See *Annual Report of the Attorney General, 1941*, p. 53, note 13. Opinions are counted, not cases; often several cases are decided by a single opinion.

Occasionally there is some doubt whether a separate opinion by one or more justices is a concurring or a dissenting opinion. In these compilations some separate opinions have been treated as dissents, although they were not so labeled by the Court reporter. This was done where the separate opinion favored a different disposition of the case than was made by the majority, or where it agreed with the disposition of the case but for reasons which revealed a fundamental divergence in judicial attitude from that of the majority. Thus in *United States* v. *Lovett* (1946), the concurring opinion of Justices Frankfurter and Reed was treated as a dissent, even though they joined in giving the judgment to Lovett, because they refused to go along with the majority in declaring unconstitutional the statutory provision at issue in that case. The use of judgment considerations of this sort in compiling these statistics may prevent them from being completely comparable with counts found in other sources.

3. *Jewell Ridge Coal Co.* v. *Local No. 6167, United Mine Workers.*

4. Motions for rehearing are customarily denied without opinion.

5. In addition to the *Jewell Ridge* case, Crampton Harris had argued another case the preceding term, *Tennessee Coal, Iron & R. Co.* v. *Muscoda Local No. 123* (1944), which he had won by a 7 to 2 vote, with Black again in the majority. Justices Jackson and Frankfurter had concurred with the majority in that decision, but had refused to accept the reasoning of the majority opinion.

6. *Congressional Record,* Vol. 92, pp. 7064-8, June 18, 1946.

7. Of course, Chief Justice Marshall went so far as to participate, and to write the Court's opinion, in the case of *Marbury* v. *Madison,* which involved one of his own official acts as Secretary of State, but judicial ethics have tightened up considerably since that day. Arthur M. Schlesinger, Jr., points out that "Jackson himself sat on cases argued by Solicitor General Charles Fahy, with whom his relations were more recent and cordial than Black's with his law partner of 1927." "The Supreme Court: 1947," 35 *Fortune* 78 (Jan. 1947). See also J. P. Frank, "Disqualification of Judges," 56 *Yale Law Journal* 605-39 (1947).

8. *Loc. cit.,* Chap. II, note 7.

9. See 306 U.S. v-vi.

10. "Our High Court Analyzed," *New York Times Magazine,* June 18, 1944, p. 17.

11. Justice Holmes, who retired from the Court early in the 1931 term, is not included in this table.

12. *Loc. cit.,* Chap. II, note 1. Schlesinger also has an interesting comment to make on Stone's leadership in his *Fortune* article. "Charles Evans Hughes kept things moving briskly and efficiently, confining discussion to issues, forbidding fruitless argument and adjourning promptly at four-thirty. Harlan Stone, a veteran dissenter with a New Englander's faith in town-meeting democracy, found it hard to cut off talk until everyone had spoken his fill. Especially in his last two years, conferences began to spill over to Monday, sometimes to Tuesday and Wednesday. As the discussion was prolonged, argument tended to degenerate into wrangling, which greatly increased opportunities for mutual irritation." *Loc. cit.,* Chap. II, note 7, p. 211.

Chapter III (Pages 46-70)

1. Dissenting in *Smith* v. *Allwright*.

2. George W. Martin, "Preface to the President's Autobiography," 188 *Harper's* 196 (1944).

3. "Common Law in the United States," 50 *Harvard Law Review* 20 (1936); quoted in Samuel J. Konefsky, *Chief Justice Stone and the Supreme Court* (Macmillan, 1945), p. 260.

4. See Malcolm Sharp, "Movement in Supreme Court Adjudication—A Study of Modified and Overruled Decisions," 46 *Harvard Law Review* 361, 593, 795 (1933).

5. "The Supreme Court and Business Planning," 24 *Harvard Business Review* 151 at 163 (1946).

6. 40 *American Political Science Review* 231 (1946).

7. *Loc. cit.*, Chap. II, note 7, pp. 211-12.

8. "The Nine Young Men," 18 *Life* 76-80 (Jan. 22, 1945).

9. Quoted by Alexander H. Pekelis, "The Supreme Court Today," 110 *New Republic* 522-5 (April 17, 1944).

10. *Ibid.*, pp. 522-3.

11. Robert H. Jackson, "The Law Is a Rule for Men to Live By," 9 *Vital Speeches* 664 at 665 (1943).

12. *Wilson* v. *Cook* (1946).

13. "And Repent at Leisure," 58 *Harvard Law Review* 930 at 943 (1945).

14. Quoted by Arthur Ballantine, *loc. cit.*, Chap. III, note 5, p. 162.

15. *Minersville School District* v. *Gobitis* (1940).

16. Jackson, *loc. cit.*, Chap. III, note 11, p. 665.

17. Dissenting in *Burnet* v. *Coronado Oil & Gas Co.* (1932).

18. *Ibid.*

19. *Bunting* v. *Oregon*.

20. *Adkins* v. *Children's Hospital*.

21. Or the reason may have been, as Curtis suggests, that these two precedents, which Roberts had voted for, and which the Court was now abandoning with the aid of Roberts' vote, were treated "somewhat delicately out of regard to Roberts's feelings." *Op. cit.*, p. 174.

22. *United States* v. *Darby Lumber Co.*

23. *Tyson* v. *Banton* (1927); *Ribnik* v. *McBride* (1928); *Williams* v. *Standard Oil Co.* (1929); *New State Ice Co.* v. *Liebman* (1932).

24. *Loc. cit.*, Chap. II, note 10.

25. Frank W. Grinnell, "The New Guesspotism," 30 *American Bar Association Journal* 507-11 (1944).

26. See list of overruled decisions on pp. 300-1.

27. *Barden* v. *Northern Pacific Rr.*

28. Stone's efforts along this line are ably analyzed by Konefsky, *op. cit.,* Chap. I.

29. *Commissioner of Internal Revenue* v. *Shamberg* (1945).

30. *Kuhn* v. *Fairmount Coal Co.*

31. This fact was underlined when the Court by an 8 to 0 vote in another case decided the same day, upheld the applicability of the Wagner Act to the insurance business. *Polish National Alliance* v. *N.L.R.B.* (1944).

32. See the interesting discussion by Charles S. Lyon, "Old Statutes and New Constitution," 44 *Columbia Law Review* 599-38 (1944).

33. *Prudential Insurance Co.* v. *Benjamin* (1946); *Robertson* v. *California* (1946).

34. See Edward S. Corwin, *The Constitution and What It Means Today* (Princeton University Press, 8th ed., 1946), pp. 180-1, for a criticism of this view of the clause.

35. *Smith* v. *Allwright* (1944).

36. *Helvering* v. *Hallock* (1940).

37. *Screws* v. *United States.*

CHAPTER IV (PAGES 71-90)

1. *Electric Bond & Share Co.* v. *S.E.C.*

2. *North American Co.* v. *S.E.C.; American Power & Light Co.* v. *S.E.C.* The former decision was unanimous, while two justices dissented from the latter, but not on the question of constitutionality of the statute.

3. *Currin* v. *Wallace* (1939); *Mulford* v. *Smith* (1939); *Wickard* v. *Filburn* (1942).

4. *Sunshine Anthracite Coal Co.* v. *Adkins* (1940).

5. *United States* v. *Bekins.*

6. *Wickard* v. *Filburn.*

7. *United States* v. *Yellow Cab Co.* (1947).

8. *Steward Machine Co.* v. *Davis; Helvering* v. *Davis.*

9. *United States* v. *Darby Lumber Co.*

10. See his dissents in *H. P. Hood and Sons* v. *United States* (1939), and *Yakus* v. *United States* (1944). The delegation of powers issue was also raised by Justice Frankfurter in *Federal Power Commission* v. *Hope Natural Gas Co.* (1944). See also Chap. VII, *infra.*

11. *Yakus* v. *United States* (1944); *Bowles* v. *Willingham* (1944). The post-war Housing and Rent Control Act of 1947 was unanimously upheld in *Woods* v. *Cloyd W. Miller Co.* (1948).

12. *United States* v. *Montgomery Ward* (1945). For a general discussion of the impact of war on federal powers, see Edward S. Corwin, *Total War and the Constitution* (Knopf, 1946).

13. *Southwestern Bell Telephone Co.* v. *Public Service Commission of Missouri* (1923).

14. *Olsen* v. *Nebraska* (1941).

15. From "Law and the Court," in *Speeches* (Little, Brown, 1934), p. 102.

16. *California* v. *Thompson.*

17. *Maurer* v. *Hamilton* (1940).

18. *Parker* v. *Brown* (1943).

19. *Cloverleaf Butter Co.* v. *Patterson* (1942); *Southern Pacific Co.* v. *Arizona* (1945); *Rice* v. *Santa Fe Elevator Corp.* (1947); *Bethlehem Steel Co.* v. *New York State Labor Relations Board* (1947).

20. *Nelson* v. *Sears, Roebuck & Co.; Nelson* v. *Montgomery Ward & Co.*

21. *Brown* v. *Maryland.*

22. *Richfield Oil Corp.* v. *State Board of Equalization* (1946); *Freeman* v. *Hewit* (1946); *Joseph* v. *Carter & Weekes Stevedoring Co.* (1947).

23. Later in the 1946 term, however, the Court refused to carry the principle of the *Freeman* and *Joseph* cases to the extreme of invalidating a local license tax on commerce grounds, although Justices Jackson and Vinson contended that the two earlier decisions required such a ruling. *Independent Warehouses* v. *Scheele* (1947).

CHAPTER V (PAGES 91-136)

1. *Minersville School District* v. *Gobitis.*

2. Carl B. Swisher, *The Growth of Constitutional Power in the United States* (University of Chicago Press, 1946), p. 165.

3. *Milk Wagon Drivers Union* v. *Meadowmoor Dairies* (1941).

4. *Thomas* v. *Collins* (1944).

5. For an account of the Jehovah's Witnesses sect and its methods of operation, see Herbert H. Stroup, *The Jehovah's Witnesses* (Columbia University Press, 1945). The Supreme Court cases in which this religious group has appeared are analyzed by Hollis W. Barber, "Religious Liberty v. the Police Power: Jehovah's Witnesses," 41 *American Political Science Review,* 226-47 (1947).

6. *Stromberg* v. *California; Near* v. *Minnesota.*

7. *Lovell* v. *Griffin.* A few months earlier the Court had refused by a per curiam decision to review a flag salute case from Georgia involving Jehovah's Witnesses, for want of a substantial federal question. *Leoles* v. *Landers* (1937).

8. *Schneider* v. *Irvington* (1939), with only McReynolds dissenting.

9. *Cantwell* v. *Connecticut.*

10. *United States* v. *Carolene Products Co.* (1938); see Konefsky, *op. cit.,* p. 195.

11. *Cox* v. *New Hampshire.*

12. *Chaplinsky* v. *New Hampshire.*

13. *Taylor* v. *Mississippi* (1943); *Jamison* v. *Texas* (1943); *Largent* v. *Texas* (1943); *Busey* v. *District of Columbia* (1943).

14. *Martin* v. *City of Struthers* (1943).

15. There have been some additional Jehovah's Witnesses cases coming up in connection with their resistance to the draft, which will be considered in Chap. VI.

16. *Prince* v. *Massachusetts* (1944). *Follett* v. *Town of McCormick* (1944) was decided the same term.

17. *Tucker* v. *Texas; Marsh* v. *Alabama.*

18. See Justice Jackson's opinion in *Douglas* v. *City of Jeanette* (1943).

19. *Op. cit.,* Chap. III, note 34, p. 194.

20. *Ibid.* The second *Ballard* decision is discussed in Chap. VI.

21. *Illinois ex rel. McCullom* v. *Board of Education of School District No. 71, Champaign County.* In the wake of the *Everson* decision the Supreme Court was asked on August 29, 1947 to review a decision of the Pennsylvania Supreme Court to the effect that public school boards need not pay for transportation of pupils to Catholic parochial schools. In this case the township school board provided free bus service for public school children, but refused to do so for parochial students; the contention was made by the father of a parochial school student that he was being denied the right of freedom of religion and equal protection of the laws. This appeal was withdrawn before the Supreme Court could accept it or reject it.

22. *Grosjean* v. *American Press Co.* (1936).

23. *Times-Mirror Co.* v. *Superior Court of California,* consolidated with the case of *Bridges* v. *California* (1941).

24. Charles P. Curtis, Jr., contends that Reed's decision in the *Pennekamp* case amounts to "a masterly job of tactful reconstruction" of Black's opinion in the *Los Angeles Times* case, relying more on the facts of the particular situation and less on Black's "dogmatized version of the First Amendment." *Op. cit.,* pp. 295-7.

25. See Robert E. Cushman, "Civil Liberties," 37 *American Political Science Review* 50 (1943).

26. *Associated Press* v. *N.L.R.B.*

27. *Associated Press* v. *United States.*

28. *Oklahoma Press Publishing Co.* v. *Walling; Mabee* v. *White Plains Publishing Co.*

29. *Whitney* v. *California* (1927).

30. *Stromberg* v. *California.*

31. *Herndon* v. *Lowry.*

32. *DeJonge* v. *Oregon.*

33. For two excellent discussions of the circumstances giving rise to this case, see Robert E. Cushman, "The Purge of Federal Employees Accused of Disloyalty," 3 *Public Administration Review* 297-316 (1943), and Frederick L. Schuman, "'Bill of Attainder' in the Seventy-Eighth Congress," 37 *American Political Science Review* 819-29 (1943).

34. *United States* v. *Lovett* (1946).

35. *Schneiderman* v. *United States* (1943).

36. *Kessler* v. *Strecker* (1939).

37. H.R. 9766, 76th Cong.

38. *Bridges* v. *Wixon* (1945).

39. *Hartzel* v. *United States* (1944).

40. *Cramer* v. *United States* (1945).

41. *Viereck* v. *United States* (1943); *Keegan* v. *United States* (1945).

42. Cushman, *loc. cit.*, Chap. V, note 25, p. 54.

43. *Baumgartner* v. *United States* (1944).

44. *Knauer* v. *United States* (1946).

45. *Hirabayashi* v. *United States* (1943).

46. For discussions of the Japanese cases, see Corwin, *Total War and the Constitution,* Chap. III, and N. Dembitz, "Racial Discrimination and the Military Judgment," 45 *Columbia Law Review* 175-239 (1945). The Court has recently made partial amends for its wartime decisions by upholding the right of a minor American citizen of Japanese ancestry to hold land in California in spite of certain restrictive state legislation. *Oyama* v. *State of California* (1948).

47. *Newberry* v. *United States*. Newberry had been convicted in the lower court of violating the federal corrupt practices act by spending more money than the statute allowed in his Michigan primary campaign against Henry Ford for the U.S. Senate. A badly divided Supreme Court Set aside the conviction. Four justices held that the Constitution gave Congress no power to regulate congressional primaries, and that Newberry consequently had not committed a federal crime. Four justices held that Congress could validly regulate congressional primaries. The ninth justice concurred in reversing the conviction on grounds unrelated to the constitutional issue. While the constitutional question had thus not been definitely determined by a Court majority, the opinion was widely taken to mean that congressional control of primaries was unconstitutional, and Congress amended the corrupt practices act in 1925 to remove primaries from its purview.

48. *Nixon* v. *Herndon* (1927).

49. *Nixon* v. *Condon* (1932).

50. *Cook* v. *Fortson.*

51. Justice Holmes once said in a Massachusetts case where a policeman was objecting to a rule prohibiting solicitation of money for political purposes: "The petitioner may have a constitutional right to talk politics, but he has no constitutional right to be a policeman." *McAuliffe* v. *New Bedford* (1892).

52. *Josephson* v. *United States.*

53. *Edwards* v. *California.*

54. *Missouri, Kansas & Texas Ry. Co.* v. *May* (1904).

55. *Federal Power Commission* v. *Natural Gas Pipeline Co.* (1942).

56. *Mr. Justice Holmes and the Supreme Court,* p. 49.

Chapter VI (pages 137-166)

1. *McNabb* v. *United States* (1943).

2. For a general discussion of recent decisions in this field, see Bennett Boskey and John H. Pickering, "Federal Restrictions on State Criminal Procedure," 13 *University of Chicago Law Review* 266-99 (1946).

3. *Powell* v. *Alabama.*

4. *Op. cit.,* Chap. III, note 34, p. 182n.

5. *Williams* v. *Kaiser* (1945); *Tomkins* v. *Missouri* (1945); *House* v. *Mayo* (1945); *Rice* v. *Olson* (1945).

6. *Carter* v. *Illinois* (1946); *Gayes* v. *New York* (1947); *Foster* v. *Illinois* (1947).

7. *Ex parte Virginia.*

8. *Strauder* v. *West Virginia.*

9. *Pierre* v. *Louisiana.*

9a. Another New York conviction involving use of a blue ribbon jury was upheld in March, 1948, by the same 5 to 4 vote. *Moore* v. *New York.*

10. *Brown* v. *Mississippi* (1936).

11. *McNabb* v. *United States.*

12. Robert K. Carr, "Screws vs. United States: The Georgia Police Brutality Case," 31 *Cornell Law Quarterly* 48-67 (1945).

13. *Nardone* v. *United States* (1937).

14. *Nardone* v. *United States* (1939).

15. *Goldman* v. *United States; Goldstein* v. *United States.*

16. *Davis* v. *United States.*

17. *Zap* v. *United States.*

18. *Harris* v. *United States* (1947).

19. *Ex parte Quirin* (1942).

20. 36 *American Political Science Review* 1091 (1942).

21. *Snyder* v. *Massachusetts* (1934).

22. *Louisiana ex rel. Francis* v. *Resweber* (1947).

CHAPTER VII (PAGES 167-197)

1. *The Administrative Process* (Yale University Press, 1938), p. 123.

2. *Panama Refining Co.* v. *Ryan.*

3. Jackson, *op. cit.,* Chap. I, note 3, p. 92.

4. *Schechter* v. *United States* (1935); *Carter* v. *Carter Coal Co.* (1936).

5. *H. P. Hood & Sons* v. *United States.*

6. *Bowles* v. *Willingham.*

7. *Springer* v. *Philippine Islands.*

8. *National Broadcasting Co.* v. *United States* (1943).

9. *Gemsco, Inc.* v. *Walling.*

10. *Gray* v. *Powell* (1941).

11. *I.C.C.* v. *Railway Labor Executives Association.*

12. *First Iowa Hydro-Electric Cooperative* v. *Federal Power Commission.*

13. *Morgan* v. *United States* (1936, 1938); *United States* v. *Morgan* (1939, 1941).

14. *United States* v. *New River Co.* (1924).

15. *Steiner* v. *Great Northern Ry.*

16. See *Ohio Valley Water Co.* v. *Ben Avon Borough* (1920); *Crowell* v. *Benson* (1932).

17. *Board of Trade of Kansas City* v. *United States* (1942).

18. *Federal Power Commission* v. *Hope Natural Gas Co.* (1944).

19. *Barringer & Co.* v. *United States* (1943); *I.C.C.* v. *Inland Waterways Corp.* (1943); *I.C.C.* v. *Mechling* (1947).

20. *McLean Trucking Co.* v. *United States* (1944).

21. *I.C.C.* v. *Jersey City* (1944). See also *North Carolina* v. *United States* (1945); *Alabama* v. *United States* (1945).

22. *Gregg Cartage Co.* v. *United States* (1942).

23. *United States* v. *Carolina Freight Carriers Corp.* (1942).

24. *Eastern-Central Motor Carriers Assn.* v. *United States* (1944).

25. *I.C.C.* v. *Columbus & Greenville Rr. Co.*

26. *Eastern-Central Motor Carriers Assn.* v. *United States.*

27. *United States* v. *Carolina Freight Carriers Corp.*

28. *Federal Communications Commission* v. *National Broadcasting Co.*

29. *Ashbacker Radio Corp.* v. *Federal Communications Commission.*

30. *Columbia Broadcasting System* v. *United States* (1942).

31. *Yakus* v. *United States* (1944).

32. *Hecht Co.* v. *Bowles* (1944).

33. *Scripps-Howard Radio* v. *Federal Communications Commission* (1942).

34. Dissenting in *Stark* v. *Wickard* (1944).

35. *Board of Governors* v. *Agnew.*

36. *Parker* v. *Fleming.*

37. *Case* v. *Bowles* (1946); *Hulbert* v. *Twin Falls County* (1946).

38. *Driscoll* v. *Edison Light & Power Co.* (1939).

39. *Columbia Broadcasting System* v. *United States* (1942).

40. *Bridges* v. *Wixon* (1945). Or as Justice Reed said for the Court's right wing in *Cox* v. *United States* (1948): "The concept of a jury passing independently on an issue previously determined by an administrative body is contrary to settled federal administrative practice; the constitutional right to jury trial does not include the right to have a jury pass on the validity of an administrative order."

41. *Elgin, J. & E. Ry. Co.* v. *Burley* (1945).

42. *Elgin, J. & E. Ry. Co.* v. *Burley* (1946). See also *Chicago & Southern Air Lines* v. *Waterman S. S. Corp.* (1948), where the Court held unreviewable orders of the

Civil Aeronautics Board approved by the President, over the protest of the predominantly left-wing group of Douglas, Black, Rutledge, and Reed.

43. See Foster H. Sherwood, "The Federal Administrative Procedure Act," 41 *American Political Science Review* 271-81 (1947); Frederick F. Blachly and Miriam E. Oatman, "Sabotage of the Administrative Process," 6 *Public Administration Review* 213-27 (1946).

44. *Scripps-Howard Radio* v. *Federal Communications Commission* (1942).

Chapter VIII (pages 198-238)

1. *Op. cit.*, Chap. III, note 34, p. viii.

2. *United States* v. *Local 807, International Brotherhood of Teamsters.*

3. *N.L.R.B.* v. *Fruehauf Trailer Co.* (1937); *N.L.R.B.* v. *Friedman-Harry Marks Clothing Co.* (1937); *Santa Cruz Fruit Backing Co.* v. *N.L.R.B.* (1938); *Consolidated Edison Co.* v. *N.L.R.B.* (1938); *N.L.R.B.* v. *Fainblatt* (1939).

4. *Polish National Alliance* v. *N.L.R.B.*

5. *N.L.R.B.* v. *Columbian Enameling & Stamping Co.; N.L.R.B.* v. *Sands Mfg. Co.*

6. *N.L.R.B.* v. *Waterman S.S. Co.*

7. *N.L.R.B.* v. *Fansteel Metallurgical Corp.*

8. *Phelps Dodge Corp.* v. *N.L.R.B.* (1941).

9. Charles O. Gregory, *Labor and the Law* (W. W. Norton, 1946), p. 300.

10. *J. I. Case Co.* v. *N.L.R.B.* (1944).

11. *Medo Photo Supply Co.* v. *N.L.R.B.* (1944).

12. *10 East 40th St. Bldg.* v. *Callus* (1945).

13. *Borden Co.* v. *Borella* (1945); *to East 40th St. Bldg.* v. *Callus.*

14. *Kirschbaum* v. *Walling* (1942); *Martino* v. *Michigan Window Cleaning Co.* (1946); *Warren-Bradshaw Drilling Co.* v. *Hall* (1942); *Overstreet* v. *North Shore Corp.* (1943); *Mabee* v. *White Plains Pub. Co.* (1946).

15. *McLeod* v. *Threlkeld* (1943); *Walling* v. *Portland Terminal Co.* (1947); *Western Union Telegraph Co.* v. *Lenroot* (1945).

16. *Anderson* v. *Mt. Clemens Pottery Co.*

17. *Tennessee Coal, Iron & R. Co.* v. *Muscoda Local.*

18. *Jewell Ridge Coal Corp.* v. *Local No. 6167, U.M.W.*

19. *Walling* v. *Portland Terminal Co.; Walling* v. *Nashville, C. & St. L. Ry.*

20. *Cudahy Packing Co.* v. *Holland.*

21. *Oklahoma Press Pub. Co.* v. *Walling.*

22. *Loewe* v. *Lawlor.*

23. *American Steel Foundries* v. *Tri-City Central Trades Council; Duplex Printing Press Co.* v. *Deering.*

24. *Coronado Coal Co.* v. *United Mine Workers* (1925).

25. *Bedford Cut Stone Co.* v. *Journeymen Stone Cutters' Assn.* (1927).

26. *Op. cit.*, p. 253.

27. *Apex Hosiery Co.* v. *Leader.*

28. *American Steel Foundries* v. *Tri-City Central Trades Council.*

29. *Op. cit.*, pp. 347-8.

30. *Milk Wagon Drivers Union* v. *Meadowmoor Dairies.*

31. *Cafeteria Employees' Union* v. *Angelos.*

32. *Op. cit.*, pp. 360-1.

33. "The Supreme Court and Organized Labor, 1941-1945," 58 *Harvard Law Review* 1018 at 1056 (1945).

34. *Hotel and Restaurant Employees' Union* v. *Wisconsin Employment Relations Board* (1942).

35. *Alabama State Federation of Labor* v. *McAdory; C.I.O.* v. *McAdory.*

36. *American Federation of Labor* v. *Watson* (1946).

37. *N.L.R.B.* v. *Virginia Electric & Power Co.*

38. *Virginia Electric & Power Co.* v. *N.L.R.B.* (1943).

39. *Steele* v. *Louisville & N. R. Co.; Tunstall* v. *Brotherhood of Locomotive Firemen and Enginemen, Ocean Lodge No. 76.*

40. *Railway Mail Assn.* v. *Corsi* (1944).

Chapter IX (pages 239-263)

1. *Op. cit.*, Chap. I, note 26, pp. 56-7.

2. *West Virginia State Board of Education* v. *Barnette* (1943).

3. "Some Aspects of American Constitutional Law," 53 *Harvard Law Review* 529 at 536 (1940).

Chapter X (pages 264-287)

1. *Op. cit.*, Chap. I, note 42, pp. 100-1.

2. "The Lost Liberals," 194 *Harper's* 386 (1947).

3. *Loc. cit.*, Chap. II, note 7.

4. *Springer* v. *Philippine Islands* (1928).

5. *Op. cit.*, pp. 175-6.

6. *Ashcraft* v. *Tennessee* (1944).

7. *Northern Securities Co.* v. *United States* (1904).

8. Gregory, *op. cit.*, p. 168.

9. *Jacobsen* v. *Massachusetts.*

10. *Buck* v. *Bell.*

11. *United States* v. *Schwimmer* (1929).

12. *Abrams* v. *United States* (1919).

13. See V. M. Barnett, Jr., "Mr. Justice Murphy, Civil Liberties and the Holmes Tradition," 32 *Cornell Law Quarterly,* 177-221 (1946).

14. *West Virginia State Board of Education* v. *Barnette.*

15. *Law and Politics,* p. 197; quoted in Henry S. Commager, *Majority Rule and Minority Rights* (Oxford, 1943), p. 71.

16. *Ibid.,* pp. 67, 75, 81.

17. Dissenting in *United States* v. *Butler.*

18. *Loc. cit.,* Chap. II, note 7, p. 202.

19. *Holmes-Pollock Letters* (Harvard University Press, 1941), Vol. II, p. 29.

20. *Pierce* v. *Society of Sisters.*

21. *Stromberg* v. *California; Near* v. *Minnesota.*

22. *Bridges* v. *California* (1941).

23. Quoted in Lerner, *Ideas for the Ice Age,* p. 110.

24. 35 *American Political Science Review* 270 (1941).

25. *Loc. cit.,* p. 208.

26. *Loc. cit.,* Chap. II, note 10.

27. 49 *American Mercury* 135 at 142 (1944).

28. Schlesinger, *loc. cit.,* p. 208.

DECISIONS OVERRULED
BY THE SUPREME COURT
1937-1946 TERMS

Previous Decision	Vote	Overruled by	Vote
Burnet v. Coronado Oil & Gas Co. (1932)	5-4	Helvering v. Mountain Producers (1938)	5-2
Gillespie v. Oklahoma (1922)	6-3	Helvering v. Mountain Producers (1938)	5-2
Swift v. Tyson (1842)	Unan.	Erie R. v. Tompkins (1938)	6-2
Dobbins v. Cmsrs. of Erie County (1842)	Unan.	Graves v. O'Keefe (1939)	7-2
Collector v. Day (1871)	7-1	Graves v. O'Keefe (1939)	7-2
N.Y. ex rel. Rogers v. Graves (1937)	8-0	Graves v. O'Keefe (1939)	7-2
Brush v. Commissioner (1937)	5-2	Graves v. O'Keefe (1939)	7-2
Proctor & Gamble v. U.S. (1912)	Unan.	Rochester Tel. Co. v. U.S. (1939)	7-2
Evans v. Gore (1920)	7-2	O'Malley v. Woodrough (1939)	7-1
Miles v. Graham (1925)	8-1	O'Malley v. Woodrough (1939)	7-1
Colgate v. Harvey (1935)	6-3	Madden v. Kentucky (1940)	6-2
Connally v. Union Sewer Pipe Co. (1902)	7-1	Tigner v. Texas (1940)	8-1
Hammer v. Dagenhart (1918)	5-4	U.S. v. Darby (1941)	8-0
Toledo Newspaper Co. v. U.S. (1918)	5-2	Nye v. U.S. (1941)	5-3
Adair v. U.S. (1908)	6-2	Phelps Dodge v. N.L.R.B. (1941)	8-0*
Coppage v. Kansas (1915)	6-3	Phelps Dodge v. N.L.R.B. (1940)	8-0*
Ribnik v. McBride (1928)	6-3	Olsen v. Nebraska (1941)	8-0
DiSanto v. Pennsylvania (1927)	6-3	California v. Thompson (1941)	8-0
Newberry v. U.S. (1921)	5-4	U.S. v. Classic (1941)	7-0*
Panhandle Oil Co. v. Mississippi (1928)	5-4	Alabama v. King & Boozer (1941)	8-0
Graves v. Texas Co. (1936)	6-2	Alabama v. King & Boozer (1941)	8-0
Supreme Tribe of Ben Hur v. Cauble (1921)	Unan.	Toucey v. N. Y. Life Ins. (1941)	6-3

First Nat. Bank v. Maine (1932)	6-3 Tax Cmsn. of Utah v. Aldrich (1942)	7-2
Haddock v. Haddock (1906)	5-4 Williams v. N. Carolina (1942)	6-2
Jones v. Opelika (1942)	5-4 Murdock v. Pennsylvania (1943)	5-4
Minersville School Dist. v. Gobitis (1940)	8-1 W. Va. State Bd. of Ed. v. Barnette (1943)	6-3
Grovey v. Townsend (1935)	Unan. Smith v. Allwright (1944)	8-1
Paul v. Virginia (1869)	Unan. U.S. v. South-Eastern Underwriters (1944)	4-3
U.S. v. Schwimmer (1929)	6-3 Girouard v. U.S. (1946)	5-3
U.S. v. Macintosh (1931)	5-4 Girouard v. U.S. (1946)	5-3
U.S. v. Bland (1931)	5-4 Girouard v. U.S. (1946)	5-3
Lupton's Sons v. Automobile Club (1912)	Unan. Angel v. Bullington (1947)	6-3

* Unanimous on the question of overruling the previous decision.

TABLE OF CASES

[Page numbers reference the original pagination of the previous printed editions. This pagination is found embedded into the text using brackets.]

Abrams v. United States, 250 U.S. 616 (1919), 274, 275

Adamson v. California, 332 U.S. 46 (1947), 164-5

Addison v. Holly Hill Fruit Products, 322 U.S. 607 (1944), 49, 207

Adkins v. Children's Hospital, 261 U.S. 525 (1923), 3, 6, 55

Akins v. Texas, 325 U.S. 398 (1945), 143

Alabama v. King & Boozer, 314 U.S. 1 (1941), 61

Alabama v. United States, 325 U.S. 535 (1945), 297, n. 21

Alabama Power Co. v. Ickes, 302 U.S. 464 (1938), 76

Alabama State Federation of Labor v. McAdory, 325 U.S. 450 (1945), 227-8

Allen Bradley Co. v. Local Union No. 3, 325 U.S. 797 (1945), 216

Allen-Bradley Local No. 1111 v. Wisconsin Employment Relations Board, 315 U.S. 740 (1942), 226

American Federation of Labor v. Swing, 312 U.S. 321 (1941), 221

American Federation of Labor v. Watson, 327 U.S. 582 (1946), 228

American Power & Light Co. v. S.E.C., 329 U.S. 90 (1946), 75

American Steel Foundries v. Tri-City Central Trades Council, 257 U.S. 184 (1921), 209, 218

Anderson v. Mt. Clemens Pottery Co., 328 U.S. 680 (1946), 205-6

Apex Hosiery Co. v. Leader, 310 U.S. 469 (1940), 210-11, 214, 215

Ashbacker Radio Corp. v. F.C.C., 326 U.S. 327 (1945), 180

Ashcraft v. Tennessee, 322 U.S. 143 (1944), 327 U.S. 274 (1946), 147-8, 270

Ashton v. Cameron County Improvement District, 298 U.S. 513 (1936), 6

Ashwander v. Tennessee Valley Authority, 297 U.S. 288 (1936), 6

Associated Press v. N.L.R.B., 301 U.S. 103 (1937), 111

Associated Press v. United States, 326 U.S. 1 (1945), 111-12

Bakery and Pastry Drivers v. Wohl, 315 U.S. 769 (1942), 221

Baldwin v. Missouri, 281 U.S. 586 (1930), 77, 78, 270

Ballard v. United States, 329 U.S. 187 (1946), 145, 261

Barden v. Northern Pacific Rr., 154 U.S. 288 (1894), 58

Barringer & Co. v. United States, 319 U.S. 1 (1943), 177

Barron v. Baltimore, 7 Pet. 243 (1833), 163

Baumgartner v. United States, 322 U.S. 665 (1944), 119-20

Bedford Cut Stone Co. v. Journeymen Stone Cutters' Assn., 274 U.S. 37 (1927), 210, 272

Bethlehem Steel Co. v. New York State Labor Relations Board, 330 U.S. 767 (1947), 292, n. 19

Betts v. Brady, 316 U.S. 455 (1942), 139

Blackstone v. Miller, 188 U.S. 189 (1903), 78

Board of Governors of Federal Reserve System v. Agnew, 329 U.S. 441 (1947), 185

Board of Trade of Kansas City v. United States, 314 U.S. 534 (1942), 174

Bob-Lo Excursion Co. v. Michigan, 333 U.S. 28 (1948), 129

Borden Co. v. Borella, 325 U.S. 679 (1945), 204

Bowles v. Willingham, 321 U.S. 503 (1944), 76, 169

Bridges v. California, 314 U.S. 252 (1941), 280

Bridges v. Wixon, 326 U.S. 135 (1945), 116-17, 195

Brown v. Maryland, 12 Wheat. 419 (1827), 86

Brown v. Mississippi, 297 U.S. 278 (1936), 146

Brush v. Commissioner, 300 U.S. 352 (1937), 60, 61

Buck v. Bell, 274 U.S. 200 (1927), 274

Bunting v. Oregon, 243 U.S. 426 (1917), 54

Burnet v. Coronado Oil & Gas Co., 285 U.S. 393 (1932), 33, 54, 59, 60

Busey v. District of Columbia, 319 U.S. 579 (1943), 293, n. 13

Cafeteria Employees Union v. Angelos, 320 U.S. 293 (1943), 223

California v. Thompson, 313 U.S. 109 (1941), 82

Cantwell v. Connecticut, 310 U.S. 296 (1940), 94-5

Carpenters and Joiners Union v. Ritter's Cafe, 315 U.S. 722 (1942), 222-3

Carter v. Carter Coal Co., 298 U.S. 238 (1936), 6, 55, 169, 268

Carter v. Illinois, 329 U.S. 173 (1946), 296, n. 6

Case v. Bowles, 327 U.S. 92 (1946), 297, n. 37

Case Co. v. N.L.R.B, 321 U.S. 332 (1944), 201

Chambers v. Florida, 309 U.S. 227 (1940), 147

Chaplinsky v. New Hampshire, 315 U.S. 568 (1942), 96-7

Chicago & Southern Air Lines v. Waterman Steamship Co., 333 U.S. 95 (1948), 297, n. 42

Cloverleaf Butter Co. v. Patterson, 315 U.S. 148 (1942), 292, n. 19

Colegrove v. Green, 328 U.S. 549 (1946), 125

Colgate v. Harvey, 296 U.S. 404 (1935), 66, 67

Collector v. Day, 11 Wall. 113 (1871), 58, 60, 61

Columbia Broadcasting System v. United States, 316 U.S. 407 (1942), 180-81, 195

Commissioner of Internal Revenue v. Shamberg, 144 F. (2d) 998 (1944), 323 U.S. 792 (1945), 62

Congress of Industrial Organizations v. McAdory, 323 U.S. 472 (1945), 227-8

Consolidated Edison Co. v. N.L.R.B., 305 U.S. 197 (1938), 199

Cook v. Fortson, 329 U.S. 675 (1946), 125

Coronado Coal Co. v. United Mine Workers, 268 U.S. 295 (1925), 209, 211

Cox v. New Hampshire, 312 U.S. 569 (1941), 96

Cox v. United States, 332 U.S. 442 (1947), 188, 297, n. 40

Craig v. Harney, 331 U.S. 367 (1947), 109

Cramer v. United States, 325 U.S. 1 (1945), 118

Crowell v. Benson, 285 U.S. 22 (1932), 195, 271, 296, n. 16

Cudahy Packing Co. v. Holland, 315 U.S. 357 (1942), 207

Currin v. Wallace, 306 U.S. 11 (1938), 75

Curry v. McCanless, 307 U.S. 357 (1939), 79

Danbury Hatters Case. *See* Loewe v. Lawlor

Davis v. United States, 328 U.S. 582 (1946), 153-4

Debs v. United States, 249 U.S. 211 (1919), 275

De Jonge v. Oregon, 299 U.S. 353 (1937), 113

Di Santo v. Pennsylvania, 273 U.S. 34 (1927), 82

Dobbins v. Commissioners of Erie County, 16 Pet. 435 (1842), 58, 60, 61

Douglas v. City of Jeanette, 319 U.S. 157 (1943), 293, n. 18

Dred Scott v. Sandford, 19 How. 393 (1857), 73

Driscoll v. Edison Light & Power Co., 307 U.S. 104 (1939), 80, 173-4, 193

Duncan v. Kahanamoku, 327 U.S. 304 (1946), 156-8

Duplex Printing Press Co. v. Deering, 254 U.S. 443 (1921), 209, 210, 213, 272

Eastern-Central Motor Carriers Assn. v. United States, 321 U.S. 104 (1944), 178

Educational Films Corp. v. Ward, 282 U.S. 379 (1931), 59, 60

Edwards v. California, 314 U.S. 160 (1941), 128

Electric Bond & Share Co. v. S.E.C., 303 U.S. 419 (1938), 75

Elgin, Joliet & Eastern Ry. v. Burley, 325 U.S. 711 (1945), 327 U.S. 661 (1946), 195-6

Erie Railroad Co. v. Tompkins, 304 U.S. 64 (1938), 62

Estep v. United States, 327 U.S. 114 (1946), 187-8

Everson v. Board of Education of Ewing Township, 330 U.S. 1 (1947), 103-6

F.C.C. v. National Broadcasting Co., 319 U.S. 239 (1943), 180

F.P.C. v. Hope Natural Gas Co., 320 U.S. 591 (1944), 176, 292, n. 10

F.P.C. v. Natural Gas Pipeline Co., 315 U.S. 575 (1942), 133-4, 174-5

F.T.C. v. Bunte Brothers, 312 U.S. 349 (1941), 76

Falbo v. United States, 320 U.S. 549 (1944), 186

Farmers' Loan & Trust Co. v. Minnesota, 280 U.S. 204 (1930), 78

Fay v. New York, 332 U.S. 261 (1947), 146, 164

First Iowa Hydro-Electric Cooperative v. F.P.C., 328 U.S. 152 (1946), 171

First National Bank of Boston v. Maine, 284 U.S. 312 (1932), 78

Fletcher v. Peck, 6 Cranch 87 (1810), 73

Follett v. Town of McCormick, 321 U.S. 573 (1944), 293, n. 16

Foster v. Illinois, 332 U.S. 134 (1947), 140, 164

Fox Film Corp. v. Doyal, 286 U.S. 123 (1932), 59, 60

Freeman v. Hewit, 329 U.S. 249 (1946), 87, 88

Friedman v. Schwellenbach, 65 F. Supp. 254, 159 F. (2d) 22 (1946), 127

Gayes v. New York, 332 U.S. 145 (1947), 140, 164

Gemsco, Inc. v. Walling, 324 U.S. 244 (1945), 170, 207

Genessee Chief, 12 How. 443 (1851), 47, 53

Gibson v. United States, 329 U.S. 338 (1946), 188

Gillespie v. Oklahoma, 257 U.S. 501 (1922), 59, 60

Girouard v. United States, 328 U.S. 61 (1946), 102-3, 135, 255

Gitlow v. New York, 268 U.S. 652 (1925), 94, 112, 164, 275

Glasser v. United States, 315 U.S. 60 (1942), 139, 143

Goldman v. United States, 316 U.S. 129 (1942), 153

Goldstein v. United States, 316 U.S. 114 (1942), 153

Graves v. New York ex rel. O'Keefe, 306 U.S. 466 (1939), 52, 61

Graves v. Texas Co., 298 U.S. 393 (1936), 59

Gray v. Powell, 314 U.S. 402 (1941), 170

Greenough v. Tax Assessors of Newport, 331 U.S. 486 (1947), 79

Gregg Cartage Co. v. United States, 316 U.S. 74 (1942), 177-8

Grosjean v. American Press Co., 297 U.S. 233 (1936), 107

Grovey v. Townsend, 295 U.S. 45 (1938), 124

Haley v. State of Ohio, 332 U.S. 596 (1948), 160-61

Hammer v. Dagenhart, 247 U.S. 251 (1918), 3, 67, 75, 168

Hannegan v. Esquire, 327 U.S. 146 (1946), 111

Harris v. United States, 331 U.S. 145 (1947), 154

Hartzel v. United States, 322 U.S. 680 (1944), 117-18

Haupt v. United States, 330 U.S. 631 (1947), 119

Hecht Co. v. Bowles, 321 U.S. 321 (1944), 182

Helvering v. Davis, 301 U.S. 619 (1937), 9, 76

Helvering v. Gerhardt, 304 U.S. 405 (1938), 60

Helvering v. Hallock, 309 U.S. 106 (1940), 69

Helvering v. Mountain Producers' Corp., 303 U.S. 376 (1938), 60

Herndon v. Lowry, 301 U.S. 242 (1937), 113

Hill v. Florida, 325 U.S. 538 (1945), 226-7

Hill v. Texas, 316 U.S. 400 (1942), 142-3

Hirabayashi v. United States, 320 U.S. 81 (1943), 121-2

Home Building & Loan Assn. v. Blaisdell, 290 U.S. 398 (1934), 4

Homma, In re, 327 U.S. 759 (1946), 156

Hood & Sons v. United States, 307 U.S. 588 (1939), 169, 292, n. 10

Hooven & Allison Co. v. Evatt, 324 U.S. 652 (1945), 86

Hotel and Restaurant Employees' Union v. Wisconsin Employee Relations Board, 315 U.S. 437 (1942), 225

House v. Mayo, 324 U.S. 42 (1945), 139

Hulbert v. Twin Falls County, 327 U.S. 103 (1946), 297, n. 37

Humphrey's Executor v. United States, 293 U.S. 602 (1935), 5

Hunt v. Crumboch, 325 U.S. 821 (1945), 217-18, 238

Hurtado v. California, 110 U.S. 516 (1884), 163, 166

I.C.C. v. Columbus & Greenville Rr. Co., 319 U.S. 551 (1943), 178

I.C.C. v. Inland Waterways Corp., 319 U.S. 671 (1943), 177

I.C.C. v. Jersey City, 322 U.S. 503 (1944), 177

I.C.C. v. Mechling, 330 U.S. 567 (1947), 177

I.C.C. v. Railway Labor Executives Assn., 315 U.S. 373 (1942), 171

Illinois ex rel. McCullom v. Bd. of Ed. of School Dist. No. 71, Champaign County, 68 S. Ct. 461 (1948), 106-7

Independent Warehouses v. Scheele, 331 U.S. 70 (1947), 293, n. 23

Indian Motorcycle Co. v. United States, 283 U.S. 570 (1931), 59

Jacobson v. Massachusetts, 197 U.S. 11 (1905), 274

Jamison v. Texas, 318 U.S. 413 (1943), 293, n. 13

Jewell Ridge Coal Co. v. Local No. 6167, U.M.W., 325 U.S. 161 (1945); rehearing denied, 325 U.S. 897 (1945), 27

Johnson v. United States, 333 U.S. 10 (1948), 155 Jones v. Opelika, 316 U.S. 584 (1942), 97, 98

Joseph v. Carter & Weekes Stevedoring Co., 330 U.S. 422 (1947), 88

Josephson v. United States, 74 F. Supp. 958 (1947), 165 F. (2d) 82 (1947), 68 S. Ct. 609, 731 (1948), 128

Keegan v. United States, 325 U.S. 478 (1945), 119

Kessler v. Strecker, 307 U.S. 22 (1939), 116

Kirschbaum v. Walling, 316 U.S. 517 (1942), 205

Knauer v. United States, 328 U.S. 654 (1946), 120

Korematsu v. United States, 323 U.S. 214 (1944), 122

Kotch v. Board of River Port Pilot Commissioners, 330 U.S. 552 (1947), 81, 90

Kuhn v. Fairmount Coal Co., 213 U.S. 349 (1910), 62

Largent v. Texas, 318 U.S. 418 (1943), 293, n. 13

Leoles v. Landers, 302 U.S. 656 (1937), 293, n. 7

Levitt, Ex parte, 302 U.S. 633 (1937), 9

Lochner v. New York, 198 U.S. 45 (1905), 54

Loewe v. Lawlor, 208 U.S. 274 (1908), 209, 217

Long v. Rockwood, 277 U.S. 142 (1928), 59

Lovell v. Griffin, 303 U.S. 444 (1938), 94

Louisiana ex rel. Francis v. Resweber, 329 U.S. 459 (1947), 159

Louisville Joint Stock Land Bank v. Radford, 295 U.S. 555 (1935), 5

Mabee v. White Plains Pub. Co., 327 U.S. 178 (1946), 112, 205

Macallen Co. v. Massachusetts, 279 U.S. 620 (1929), 59

McAuliffe v. New Bedford, 155 Mass. 216 (1892), 295, n. 51

McCarroll v. Dixie Greyhound Lines, 309 U.S. 176 (1940), 84, 87

McCulloch v. Maryland, 4 Wheat. 316 (1819), 58, 74

McGoldrick v. Berwind-White Coal Co., 309 U.S. 33 (1940), 85

McLean Trucking Co. v. United States, 321 U.S. 67 (1944), 177

McLeod v. Dilworth Co., 322 U.S. 327 (1944), 86

McLeod v. Threlkeld, 319 U.S. 491 (1943), 205

McNabb v. United States, 318 U.S. 332 (1943), 138, 148

Madden v. Kentucky, 309 U.S. 83 (1940), 67

Marbury v. Madison, 1 Cranch 137 (1803), 73

Marsh v. Alabama, 326 U.S. 501 (1946), 99

Martin v. City of Struthers, 319 U.S. 141 (1943), 99

Martino v. Michigan Window Cleaning Co., 327 U.S. 173 (1946), 205

Maurer v. Hamilton, 309 U.S. 598 (1940), 83

Maxwell v. Dow, 176 U.S. 581 (1900), 163

Medo Photo Supply Co. v. N.L.R.B., 321 U.S. 678 (1944), 201

Meyer v. Nebraska, 262 U.S. 390 (1923), 279

Milk Wagon Drivers Union v. Meadowmoor Dairies, 312 U.S. 287 (1941), 92, 221

Milligan, Ex parte, 4 Wall. 2 (1866), 189

Minersville School District v. Gobitis, 310 U.S. 586 (1940), 52, 91, 95-6, 280-81

Missouri, Kansas & Texas Ry. v. May, 194 U.S. 267 (1904), 132

Moore v. New York, 68 S. Ct. 705 (1948), 296, n. 9a.

Morehead v. New York ex rel. Tipaldo, 298 U.S. 587 (1936), 6

Morgan v. United States, 298 U.S. 468 (1936), 304 U.S. 1 (1938), 171-2

Morgan v. Virginia, 328 U.S. 373 (1946), 128-9

Mulford v. Smith, 307 U.S. 38 (1939), 75

Munn v. Illinois, 94 U.S. 113 (1877), 55, 56, 80

Murdock v. Pennsylvania, 319 U.S. 105 (1943), 98

N.L.R.B. v. Columbian Enameling & Stamping Co., 306 U.S. 292 (1939), 200

N.L.R.B. v. Donnelly Garment Co., 330 U.S. 219 (1947), 288, n. 7

N.L.R.B. v. Fainblatt, 306 U.S. 601 (1939), 199

N.L.R.B. v. Fansteel Metallurgical Corp., 306 U.S. 240 (1939), 200

N.L.R.B. v. Friedman-Harry Marks, 301 U.S. 58 (1937), 199

N.L.R.B. v. Fruehauf Trailer Co., 301 U.S. 49 (1937), 199

N.L.R.B. v. Jones & Laughlin Corp., 301 U.S. 1 (1937), 9, 55, 75, 199, 268-9

N.L.R.B. v. Sands Mfg. Co., 306 U.S. 332 (1939), 200

N.L.R.B. v. Virginia Electric & Power Co., 314 U.S. 469 (1941), 229-30

N.L.R.B. v. Waterman Steamship Co., 309 U.S. 206 (1940), 200

Nardone v. United States, 302 U.S. 379 (1937), 308 U.S. 338 (1939), 153

National Broadcasting Co. v. United States, 319 U.S. 190 (1943), 170

Near v. Minnesota, 283 U.S. 697 (1931), 94, 107, 274, 280

Nebbia v. New York, 291 U.S. 502 (1934), 5, 56, 80

Nelson v. Montgomery Ward & Co., 312 U.S. 373 (1941)1 85

Nelson v. Sears, Roebuck & Co., 312 U.S. 359 (1941), 85

Newberry v. United States, 256 U.S. 232 (1921), 123

New State Ice Co. v. Liebman, 285 U.S. 262 (1932), 56

New York ex rel. Rogers v. Graves, 299 U.S. 401 (1937), 60, 61

New York v. United States, 326 U.S. 572 (1946), 179-80

Nippert v. City of Richmond, 327 U.S. 416 (1946), 86, 90

Nixon v. Condon, 286 U.S. 73 (1932), 123-4

Nixon v. Herndon, 273 U.S. 536 (1927), 123

Norman v. Baltimore & Ohio Rr. Co., 294 U.S. 240 (1935), 5, 16

Norris v. Alabama, 294 U.S. 587 (1935), 142

North American Co. v. S.E.C., 327 U.S. 686 (1946), 75

North Carolina v. United States, 325 U.S. 507 (1945), 297, n. 21

Northern Securities Co. v. United States, 193 U.S. 197 (1904), 270

Northwest Airlines v. Minnesota, 322 U.S. 292 (1944), 85-6, 87

Nye v. United States, 313 U.S. 33 (1941), 107

Ohio Valley Water Co. v. Ben Avon Borough, 253 U.S. 287 (1920), 296, n. 16

Oklahoma Press Publishing Co. v. Walling, 327 U.S. 186 (1946), 112, 207

Oliver, In re, 68 S. Ct. 499 (1948), 165

Olmstead v. United States, 277 U.S. 438 (1928), 152-3

Olsen v. Nebraska, 313 U.S. 236 (1941), 81

Overstreet v. North Shore Corp., 318 U.S. 125 (1943), 205

Oyama v. California, 332 U.S. 633 (1948), 295, n. 46

Packard Motor Co. v. N.L.R.B., 330 U.S. 485 (1947), 201-2

Palko v. Connecticut, 302 U.S. 319 (1937), 163

Panama Refining Co. v. Ryan, 293 U.S. 388 (1935), 5, 168

Panhandle Oil Co. v. Mississippi, 277 U.S. 218 (1928), 59, 60, 61

Parker v. Brown, 317 U.S. 341 (1943), 83

Parker v. Fleming, 329 U.S. 531 (1947), 185-6

Passenger Cases, 7 How. 283 (1849), 53

Paul v. Virginia, 8 Wall. 168 (1869), 63, 65

Penfield Co. v. S.E.C., 330 U.S. 585 (1947), 195

Pennekamp v. Florida, 328 U.S. 331 (1946), 108

Phelps Dodge Corp. v. N.L.R.B., 313 U.S. 177 (1941), 57, 200-201

Pierce v. Society of Sisters, 268 U.S. 510 (1925), 280

Pierre v. Louisiana, 306 U.S. 354 (1939), 142

Polish National Alliance v. N.L.R.B., 322 U.S. 643 (1944), 200, 291, n. 31

Pollock v. Farmers' Loan & Trust Co., 158 U.S. 601 (1895), 58

Powell v. Alabama, 287 U.S. 45 (1932), 138

Prince v. Massachusetts, 321 U.S. 158 (1944), 99

Prudential Insurance Co. v. Benjamin, 328 U.S. 408 (1946), 66

Quirin, Ex parte, 317 U.S. 1 (1942), 155-6

Railroad Retirement Board v. Alton R. Co., 295 U.S. 330 (1935), 5

Railway Mail Assn. v. Corsi, 326 U.S. 88 (1945), 231

Rathbun v. United States. *See* Humphrey's Executor v. United States

Ribnik v. McBride, 277 U.S. 350 (1928), 3, 56, 80

Rice v. Elmore, 72 F. Supp. 516, 165 F. (2d) 387 (1947), 68 S. Ct. 905 (1948), 124

Rice v. Olson, 324 U.S. 786 (1945), 139

Rice v. Santa Fe Elevator Corp., 331 U.S. 218 (1947), 292, n. 19

Richfield Oil Corp. v. State Board of Equalization, 329 U.S. 69 (1946), 293, n. 22

Robertson v. California, 328 U.S. 440 (1946), 66

Rogers v. Graves. *See* New York ex rel. Rogers v. Graves

S.E.C. v. Chenery Corp., 318 U.S. 80 (1943), 332 U.S. 194 (1947), 193-4

St. Joseph Stockyards Co. v. United States, 298 U.S. 38 (1936), 271

Santa Cruz Fruit Packing Co. v. N.L.R.B, 30) U.S. 453 (1938), 199

Schechter Corp. v. United States, 295 U.S. 495 (1935), 5, 55, 169, 268

Schenck v. United States, 249 U.S. 47 (1919), 275

Schneider v. Irvington, 308 U.S. 147 (1939), 94

Schneiderman v. United States, 320 U.S. 118 (1943), 113

Scottsboro Case. *See* Powell v. Alabama

Screws v. United States, 325 U.S. 91 (1945), 48, 70, 150-52, 163

Scripps-Howard Radio v. F.C.C., 316 U.S. 4 (1942), 182, 197

Second Coronado Case. *See* Coronado Coal Co. v. United Mine Workers

Senn v. Tile-Layers' Protective Union, 301 U.S. 468 (1937), 219, 220

Shelley v. Kraemer, 68 S. Ct. 836 (1948), 129

Shreveport Case, 234 U.S. 342 (1914), 76

Slaughter House Cases, 16 Wall. 36 (1873), 67

Smith v. Allwright, 321 U.S. 649 (1944), 46, 68, 124

Smith v. Texas, 311 U.S. 128 (1940), 142

Smyth v. Ames, 169 U.S. 466 (1898), 80, 175

Snyder v. Massachusetts, 291 U.S. 97 (1934), 159

South Carolina Highway Dept. v. Barnwell Brothers, 303 U.S. 177 (1938), 82, 83

Southern Pacific Railroad Co. v. Arizona, 325 U.S. 761 (1945), 83, 90

Southwestern Bell Telephone Co. v. Public Service Commission of Missouri, 262 U.S. 276 (1923), 271, 292, n. 13

Springer v. Philippine Islands, 277 U.S. 189 (1928), 169, 267

Stark v. Wickard, 321 U.S. 288 (1944), 183-5

State Tax Commission of Utah v. Aldrich, 316 U.S. 174 (1942), 79

Steele v. Louisville & N. R. Co., 323 U.S. 192 (1944), 231

Steiner v. Great Northern Ry., 72 N.W. 713 (1897), 173

Steward Machine Co. v. Davis, 301 U.S. 548 (1937), 9, 76

Strauder v. West Virginia, 100 U.S. 303 (1880), 142

Stromberg v. California, 283 U.S. 359 (1931), 94, 113, 280

Summers, In re, 325 U.S. 561 (1945), 101-2, 103

Sunshine Anthracite Coal Co. v. Adkins, 310 U.S. 381 (1940), 75

Swift v. Tyson, 16 Pet. 1 (1842), 62

Switchmen's Union v. National Mediation Board, 320 U.S. 297 (1943), 182-3, 184

Taylor v. Mississippi, 319 U.S. 583 (1943), 293, n. 13

10 East 40th St. Bldg. v. Callus, 325 U.S. 578 (1945), 204, 205

Tennessee Coal, Iron & R. Co. v. Muscoda Local No. 123, 321 U.S. 590 (1944), 290, n. 5

Thiel v. Southern Pacific Co., 328 U.S. 217 (1946), 144

Thomas v. Collins, 323 U.S. 516 (1945), 93, 225-6, 230, 276

Thornhill v. Alabama, 310 U.S. 88 (1940), 218-19, 276

Times-Mirror Co. v. Superior Court of California, 314 U.S. 252 (1941), 108

Toledo Newspaper Co. v. United States, 247 U.S. 402 (1918), 107, 109

Tomkins v. Missouri, 323 U.S. 485 (1945), 139

Tucker v. Texas, 326 U.S. 517 (1946), 99

Tunstall v. Brotherhood of Locomotive Firemen, Ocean Lodge No. 76, 323 U.S. 210 (1944), 231

Twining v. New Jersey, 211 U.S. 78 (1908), 163, 164-5

Tyson v. Banton, 273 U.S. 418 (1927), 56

United Brotherhood of Carpenters v. United States, 330 U.S. 395 (1947), 216

United Public Workers v. Mitchell, 330 U.S. 75 (1947), 125-7

United States v. Appalachian Electric Power Co., 311 U.S. 377 (1940), 75

United States v. Ballard, 322 U.S. 78 (1944), 101

United States v. Bekins, 304 U.S. 27 (1938), 75

United States v. Butler, 297 U.S. 1 (1936), 6, 7, 15, 52, 75

United States v. Carolene Products Co., 304 U.S. 104 (1938), 96

United States v. Carolina Freight Carriers Corp., 315 U.S. 475 (1942), 178, 179

United States v. Classic, 313 U.S. 299 (1941), 70, 123, 124, 150

United States v. Darby Lumber Co., 312 U.S. 100 (1941), 55, 68, 75, 76, 203

United States v. Di Re, 332 U.S. 581 (1948), 155

United States v. Hutcheson, 312 U.S. 219 (1941), 212-14, 283

United States v. Local 807, International Brotherhood of Teamsters, 315 U.S. 521 (1942), 198

United States v. Lovett, 328 U.S. 303 (1946), 113-15, 169-70

United States v. Macintosh, 283 U.S. 605 (1931), 102

United States v. Montgomery Ward, 58 F. Supp. 408 (1945), 150 F. (2d) 369 (1945), 76

United States v. Morgan, 307 U.S. 183 (1939), 313 U.S. 409 (1941), 171-2

United States v. New River Co., 265 U.S. 533 (1924), 173

United States v. Petrillo, 332 U.S. 1 (1947), 236-7

United States v. Schwimmer, 279 U.S. 644 (1929), 102, 274

United States v. South-Eastern Underwriters Assn., 322 U.S. 533 (1944), 64

United States v. United Mine Workers, 330 U.S. 258 (1947), 232-6, 273

United States v. Yellow Cab Co., 332 U.S. 218 (1947), 76

Vegelahn v. Guntner, 167 Mass. 92 (1896), 271-2

Viereck v. United States, 318 U.S. 236 (1943), 119

Virginia, Ex parte, 100 U.S. 339 (1880), 141

Virginia Electric & Power Co. v. N.L.R.B., 319 U.S. 533 (1943), 230

Wallace Corp. v. N.L.R.B., 323 U.S. 248 (1944), 202-3

Walling v. Nashville, C. & St. L. Ry., 330 U.S. 158 (1947), 207

Walling v. Portland Terminal Co., 330 U.S. 148 (1947), 205, 207

Ward v. Texas, 316 U.S. 547 (1942), 147

Warren-Bradshaw Drilling Co. v. Hall, 317 U.S. 88 (1942), 205

West Coast Hotel Co. v. Parrish, 300 U.S. 379 (1937), 9

West Virginia State Board of Education v. Barnette, 319 U.S. 624 (1943), 98, 132-3, 134-5, 276, 281, 284

Western Union Telegraph Co. v. Lenroot, 323 U.S. 490 (1945), 205

Whitney v. California, 274 U.S. 357 (1927), 113, 280

Wickard v. Filburn, 317 U.S. 111 (1942), 75

Williams v. Kaiser, 323 U.S. 471 (1945), 139, 163

Williams v. Standard Oil Co., 278 U.S. 235 (1929), 56

Wilson v. Cook, 327 U.S. 474 (1946), 51

Woods v. Cloyd W. Miller Co., 333 U.S. 138 (1948), 292, n. 11

Yakus v. United States, 321 U.S. 414
(1944), 76, 181-2, 292, n. 10

Yamashita, Application of, 327 U.S. 1
(1946), 156

Yick Wo v. Hopkins, 118 U.S. 357
(1886), 81

Zap v. United States, 328 U.S. 624
(1946), 330 U.S. 800 (1947), 154

INDEX

[Page numbers reference the original pagination of the previous printed editions. This pagination is found embedded into the text using brackets.]

Adams, Brooks, quoted, 1, 2, 20, 286

Adams, Henry, 1

Administrative Procedure Act, 196

Agricultural Adjustment Act, 6, 7, 15, 75

Agricultural Marketing Agreement Act, 169, 183-4

Agriculture, Department of, 171-2

Anti-Petrillo Act, 224, 237

Anti-Racketeering Act, 224

Arnold, Thurman, 212

Associated Press, 111-12

Ballantine, Arthur, quoted, 48

Biddle, Francis, 116

Bill of attainder, 114, 170

Bituminous Coal Act, 75

Bituminous Coal Conservation Act, 6

Bituminous Coal Division, 170

Black, Hugo L., appointment, 9-10; Jackson's charges against, 26-9; on civil liberties, 130; appraisal of voting record, 258; on judicial restraint, 282-3; quoted, 64, 83, 87, 92, 104, 129, 194

Bradford Act, Alabama, 227

Brandeis, Louis D., retirement, 10; appointment, 17; on stare decisis, 53, 54; liberalism, 266, 271-2; quoted, 219; and McReynolds, 29

Bridges, Harry, 115-17, 195

Bridges, Styles (Senator), 28

Bryce, Lord, quoted, 15

Burton, Harold, appointment, 11; civil liberties, 132; appraisal of voting record, 261

Butler, Pierce, 3, 4, 10

Byrnes, James F., appointment, 10; resignation, 11, 29

Cardozo, Benjamin N, appointment, 3; death, 10; quoted, 159

Carr, Robert K., 152

Chain broadcasting regulations, 181

Chamberlain, John, quoted, 50

Child labor act, 3

Choate, Joseph H, 18

Civil Rights Section, Department of Justice, 149, 152

Clayton Act, 209 ff.

Clear and present danger, 108-9, 275-6

Closed shop, constitutionality of laws against, 228

Commager, Henry S., 277, 284

Commerce power, expansion of, 75-6; and state laws, 81-89; and personal liberties, 128-29; and Wagner Act, 199-200; and Wage and Hour Act, 203-5; conceptual versus pragmatic interpretation of, 268-9

Communism, 113, 115-17, 128

Concurring opinions, 48

Confessions, in criminal cases, 146-8

Conscientious objectors, 101-3

Constitutional facts, 173

Contempt of court, newspaper editors, 107-10; John L. Lewis case, 232 ff.

Corwin, Edward S., quoted, 101, 139, 198

Counsel, in criminal cases, 138-41

Curtis, Charles P., Jr., quoted, 4, 269

Cushman, Robert E., quoted, 48, 150

Daniels, Jonathan, 23, 40

Delegation of legislative power, 5, 76, 168-9

Denaturalization, 115, 119-21

Dissenting opinions, growth of, 25-6; attitude toward, 49; uses of, 50-2

Dodd, E. M., 223, 225

Double jeopardy, 159

Douglas, William O, appointment, 10; political interests, 29; civil liberties, 130; appraisal of voting record, 258-9; quoted, 70, 176, 177-8, 187

Due process, and state legislation, 77 ff.; labor legislation, 225

Edmunds, George F., 18

Election cases, 123-5

Equal protection, 81

Espionage Act, 117, 276

Establishment of religion, 103-7

Ewing, Cortez A. M., quoted, 14-15

Fair hearing, 180

Fair Labor Standards Act, 75, 170, 203-8

Fair value theory, 80, 175

F.B.I., 154

Federal Communications Commission, 170, 180-1, 182, 189

Federal Power Commission, 171, 174-6, 189

Federal Reserve System, 185

Federal Trade Commission, Humphrey case, 5; 76, 167, 189

Federal-state controversies, 163, 262

Field, Stephen, 57-8

Final order rule, 180

Fischer, John, 265, 273

Flag salute, 91, 95-6, 98-9

Foreign Agents Registration Act, 119

Foremen, unionization of, 201-2

Fourteenth Amendment, relation to Bill of Rights, 164-6

Frankfurter, Felix, appointment, 10; flag salute, 95, 99; civil liberties, 132-3, 134-5; personal basis of decisions, 159—61; on administrative law, 192-5; appraisal of voting record, 260; liberalism, 276-7; judicial restraint, 280-4; quoted, 15, 52, 69-70, 87-8, 95, 174, 176, 179-80, 185, 188, 217, 222

Frazier-Lemke Act, 5

Freight rates, 179

Gold clause cases, 5, 16

Gregory, Charles O., quoted, 201, 210, 220, 223

Hamilton, Alexander, quoted, 239

Harding, President Warren G., appointment of Taft as chief justice, 8

Harris, Crampton, 27

Hatch Act case, 125-7

Hawaii Organic Act, 157

Holmes, Oliver Wendell, liberalism, 266; judicial pragmatism, 267; economic liberalism, 270-1; individual liberties, 274-5; judicial restraint, 277-82; quoted, 60, 62, 77, 82, 102,. 169

Hoover, Herbert, 8, 18

Hughes, Charles Evans, appointment, 3; resignation, 10; advised Truman, 26; quoted, 52, 269

Insurance, regulation of, 63-6

Intergovernmental tax immunity, 58-62

Interstate Commerce Commission, 167, 171, 177-80, 189, 191

Involuntary servitude, 237

Jackson, Andrew, 7

Jackson, Robert H., appointment, 11; charges against Black, 26-9; on civil liberties, 131, 133; appraisal of voting record, 260-1; quoted, 2, 4, 7, 12, 21, 30, 50-1, 53, 66, 98, 203, 207, 238, 284

Japanese evacuation, 121-2

Jefferson, Thomas, 7

Jehovah's Witnesses, 30, 91, 92, 93-101, 187

Jurisdictional facts, 173, 188, 195

Jury trial, 141-6

Krock, Arthur, 50

Krug, Julius, 232

LaFollette, Robert M., 7

Landis, James M., 116, 167

Lerner, Max, quoted, 16, 19, 264

Lewis, John L., 232 ff., 273

Lincoln, Abraham, 7

Loyalty investigation, 127

Madison, James, quoted, 21

Marshall, John, quoted, 73, 74, 267

Martial law, 156-8

McCune, Wesley, quoted, 255

McIlwain, Charles H., quoted, 21

McReynolds, James C., appointment, 2; resignation, 10; attitude, 29

Milk price control law, 5, 56, 80

Minimum wage laws, District of Columbia, 3; New York, 6; Washington, 9

Mortgage moratorium law, 4

Municipal Bankruptcy Act, 6, 75

Murphy, Frank, appointment, 10; on civil liberties, 130; Civil Rights Section, 149; appraisal of voting record, 259; extremism, 285; quoted, 97, 229

National Industrial Recovery Act, 5

National Labor Relations Act, 9, 168, 199-203, 226-7

National Labor Relations Board, 189, 199-203, 229

National Mediation Board, 182, 183

National Railroad Adjustment Board, 196

New Deal, and the Court, 265-6

New York Civil Rights Law, 231

New York Criminal Anarchy Act, 112, 275

Nonunanimous decisions, growth of, 25-6; judicial attitudes, 240

Norris-LaGuardia Act, 210 ff., 233

O.P.A., 153-4, 185, 189

Original package doctrine, 86

Overruling of decisions, 54-58, 300-1

Pegler, Westbrook, 198

Pekelis, Alexander, quoted, 50

Pepper, George Wharton, quoted, 18

Perkins, Frances, 206

Picketing, 218-24

Portal-to-portal cases, 205-6

Post Office Department, and second-class privileges, 110-11

Powell, Thomas Reed, quoted, 32, 51, 56-7, 262, 282

Price Control Act, 169, 181, 182, 185

Primary elections, 123

Public Utility Act, 75

Railroad Retirement Act, 5, 75

Railway Labor Act, 183, 196, 231

Rate regulation, 80, 174-6

Reed, Stanley, appointment, 10; appraisal of voting record, 260; quoted, 184, 223

Reproduction cost, 80, 175

Restrictive covenants case, 129

Roberts, Owen J., appointment, 3; advisor to Truman, 26; on civil liberties, 131; appraisal of voting record, 261; quoted, 15, 46, 69, 170

Rodell, Fred, 282-3

Roosevelt, Franklin D., Court reorganization proposal, 7-8; judicial appointments, 9-10; appraisal of appointments, 11-14

Roosevelt, Theodore, 7, 16

Rutledge, Wiley B., appointment, 11; civil liberties, 130; appraisal of voting record, 259-60; quoted, 93, 185

Schlesinger, Arthur M., Jr., quoted, 28, 49, 266, 278, 281, 282, 283, 284

Search and seizure cases, 152-5

Securities and Exchange Commission, 189, 193, 195

Selective service cases, 186-8

Self-incrimination, 164-5

Sherman Act, insurance, 63-6; labor, 208-18

Smith-Connally Act, 233-4, 236

Social Security Act, 9, 76

Stare decisis, 53-6

Stone, Harlan F., appointment, 3; as chief justice, n; lack of skill as presiding officer, 40, 290; flag salute case, 95-6; civil liberties, 130; appraisal of voting record, 261; quoted, 47, 68, 71, 172, 174, 181

Sutherland, George, appointment, 3; retirement, 10; quoted, 268

Swisher, Carl B., 72, 92

Taft, William H., appointments to Court, 8; opposition to Brandeis, 17; 1920 election, 17; appointment as chief justice, 17-18; quoted, 55

Taft-Hartley Act, 202, 224, 238

Taney, Roger B., quoted, 53-4

Taxation, inheritance, 78-9; state, 84 ff.; federal, 262

Tennessee Valley Authority, 6

Thomas, R. J., 225

Treason, 118-19

Truman, Harry S., appointments to Court, 11, 26

Unconstitutional, power to declare acts of Congress, 72-4

United Mine Workers, 27, 232 ff.

VanDevanter, Willis, appointment, 2; retirement, 9

Vinson, Fred M., appointment, 11, 26; civil liberties, 132; appraisal of voting record, 261

Wage and Hour Administrator, 170, 189, 204, 206, 207

Wagner Act, see National Labor Relations Act

War Labor Disputes Act, see Smith-Connally Act

Wheeler, Burton K., 7

White primaries, 46, 123-4

Wire-tapping, 152-3

Wisconsin Employment Peace Act, 224

Wisconsin Employment Relations Board, 225

qp

Visit us at *www.quidprobooks.com.*